HUMAN RESOURCE MANAGEMENT

Palgrave Business Briefing

The *Business Briefings* series consists of short and authoritative introductory textbooks in core business topics. Written by leading academics, they take a no-nonsense, practical approach and provide students with a clear and succinct overview of the subject.

These textbooks put the needs of students first, presenting the topics in a meaningful way that will help students to gain an understanding of the subject area. Covering the basics and providing springboards to further study, these books are ideal as accessible introductions or as revision guides.

Other books in the Business Briefings series:

Quantitative Methods, by Les Oakshott

Research Methods, by Peter Stokes

Marketing, by Jonathan Groucutt

Organizational Behaviour, by Mike Maughan

Financial Accounting, by Jill Collis

Management Accounting, by Jill Collis

The Business Briefings Series

Series Standing Order ISBN 978–0–230–36385–4

You can receive future titles in this series as they are published by placing a standing order. Please contact your bookseller or, in the case of difficulty, write to us at the address below with your name and address, the title of the series and the ISBN quoted above.

Customer Services Department, Macmillan Distribution Ltd, Houndmills, Basingstoke, Hampshire, RG21 6XS, UK

HUMAN RESOURCE MANAGEMENT

MICHAEL L. NIETO

PRINCIPAL LECTURER AND HEAD OF THE DEPARTMENT OF MANAGEMENT, HUMAN RESOURCES AND ORGANISATIONS, REGENTS UNIVERSITY LONDON, UK

palgrave
macmillan

First published 2014 by
PALGRAVE MACMILLAN

Palgrave Macmillan in the UK is an imprint of Macmillan Publishers Limited, registered in England, company number 785998, of Houndmills, Basingstoke, Hampshire RG21 6XS.

Palgrave Macmillan in the US is a division of St Martin's Press LLC, 175 Fifth Avenue, New York, NY 10010.

Palgrave Macmillan is the global academic imprint of the above companies and has companies and representatives throughout the world.

Palgrave® and Macmillan® are registered trademarks in the United States, the United Kingdom, Europe and other countries.

ISBN 978–1–137–28227–9

This book is printed on paper suitable for recycling and made from fully managed and sustained forest sources. Logging, pulping and manufacturing processes are expected to conform to the environmental regulations of the country of origin.

A catalogue record for this book is available from the British Library.

Library of Congress Cataloging-in-Publication Data
Nieto, Michael L.
Human resource management / Michael L. Nieto, Deputy Head of Department Management and HRM, Regents College London.

pages cm
ISBN 978–1–137–28227–9
1. Personnel management. I. Title.
HF5549.N4734 2014
658'.3—dc23   2014022984

Typeset by MPS Limited, Chennai, India.

Printed in China.

CONTENTS

LIST OF FIGURES

PREFACE

Dedications

This book is dedicated to family, friends, mentors and colleagues. Many people have contributed to the development of the ideas you are about to read.

With special gratitude to my mum and Winnie Dent, Trudy, Beryl, Mary, Henry and Fred for believing in me. Thank you.

Employability

In a competitive job market it is essential that you develop your employability so that you can present yourself effectively to employers and secure a permanent job when you graduate. In the chapters which follow, you will find practical guidance on writing a CV and making an interview presentation. There are also self-development guides from consultants, and management insights from successful professionals who have informed the case studies and content of this book on current organizational life and their experiences of working and managing people.

Practical academic research

The purpose of this book is to provide a student-focused, academically rigorous, HR course for management students. The philosophy of this book is that it's people who make organizations successful. The underpinning research includes studies with large organizations, small businesses, public-sector and not-for-profit organizations. The examples and learning materials also reflect the diversity and global nature of the modern workplace.

International

More than ever we are global citizens with job opportunities available for those who wish to move locations. This book is designed to provide a contemporary view of managing people within the international environment.

More and more students are telling me that they plan to work away from their home country, at least for a few years, to build their international experience. The research and activities you find in this book have been developed through both UK and international Master's and undergraduate programmes. There are also contributions from people whose consultancy work and research focus are international.

Contributors

There are some really interesting and helpful contributions. Look out for Nicholas Bowen's international overview. Duncan Christie Miller is an international consultant who shares some insightful guidance on self-development and leadership. Nina Seppala researches ethics and corporate social responsibility, and has commented on the influence this can have on successfully recruiting talented people. Bradley Saunders shares his thoughts on the development of e-learning. And for the legal overview, Danielle Wootton gives us a concise and easy-to-understand summary of HR law for non-legal managers in the UK (at the time of publication).

I would like to thank each of them for some really interesting and practical insights into their specialist areas of academic research and consultancy.

Nicholas Bowen has international standing as an author on international business and has been a member of the Editorial Advisory Board of the *Euro Asia Journal of Management* since 2008.

Duncan Christie Miller leads a consulting and personal leadership consultancy. After a first career in the Royal Marines and Special Forces, Duncan established CM Ltd in 1986, having previously been part of the initial management team of Textainer – a global containers leasing company.

Nina Seppala is Associate Dean of Business and Management, Regent's University London.

Bradley Saunders manages e-learning delivery for Derby Business School, University of Derby.

Danielle Wootton, LLB (Hons) Law. Danielle has experience in working in the public and private sectors and lecturing in UK universities.

And thank you, for choosing this book.

ABOUT THE AUTHOR

Michael L. Nieto Cert Ed, B Ed (Hons), MA, Adv Dip Consultancy (Henley), FCMI, Academic FCIPD, FHEA.

Michael is Head of Department of Management and HRM, Regent's University London.

His academic management experience includes: leading a Management and HR Department of over 50 academic staff; MBA director for both Executive and International MBAs; International officer. Michael's lecturing experience includes international Master's, MBA and undergraduate programmes in several leading universities, in the areas of Human Resources, Leadership and Organizational Behaviour. This includes invitations to lecture to students at: Marymount University, US; the ACI Paris; and Valencia University, Spain. He is currently an external examiner to the postgraduate programme with Kingston University and with Buckingham University, overseeing postgraduate programmes with the European School of Economics campuses in London, New York, Madrid, Florence and Milan.

Michael has also led academic groups within several universities, developing postgraduate and undergraduate programmes including; MBA; HR (CIPD accredited); Master's in Voluntary Action Management and a Pre-Master's programme for international students. Michael was a member of Bournemouth University's centre for corporate social responsibility. He was also a founding member of Surrey University's Centre for Applied Business Ethics and has published academic papers on HR and related research areas. His current research is in leadership for a doctorate with the University of Birmingham, supervised by Professor Chris Mabey and Doctor Tom Bisschoff. Michael's consultancy experience includes working with international companies, SMEs, distributor networks and not-for-profit and family businesses.

ABOUT THIS BOOK

The content of this book provides students with an overview of HRM theory and practice. The materials for this book have been formatted to offer an accessible and concise general HRM textbook.

There are 12 chapters: ideal for use on one-semester, 12-week modules. The chapters can also be used as in different order to meet the needs of specialized modules.

Each chapter contains the following:

- **Stand-alone chapters**

  Each chapter is written as a stand-alone chapter to enable use in any order so that the chapters can be rearranged to meet modular requirements.

- **Introduction to the chapter**

  The key learning outcomes are listed in order to provide both the lecturer and the students with an overview of the key learning areas for the chapter.

- **Practical examples of the chapter topics in the real world**

  This includes short cases from consultancy and research with organizations. Where appropriate, a short learning note will be added from a graduate student who has done well in the area and/or an academic who is currently delivering the materials or professionals commenting on how HR works in their organization. These additional materials add learning experiences and practical applications of theory to practice.

- **Key Points**

  These appear throughout the text to alert students to their importance.

- **Summary**

  Each chapter has a summary of key points.

- **Taking it further**

  This section has a list of short list of books and or journal articles.

- **Revision**

  Each chapter has revision questions

1

The Development and History of Human Resource Management

INTRODUCTION

Welcome to human resource management (HRM)!

This book in the series focuses on the most important part of every organization; *the people*. An organization's key asset is its people. Through people strategies are formed, financial plans are shaped, innovations are created and products and services are made and delivered.

> **Key Point:** Since the late twentieth century, an individual's employment future has become a matter of personal employability within the employment environment. Consequently, people are likely to work for many different employers (possibly within different sectors) rather than just five or six organizations throughout a career.

The way in which people are managed has evolved during two centuries of transformational changes in organizational structures and employee and employer expectations. During the early twentieth century, industrialization and trade unionism led to the emergence of industrial relations with the collectivist approach to employment, where many employees were represented by a trade union. This led in turn to the growth of personnel management (Ulrich 2011). By the later part of the twentieth century, collectivism was being replaced by the trend towards individual employment contracts. Those changes led towards more individualistic employer and employee relationships replacing the intercessions of trade unions on behalf of employees. The individual employment trend of the late twentieth century thereby shifted the employee–employer relationship environment away from Weber's paternalistic bureaucracy, where employees had tended to stay with one employer for many years with more individualistic pragmatism on the part of both employers and employees (Eisenstadt 1968; Emmott 2005).

The retention of talent within the global employment market places human resource at the centre of enabling organizations to build a sustainable employment strategy for both recruiting and retaining talent (Saunders and Nieto in Al Ariss 2014).

> **Key Point:** Retaining and promoting your staff builds a *competitive* organization.

It is cost non-effective to recruit talent from outside an organization without simultaneously developing and promoting the people you already have and encouraging them to stay with the organization. This is because it is vital to have a committed and engaged team of staff to build organizational success within an international marketplace that is continually evolving and changing (Pilenzo 2009; Woolever et al. 2010; Ulrich 2011).

> **Key Point:** Every manager's primary task is building the motivation and engagement of his/her team.

For twenty-first century managers, many of the tasks, which may have been traditionally regarded as the domain of a human resource (HR) person, have become part of the modern manager's job role (Nieto 2006; Van Eynde et al. 2011). Furthermore, in the contemporary environment, an organization may decide to out-source (use external providers) to manage part of the human resource function. There are also many SMEs (small to medium-size enterprises) that cannot afford to employ a full-time human resource specialist (Nieto 2006; Conway and Jones 2012). This means that contemporary managers need to have the appropriate attitudes, knowledge, and skills to manage their people. Hence, HRM is for every manager, not just the specialists (Nieto 2006; Van Eynde et al. 2011).

LEARNING OBJECTIVES

The key learning outcomes for the chapter are below:

- Understand the context and historical development of HRM.
- Transition from personnel management to HRM.
- Defining what is understood by HRM in the contemporary organizational context. Integrated HRM.
- Critically evaluate the relevance and applications of HRM to modern organizations.
- Scientific management (Taylor 1947) and human relations approaches (Mayo 1933). How are they applied into the current workplace environment?
- Hawthorne experiments.
- Modern applications of human relations and scientific management.
- Summary of the role and contribution of HRM to organizational management.

UNDERSTAND THE CONTEXT AND HISTORICAL DEVELOPMENT OF HRM

In pre-industrial society, the employment relationship was conditioned by tradition and custom. As can be seen in Figure 1.1, the pre-industrial forms of custom were eventually replaced as workers sought collective representation. It was after the Industrial Revolution that workers joined together into trade unions, so that they had a voice through which they could negotiate their pay and working conditions. This was a collectivist approach so that whole groups of employees negotiated with their employers via the trade unions.

The larger industrial and commercial employers also found it necessary to employ specialist staff who could manage the processes of recruitment,

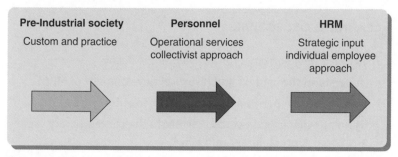

Figure 1.1 From pre-industrial society to personnel management and HRM

Source: Nieto (2006: 3).

development and training, and serve as a point of contact for staff and their trade union representation. Hence, in Figure 1.1 there is a transition from the custom and practices of the pre-industrial environment into collectivism, where the corporate personnel departments oversaw the operational delivery of staff services, such as recruitment, selection, induction, training, retention and disciplinary procedures (Ulrich 2011).

TRANSITION FROM PERSONNEL MANAGEMENT TO HRM

Key Point: Pre-industrial society's custom and practice (traditions in local communities and social responsibility) was replaced by national trade unions and personnel management (collective bargaining by employees with bureaucratic organizations). This was replaced by individual employment contracts and management-centred HRM (see Figure 1.1).

Twentieth-century personnel departments generally served their organizations' functional departments with recruitment, selection, induction, training, retention and personnel management procedures.

Within large functionally structured organizations, the personnel departments provided a comprehensive range of services (Legge 1993; Ulrich 2011). By the nature of their structure and culture, large public or private bureaucracies tended to focus on the adherence to regulations, whether externally imposed of internally constituted.

The reformation of personnel management into HRM marked a significant change in employee relations (Sisson 1993; Ulrich 2011). The workplace was becoming more orientated to individual employee contracts as the trade union membership receded in the later part of the twentieth century. Hence, by the twenty-first century, employee relations are more about individual contracts than collective national agreements with large trade unions (Nieto 2006).

As can be seen in the figure above, HRM has been evolving and changing in response to the work environment. Furthermore, as employees have become less unionized, each employer has had to manage employment contracts. For many non-HR managers, this has added additional responsibilities in employee management as well as their functional managerial role.

> **Key Point:** The integrated approach (Nieto 2006) is where managers are responsible for HRM.

In the contemporary organizational environment, managers conduct many of the HR functions, hence integrated HRM (Nieto 2006; Morgan and Jardin 2010; Woolever et al. 2010). Alternatively, SMEs may not wish to employ a department of professional HRM specialists. Instead they can use out-sourced firms which specialize in areas such as recruitment, employee development, pay roll, legal matters, standards compliance or incentive schemes. Indeed, small entrepreneurial businesses may draw upon expertise by building networks with other businesses (Jones et al. 2001; Conway and Jones 2012). This does not mean that organizations do not need HRM people; it *does* require the managers to be trained in HR so that they can guide and support their staff and understand what kind of external support they require. Accordingly, HR services may be provided internally, externally or by a balanced combination of both (Davies 2008).

As with any other service to an organization, HR needs to be value-adding. The modern HR professional should therefore be more proactively involved with their organization's policy making and management. The case for the value-adding benefits of HR is persuasive if it is seen as an integrated part of whatever the organization is planning to achieve. Modern research has indicated that effectiveness of HR practices can add significantly to organizational performance. Referring to the substantial weight of research evidence regarding the value of HR activities, Alberg (2002: 23) observed that over 30 studies conducted in both Britain and the US during the 1990s found a positive correlation between people management and organizational performance. However, during the course of researching this book I still found evidence from a wide range of sectors and in international companies indicating varying levels of acceptance as to the value of managing talent and encouraging the motivation of their employees.

> **Key Point:** Value existing staff, manage their talent and encourage the motivation of employees.

CRITICALLY EVALUATE THE RELEVANCE OF HRM TO MODERN ORGANIZATIONS

HR serves the situation-specific needs of the organization. For example, if it is a for-profit organization, then HR people should set themselves the task of improving the delivery of agreed objectives with their operational colleagues. In the public and not-for-profit sectors, the objectives may be centred upon improvements in service delivery whether this be education, healthcare or the delivery of charitable aid (Billis and Harris 1996; Davies 2008; Cunningham 2010).

Operational managers, team leaders and executives are often preoccupied with their core tasks and so they usually welcome productive input to motivate their staff and develop their skills. Under such circumstances, HR people can deliver value-adding input by providing a strategic planning overview that can lead to performance-enhancing interventions (Paauwe 2009). Essentially this requires studying the local management situations (micro) and advising on how best to enhance performance in relation to the organization's broader (macro) objectives. These kinds of micro/macro initiatives require a range of managerial attributes and the HR person should be encouraged to develop sound research and communication attitudes, knowledge and skills in order to critically evaluate situations and discuss possibilities empathetically with colleagues.

> **Key Point:** The local managers are best placed to maximize opportunities in their area.
> This is particularly relevant for companies with international offices.

The design detail and local implementation of initiatives should ideally be directed by the operational managers who are best placed to manage local operational matters because they are close to the opportunities and problems in their area. This is particularly relevant to companies with international offices where local managers can respond to market requirements on a local basis. In modern organizational environments, initiatives need to meet situation-specific requirements. This means designing initiatives that serve the particular organizational structure and culture.

Research into a one-size-fits-all approach for organizations indicates that it is not an effective way to deliver HR (O'Neill 2002; Roberts 2003). For example, interventions, such as performance targets, or competencies which may have been useful elsewhere, could require extensive consultation and adaptation to meet the situation-specific requirements and needs of a different organization. Furthermore, each organization has its own style of management and ethos, which in turn influences employees' psychological contracts (Guest and Conway 2001). For example, employee expectations in public and private sectors may be quite different, as may the customs and practices in different countries (O'Neill 2002). Accordingly, international managers can benefit from courses which develop their international awareness. This can be achieved through assignments that require initiatives to be planned via a cross-cultural/ nationality study group.

> **Key Point:** Be situation-specific. Transferring interventions such as performance targets or competencies or procedures from one organization to another may not work. There is no one best practice, and one 'size' of policy does not fit all organizations.

Similarly, the use of management approaches normally associated with the for-profit sector may not always sit comfortably with the cultural norms of the not-for-profit environment (Davies 2008). For example, a doctor whose primary interest is to care for patients may be less than motivated by terms such as 'unit cost minimization' (spend less on each patient) or an aid worker whose work is focused on helping to organize food for starving people might be forgiven for failing to respond to a 'management by objectives' drive. Thus modern, integrated HR is situation-specific, actively recognizing and responding to the needs and values of those it serves (Nieto 2006; Pilenzo 2009; Woolever et al. 2010).

SCIENTIFIC MANAGEMENT (TAYLOR 1947) AND HUMAN RELATIONS APPROACHES (MAYO 1933): HOW ARE THEY APPLIED INTO THE CURRENT WORKPLACE ENVIRONMENT?

Within the area of managing people there are prominent differences among the various theoretical protagonists. Some academics favour the view that management is a 'science', a concept first propagated by Taylor (1947). Others have taken the human relations approach, which was initiated by the Hawthorne experiments and the work of Mayo (1933). This debate is interesting to management students in that both approaches sought to observe and interpret the role people play in organizational performance.

Key Point: The integrated approach recommends a 'fitness to purpose' approach. Accordingly, both the scientific and human relations schools have a role to play in modern HR (Nieto 2006; Van Eynde et al. 2011).

In the case of Taylor's (1947) experiments, the results concluded that segmenting work activities into tightly controlled elements enabled the more efficient movement of pig iron in an early twentieth-century factory. Interestingly, the original writings of Taylor were concerned with addressing the exhaustive conditions under which workers toiled and his aim was to improve both working conditions and efficiency. Therefore, although Taylor's work has become associated with managing processes, his intentions were also to improve working conditions. Indeed, during the nineteenth and twentieth centuries workers were exposed to sometimes life-threatening dangers, even on the leading technological projects such as the construction of the Brooklyn Bridge or the Hoover Dam (Cadbury 2003). Part of Taylor's vision was therefore to apply scientific methodology and thereby improve working processes and conditions.

One of the first corporations to recognize the advantages of scientific management to productivity was Ford, who adopted Taylor's (1947) methods to replace craft-like working practices with the first of the modern car production lines. The scientific method of segmenting work into a series of allocated tasks enabled the company to employ a less skilled workforce because they were only required to learn how to complete their allocated task, rather than to work as automotive engineers. It was therefore possible for a person with no knowledge of how to build a complete car to successfully work on a production line. The scientific approach thereby reduced the cost of manufacture by increasing efficiency and the number of cars produced per day. Ford also made precise calculations of the productivity and price needed to make the required profit level (Pickard 2003). The manufacturing process was very effective at mass production, as the late Henry Ford is reported to have said that customers could have any colour, as long as it was black. (The original Models T Fords were all painted black.)

Essentially, the scientific approach to task management dissects work into managed elements, thereby reducing the autonomy of the human input in favour of the systematically organized process. This is why the scientific approach and its derivatives are still an integral part of the modern workplace. For example, burger restaurants can produce the same product in New York, London, Paris and Tokyo by specifying the exact ingredients, cooking method and delivery in every outlet. A similar approach can be utilized in other organizational activities such as call centres where the client is led through a series of pre-set questions and their answers are inputted into a computer programme which can then offer a response such as a credit rating, an insurance quotation and so forth.

The advantage of Taylor's scientific systems (1947) is that employees can be trained to operate and deliver a standard service package. It thereby follows that the interaction between the service provider and client can be scripted so that the organization retains uniformity and conformity to its service parameters. The scientific approach can be taken further by the client simply pressing buttons on a telephone to receive services. Full automation can remove all direct human contact, with the customer interface being the service provider's computer system direct via the Internet. Interestingly, the use of the Internet thereby shifts the workload onto the customer. Indeed, the customer may then be sent documents electronically to print out which then saves costs in both printing and postage.

Scientific management therefore has a major place in today's organizations. Fortunately for human beings, there are many tasks where human input is preferable. Even when a service can be fully automated there are likely to be situations where some clients prefer to talk to a human being rather than a computer. Furthermore, sophisticated levels of service delivery are likely to require a greater depth of knowledge than just pre-prepared answers. Interestingly, the original work of Taylor (1947) also recognized the implicit contribution and necessity of human motivation in enabling the system to work. So, the scientific model and its later derivatives – apart from those completely led by computers – are at least in part dependent upon human input, thereby implicitly accepting the importance of HR for their successful operation.

The work of Mayo (1933, 1945) – referred to as the Hawthorne Experiments – offered a more holistic view of employees as complex human beings with beliefs, loyalties and personal motivations. In a series of experiments at the Western Electric Company, researchers found no evidence that minor changes in the working environment changed behaviour, while conversely taking an interest in employee welfare did produce productivity improvements. These experiments thereby highlighted that even in an industrial production environment where a scientific approach might have been employed, performance could be improved when people were more involved and consulted about the work they were engaged with.

The Hawthorne experiments

1. *Illumination room experiments*. These studies were carried out in an assembly area of the factory. The levels of lighting were varied to evaluate any potential correlation between the general environment and work output. No significant or conclusive correlation was established.

2. *Relay room experiments*. These experiments were conducted in an area where electrical relays were being assembled. In this experiment a group of employees were encouraged to discuss their working conditions, such as break periods and working hours. The researchers listened and were empathetic to the needs of the employees who were provided with more breaks and rest periods than was the norm. Productivity increased.

3. *Interviewing experiments*. As the subtitle suggests, employees were interviewed about their attitudes to work. As the experiment progressed, the interviewing techniques became less structured, allowing respondents to express their views on a wider range of issues, through which the researchers found some evidence indicating influence of informal groups. This is arguably the genesis of modern HR.

4. *Wiring room experiments*. The influence of peer groups was found to have an influence on workplace behaviour. Employees tended to conform to the work rates and norms of colleagues rather than those promoted by management, even when additional incentives were provided to produce more work.

As with the scientific approach, it is possible to criticize the academic methodological rigour of the Hawthorne experiments, with regard to the extent to which their findings can be generalized across other organizations. Modern academic writers usually research a wider spectrum of sectors to underpin the validity and reliability of their studies. Conversely, the place of the experiments has been assured, in that they have provided a point for further academic debate on the place of human relations in the workplace. Further critical evaluations of the Hawthorne experiments can be found in Sonnenfeld (1985) and Franke and Kaul (1978).

Key Point: The research by Mayo (1945) and the Hawthorne experiments provided modern academics and practitioners with some useful points of reference from which to continue studying aspects of human behaviour in organizations. For example, Mayo (1945) also recognized the importance of groups and how organizations could prosper when individuals were joined into teams that interacted with each other to form an environment where people attained a sense of belonging and identification with the organization's mission and objectives.

Both the Hawthorne experiments and Taylor's experiments on scientific management are therefore still relevant to the on-going discourse on how people are best managed and motivated. Indeed, most management texts usually make some reference to these two contrasting pieces of research because of their enduring influence. The workplace reality is that work has to be done efficiently and this involves the motivations of people. It may therefore be surmised that it is more useful to argue for the application of either the scientific approach or the human relations approach on the basis of fitness to purpose rather than philosophical preferences for one or other theoretical methodology. However, in all cases, the motivation of workers is central to successful performance. (Performance and rewards are discussed in Chapter 5.)

SHORT CASES FROM CONSULTANCY AND RESEARCH: FORDISM

The Ford car company was one of the first to apply Taylor's scientific management (1947). The importance to a national economy of having a workforce which can afford to buy goods and services was as evident in the early twentieth century as it is today in the twenty-first century.

There is an interesting story (which may or may not be factual but is nevertheless informative) that Henry Ford II had a discussion with the union boss Walter Reuther, leader of the United Automobile Workers.

Ford allegedly asked the union boss how he would collect union funds if robots built the cars? Reuther allegedly replied, 'How are you going to get them [the robots] to buy your cars?'

According to Pickard's research (2003: 30), Henry Ford had recognized the importance of an affluent workforce. Accordingly, Ford doubled his workers' pay to ensure they could afford the cars they made and in recognition that affluent workers created more customers. A modern equivalent for pay comparison would be a rate of pay which was above the average level and enabled workers to buy new cars.

Activity: Individual or Group seminar presentation on the productivity benefits of having a well-paid and cared for workforce.

MODERN APPLICATIONS OF HUMAN RELATIONS AND SCIENTIFIC MANAGEMENT

The human relations approach originated by Mayo (1945) has adapted and evolved, and new theories have been introduced to observe human relations in organizations. What appears to be constant is the recognition that there is value in involving people in how their work is organized. This is evident in the work of many modern writers, a small sample of which could include: Drucker 1989; Kotter 1990; Moss Kanter 1990; Pascale 1990; Morgan 1993; Peters 1994; Semler 1994; Senge et al. 1994; Handy 1997; Covey 1989; Bell 2002; Fuller 2005; Mabey and Finch-Lees 2008; to name just a few. Further discussion of key changes in twentieth-century management thinking can be seen in Crainer (1996).

The scientific management approach is currently applied in many organizations which redesign jobs into components. According to Wilson (1995), many modern initiatives are in fact derived from the earlier work conducted in Ford's factories. Furthermore, Boje and Winsor (1993) have observed that the work of Taylor (1947) has been resurrected by the new scientific methodologies (Wilson 1995). For example, the late twentieth century saw interventions such as: re-engineering (Hammer and Champy 1993; Champy 1995). This systematic approach to management has a heritage in scientific management including processes such as Just In Time

(JIT), whereby materials are delivered just as they are required, instead of storing stocks of components (Taylor 1947; Jones 1997).

In common with the early twentieth-century scientific management system, the new scientific methods have often been associated with the pursuit of greater efficiency and performance through costs reductions and greater control of employee behaviour. The new variants also share scientific management's predisposition to control the detail of working processes.

These methods might be criticized for overt micro management. Hence they usually increase management control on job content, working practices, monitoring and supervision, and take away autonomy from the people closest to the work, be they factory workers, teachers or doctors. Thus, where management micro-manages the detail of work, employees have less autonomy in their interpretations of how to do their jobs. This may be counter-productive to employee motivation.

SUMMARY OF THE ROLE AND CONTRIBUTION OF HRM TO ORGANIZATIONAL MANAGEMENT

(a) In the early twentieth century, industrialization and trade unionism led to the emergence of industrial relations with the collectivist approach to employment, whereby many employees were represented by a trade union.

(b) Contemporary managers need to have the appropriate attitudes, knowledge and skills to manage their people. Hence, human resources are for every manager, not just the specialists.

(c) Figure 1.1: From Pre-industrial society to personnel management and HRM.

(d) Twentieth-century personnel departments generally served their organizations' functional departments with recruitment, selection, induction, training, retention and personnel management procedures.

(e) With fewer unionized employees, each employer has to manage employment contracts. For many non-HR managers, this has added additional responsibilities in employee management as well as their functional managerial role.

(f) As with any other service to an organization, HR needs to be (and be seen to be) value-adding.

(g) The design detail and local implementation of initiatives should ideally be directed by the operational managers who are best placed to manage local operational matters because they are close to the opportunities and problems in their area.

(h) A 'one-size-fits-all' approach may meet with employee resistance and be less effective than the alternative, integrated, tailored approach.

(i) The integrated approach recommends a 'fitness to purpose' approach where both the scientific and human relations schools have a role to play.

(j) One of the first corporations to recognize the advantages of scientific management to productivity was Ford.

(k) Essentially, the scientific approach to task management dissects work into managed elements, thereby reducing the autonomy of the human input in favour of the systematically organized process.

(l) The advantage of Taylor's scientific systems (1947) is that employees can be trained to operate and deliver a standard service package.

(m) The Hawthorne experiments began the development of twentieth-century personnel management which focused on involving staff in discussing how to organize their work.

(n) The new scientific methods have often been associated with the pursuit of greater efficiency and performance through costs reductions and greater control of employee behaviour. The new variants also share scientific management's predisposition to control the detail of working processes.

REVISION SECTION

1. What is integrated HRM (Nieto 2006)?

2. Why is a situation-specific management approach preferable to adopting systems from other organizations?

3. What can we learn from both the scientific approach and the Hawthorne experiments in managing the way people work?

4. Would you prefer to work in an organization where the managerial system was predominantly process-orientated (scientific) or people-orientated (Hawthorne experiments)? Why?

TAKING IT FURTHER

Key texts to look up:

Davies, S. (2008) 'Contracting out Employment Services to the Third and Private Sectors: A Critique', *Critical Social Policy*, 28(2), pp. 136–164.

Morgan, H. and Jardin, D. (2010) 'Integrated Talent Management', OD Practitioner: *Journal of the Organization Development Network*, 42(4), pp. 23–29.

Nieto, M. L. (2006) *An Introduction to Human Resource Management: An Integrated Approach*. Basingstoke: Palgrave Macmillan.

Refer to the books and journals in this references section. Each one can take you to new sources and information.

REFERENCES

Alberg, R. (2002) Counting with Numbers, *People Management*, 10 January, CIPD.

Bell, D. (2002) *Ethical Ambition: Living a Life of Meaning and Worth*. London: Bloomsbury.

Billis, D. and Harris, M. (1996) *Voluntary Agencies: Challenges of Organisation and Management*. Basingstoke: Palgrave Macmillan.

Boje, D. M. and Winsor, R. D. (1993) 'The Resurrection of Taylorism: Total Quality Management's Hidden Agenda', *Journal of Organizational Management Change*, 6(4), pp. 57–70.

Cadbury, D. (2003) *Seven Wonders of the Industrial World*. London: Forth Estate.

Champy, J. (1995) *Reengineering Management: The Mandate for New Leadership.* Harper Collins: New York.

Conway, S. and Jones, O. (2012) *Entrepreneurial Networks and the Small Business.* In: Carter, S. and Jones-Evans, D. (eds), *Enterprise and Small Business: Principles, Practices and Policies.* London, FT Prentice Hall.

Covey, S. (1989) *The Seven Habits of Highly Successful People.* London: Simon & Schuster.

Crainer, S. (1996) *Key Management Ideas: Thinkers that Changed the Management World.* London: Financial Times, Pitman.

Cunningham, I. (2010) 'Drawing from a Bottomless Well? Exploring the Resilience of Value-based Psychological Contracts in Voluntary Organizations', *The International Journal of Human Resource Management,* 21(5), pp. 699–719.

Davies, S. (2008) 'Contracting out Employment Services to the Third and Private Sectors: A Critique', *Critical Social Policy,* 28(2), pp. 136–164.

Drucker, P. F. (1989) *The Practice of Management.* London: Heinemann.

Eisenstadt, S. N (ed.) (1968) *Weber on Charisma & Institution Building.* Chicago: University of Chicago Press.

Emmott, M. (2005) *What Is Employee Relations? Change Agenda.* London: Chartered Institute of Personnel and Development.

Franke, R. H. and Kaul, J. D. (1978) 'The Hawthorne Experiments: First Statistical Interpretation', *American Sociological Review,* 43, pp. 623–643.

Fuller, S. (2005) *The Intellectual.* Cambridge: Icon Books.

Guest, D. E. and Conway, N. (2001) *Public and Private Sector Perspectives on the Psychological Contract.* Results of CIPD Survey. London: CIPD.

Hammer, M. and Champy, J. (1993) *Reengineering the Corporation: A Manifesto for Business Revolution.* New York: Harper Collins.

Handy, C. B. (1997) *The Hungry Spirit.* London: Hutchinson.

Jones, O. (1997) 'Changing the Balance? Taylorism, TQM and Work Organisation', *New Technology Work and Employment,* 12(1), pp. 13–24.

Jones, O., Conway, S. and Steward, F. (eds) (2001) *Social Interaction and Organisational Change: Aston Perspectives on Innovation Networks*. London: Imperial College Press.

Kotter, J. P. (1990) *A Force for Change: How Leadership Differs from Management*. London: Collier Macmillan.

Legge, K. (1993) *The Role of Personnel Specialist: Centrality or Marginalisation*. In: Clark (ed.), *Human Resource Management and Technical Change*. London: Sage.

Mabey, C. and Finch-Lees, T. (2008) *Management and Leadership Development*. London: Sage.

Mayo, E. (1933) *The Human Problems of an Industrial Civilisation*. New York: Macmillan.

Mayo, E. (1945) *The Social Problems of an Industrial Civilisation*. Cambridge: Harvard University Press.

Morgan, G. (1993) *Imaginization: The Art of Creative Management*. London: Sage.

Morgan, H. and Jardin, D. (2010) 'Integrated Talent Management', OD Practitioner: *Journal of the Organization. Development Network*, 42(4), pp. 23–29.

Moss Kanter, R. (1990) *The Change Masters: Corporate Entrepreneurs at Work*. London: Unwin.

Nieto, M. L. (2006) *An Introduction to Human Resource Management: An Integrated Approach*. Basingstoke: Palgrave Macmillan.

O'Neill, O. (2002) *Is Trust Failing?* Reith Lecture. *BBC Radio 4*. 17 April.

Paauwe, J. (2009) 'HRM and Performance: Achievements, Methodological Issues and Prospects', *Journal of Managerial Studies*, 46(1), pp. 129–142.

Pascale, R. T. (1990) *Managing on the Edge: How Successful Companies Use Conflict to Stay Ahead*. London: Viking.

Peters T. (1994) *The Tom Peters Seminar: Crazy Times Calls for Crazy Organizations*. London: Macmillan.

Pickard, J. (2003) 100 Years of Ford, *People Management*, November, CIPD.

Pilenzo, R. C. (2009) 'A New Paradigm for HR', *Organizational Development Journal*, 27(3), pp. 63–75.

Roberts, Z. (2003) Culture Key to Global HRM, *People Management*, December, CIPD.

Saunders, B. and Nieto M. L. (Ed Al Ariss, A.) (2014) *Global Talent Management – Challenges, Strategies, and Opportunities*. Université de Toulouse, Basel: Springer– Series Management for Professionals.

Semler, R. (1994) *Maverick! The Success Story Behind the Worlds Most Unusual Workplace*. London: Arrow.

Senge, P. M., Roberts, C., Ross, R. B., Smith, B. J. and Kleiner, A. (1994) *The Fifth Discipline Fieldbook Strategies and Tools for Building a Learning Organization*. London: Nicolas Brearley.

Sisson, K. (1993) 'In search of HRM', *British Journal of Industrial Relations*, 31(2), pp. 201–210.

Sonnenfeld, J. A. (1985) 'Shedding Light on the Hawthorne Studies', *Journal of Occupational Behaviour*, April, 6(2).

Taylor, F. W. (1947) *Scientific Management*. New York: Harper & Brothers.

Ulrich, D. (2011) 'Personnel: An Anniversary Reflection', *Human Resource Management*, January/February, 50(1), pp. 3–7.

Van Eynde, D. F. and Burr, R. M. (2011) 'Human Resource Knowledge and Skills Needed by Non-HR Managers: Recommendations From Leading Senior HR Executives', *Organization Development Journal*, Winter, 29(4), pp. 67–80.

Wilson, J. M. (1995) 'Henry Ford: A Just in Time Pioneer', *Production and Inventory Management Journal*, 37(2), pp. 26–31.

Woolever, N. A., Cohen, D., Benedict, A., Williams, S., Schaefer, B. and Bergman, S. (2010) SHRM Human Resource Curriculum: An Integrated Approach to HR Education. *SPHRS Society for Human Resource Management*. Society for Human Resource Management. Alexandria, VA.

2

HRM and Organizational Structures

INTRODUCTION

Contemporary people management needs to be adaptive. When I was leading the Executive MBA at Bournemouth University, part of the management programme was called the 'Adaptive Manager', and with good reason. For many mid-career managers the purpose of joining the programme was to build their general employability, possibly for a senior management role in a different sector or industry. Therefore, learning how to adapt to working within different organizational structures is a valuable part of becoming a flexible and adaptable person who can secure employment.

Developing the ability to adapt and thereby work with managers who have differing personalities and management styles can be a challenge to our sense of security. The behaviours which may be rewarded by one manage, may be of lesser value to another. Accordingly, this chapter explores how to respond to different and often fast-moving organizational environments. In reading this chapter you will begin to develop the knowledge and skills to identity how organizational structure influences the way people behave in different organizational contexts and thereby reflect upon how you can adapt in different situations.

LEARNING OBJECTIVES

The key learning outcomes for the chapter are below:

• Identify organizational structures and the influence structure has on how organizations function.

- The Matrix model of structure. Advantages and disadvantages.
- Departmental model of structure with international, national and regional variants. Implications for HRM.
- Evaluate how and why HR is adapting to meet the needs of modern organizational management structures.
- Analysing organizational context and environment with the REACT model.

IDENTIFY ORGANIZATIONAL STRUCTURES AND THE INFLUENCE THEY HAVE ON HR

In Chapter 1, the twentieth-century paradigms of HR and large personnel departments were discussed within the context of larger organizations. Although many of the human relations practices established in the twentieth century are still relevant today, there is also a need for HR professionals to serve modern organizations with new strategies that are appropriate to the present workplace environment. HR in the twenty-first century has continued to become an increasingly integrated discipline (Nieto 2006; Morgan and Jardin 2010). It encompasses elements of the former personnel, organizational development.

There has been paradigm shift in HRM philosophy, away from employee relations, with its tendency to paternalism, towards employee partnership (Nieto 2003). This has meant that the trend is for the former large bureaucratic personnel management departments to evolve into smaller teams of HR partners, providing strategically focused recommendations to their organizations' departmental managers. Accordingly, Hall (2000) observed that by being released from some of the administrative

Key Point: By the twenty-first century the integrated approach to managing staff had replaced many of the former HR department activities such as training, development, recruitment, induction, and appraisals.

responsibilities, HR people can invest their time working with other departments. According to research involving 1,188 professionals, reported by Higginbottom (2003), the majority of respondents reported that their chief executives are recognizing HR as the key to achieving their organizations' aims and objectives. There had also been a movement by the late twentieth and early twenty-first century towards locally constructed HR initiatives (Das and Sen 1991; Farnham and Horton 1996; Farnham 1997; Nieto 2006).

According to Tiller (2012), how an organizational structure is designed can have a significant influence on the success of organizations within the context of the competitive business environment. Furthermore, organizational structure can enhance or inhibit the internal communications which enable people to respond appropriately to what can often be a fast-moving external environment.

> **Key Point:** An organizational structure, which encourages the flow of information, is more likely to produce creative inputs and thereby be responsive to changing circumstances. This can also help an organization to become more adaptable within a changing environment. Conversely, if the management approach discourages access to senior colleagues, then it could dampen the free flow of new ideas and creativity.

So, to in order to evaluate what management initiatives are practical, the first step is to recognize how the organizational structure is influencing working relationships. According to the research by Berends et al. (2003), organizational learning involves the distribution of social practices, so that implies an organizational structure and approach where information is accessible. Hence, successful communications depend upon the exchange of ideas throughout the organization.

THE MATRIX MODEL OF STRUCTURE: ADVANTAGES AND DISADVANTAGES

The matrix structure uses multidisciplinary teams instead of the linear and departmentally organized functional model (see Figures 2.1, 2.2). A matrix

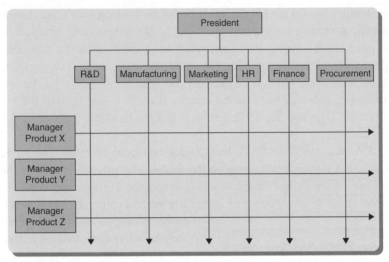

Figure 2.1 A matrix model

structure is usually organized, but not always, around project teams. The team members can be drawn into a project because of their functional specialist knowledge. So, it is possible for a person to be in several project teams at the same time. For example, within a university setting, an HR lecturer could be a member of teams developing a new: MBA; MA International Business; MA HRM; and a BA undergraduate programme. It is therefore possible for conflicts to arise when several project teams are competing for a member's time.

The positive benefits of a matrix are that the overlapping commitments which arise in a project-based structure can have synergetic advantages; learning is transferred from one team to another. However, the disadvantage is that the team members have multiple tasks competing for their attention at any one time. The differing demands of each project timescale may thereby produce conflicts of prioritization. Hence, which project should a person prioritize? Each project coordinator is likely to regard their work as the one which requires attention. It is for these reasons that people working within a matrix structure may feel unsure as how to structure their work. Hence, role conflicts may arise regarding what work should be progressed first.

In the matrix model, each person can be involved with several interdisciplinary projects simultaneously. Instead of the organization's expertise being concentrated in departments, it is redistributed into the project teams.

> **Key Point:** In the matrix model, each person can be involved with several interdisciplinary projects simultaneously. Instead of the organization's expertise being concentrated into departments, it is redistributed into the project teams.

While the matrix approach may be empowering for employees, it can also generate confusion for management and reporting. This is where disaffection may arise regarding competing project management priorities. Managers may also complain of having the responsibility to complete projects without the necessary authority to control the resources, as it is quite possible that people are involved in several projects simultaneously. Therefore, instead of a harmonious interaction, employees may experience several project leaders requesting their input and commitment. Hence, according to Kotter (2001: 89), leadership emanating from several directions can produce conflicts.

Unlike systems based on departments, the matrix structure offers the possibility of freer deployment and redeployment of people to whatever project requires their skills.

> **Key Point:** The matrix system requires higher levels of team-working awareness from all employees, which may highlight the need for some specific training in team-working skills. These require training and staff development.

This approach can require managers to trust that their teams are getting on with their assignments even when they are not monitoring their every action (Handy 1995). The antithesis of trust is arguably the imposition of strict compliance regulations (O'Neill 2002). The multiple project nature of a matrix also means that a person may be reporting to several project coordinators at the same time, instead of one department manager. To guide people in planning their work, it is possible to give the prioritizing decisions to each functional department manager, who can then liaise with the various project coordinators. The question then arises as to whom the project coordinators should report to. Are they at a similar or subordinate level to the departmental managers? If the project coordinators are at a similar level to the departmental managers, then who has ultimate responsibility for the allocation of staff to the various projects? In practice, the departmental managers would have to make the choice about where the specialist team members are deployed and for how long on each project.

DEPARTMENTAL MODEL OF STRUCTURE WITH INTERNATIONAL, NATIONAL AND REGIONAL VARIANTS: IMPLICATIONS FOR HRM

The functional structure is one of the most common forms of organizational formations. It is designed to provide departments of specialist knowledge which interact with each other (Figure 2.2). The formal lines of management control from CEO to other employees are clearly specified. In multidivisional organizations the functional structure often includes directors for each area of operation.

Product, market sector, or regions can be the basis of how an organization is structured. (In Figures 2.2 and 2.3 the HR function may be based in either the corporate headquarters or the divisions of the organization or both.) If no central HR presence exists in the head office, then it would be for the divisions to produce a coordinated approach by sharing information and good practices.

According to Peters (1994), smaller numbers of staff in each division (in larger organizations) can encourage adaptability. For example, departments of 50 or 60 people facilitate a pool of talent from which to build project teams. The teams can be formed and reformed according to requirements from within the department. This provides the opportunity to offer a range of interesting assignments and varied portfolios of work to staff.

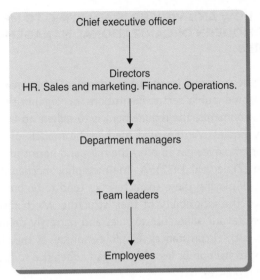

Figure 2.2 Functional structure

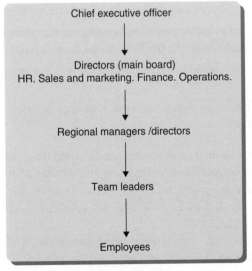

Figure 2.3 Functional structure (regional model)

EVALUATE HOW AND WHY HR IS ADAPTING TO MEET THE NEEDS OF MODERN ORGANIZATIONAL MANAGEMENT STRUCTURES

A personnel department traditionally served a functional system. For example, in some public-sector institutions or organizations in highly regulated environments, the requirement is to adhere to the stipulations of regulatory bodies. Within rigid mechanistic models of organization, the worker or employee has to obey the rules and norms of the organizational system (Zijderveld 1972). As the metaphor mechanistic describes, organizations displaying these characteristics tend to be bureaucratic and constrained by the inflexibility of their structure. Mechanistic organizations therefore favour adherence to rules and narrowly defined job roles and tasks. In such circumstances, employee initiatives may be more difficult to bring to fruition or less valued than adherence to predetermined procedures and policies.

The twentieth-century German sociologist Max Weber (Eisenstadt 1968) believed that bureaucracies were characterized by the following factors:

1. Control – employees are required to perform standardized tasks.
2. Hierarchy – the managerial structure ensures compliance and subordinate accountability to the strictures of the bureaucracy.
3. Rules – strictly defined policies/procedures and documentary reporting systems.
4. Equity – employee rights and responsibilities are clearly defined for each situation.

Weber recognized that in long-term stable conditions, employees were more likely to be compliant in accepting the dictates of the bureaucracy in return for employment security (Eisenstadt 1968: 69). Hence these organizations tended to be inflexible, but predictable and secure work environments (Blau 1955).

Organizations may also have a structure which combines elements of different approaches such as a combination of both a functional and matrix structure. In a study using a sample of 82 German multinational

> **Key Point:** The bureaucratic structures were a significant part of the organizational environment until the later part of the twentieth century when the increasing rate of change in the work environment placed inflexible bureaucracies at a disadvantage to their more responsive competitors.

companies, Joachim and Egelhoff (2012) observed that organizations which had a matrix structure and functional divisions (departments) tended to experience similar levels of organizational conflict as those organizations without a matrix structure. This may indicate that an organization's structure is less significant in how it functions than the interpersonal interactions and emotional climate of the staff. In other words, if the senior management team can work towards an HR approach which builds the sense of security, commitment and well-being, then the organization is more likely to function well. Conversely, by restructuring an organization, albeit with good intentions, the actual outcome might be to disturb and undermine the staff's sense of security, commitment and well-being, and thereby bring about the unintended consequence of reducing organizational performance.

The extent to which a structure can encourage or inhibit an organization's strategic plans are dependent upon the motivations and commitment of the staff. The area of staff motivation and team working is discussed in other chapters. It is worthwhile noting here that within the context of employee commitment, motivation and the social cohesiveness of the staff, a particular organizational structure is probably of lesser importance than the enhancement of those aforementioned employee attitudes (Argyris 1990; Nieto 2006). Hence, a new organizational structure is unlikely to resolve underlying human resources issues which are inherently about organizational human relations. Conversely, the uncertainty and disturbance of a new organizational structure could disturb trust, employee commitment, motivation and social cohesiveness to the detriment of organizational performance.

The history of enterprise has numerous examples of poor strategic decisions which had more to do with the strategic direction than the structure of staff reporting and management. For example, the record company that saw no future in signing a new pop band called the Beatles in the 1960s; the UK car company which ceased the manufacture of affordable sports cars in the 1980s because it could see no market for them; or the mobile phone company which saw its competitors take their market with innovative new products in the 2000s. In a global marketplace supported by easy access communications, consumers can be reached by a much larger range of alternative goods and service providers. Hence, responding quickly to the market has become the new norm, whether you work for a car company, a mobile phone producer, or a charity (Den Hartog and Verburg 2004). The responsiveness is dependent upon the proactive engagement and enthusiasm of the people who are in the organization. This consequently places HR front and centre in developing people and encouraging a climate of innovation and engaged organizational citizenship. This kind of organizational climate has promoted a more integrated approach to HR which combines with organizational development (Ruona and Gibson 2004).

Although the arrows in figure 2.4 denote progressions, the reality of people and management is that all of these models may exist, even coexist in organizations. There have been changes and potential conflicts during the last three centuries of industrial development (Touraine 1974; Watson 1994). The contemporary integrated HR approach fully involves HR in the organizational strategic decisions (Nieto 2006; Morgan and Jardin 2010).

Figure 2.4 Progression of HR into the twenty-first century

ANALYSING ORGANIZATIONAL CONTEXT AND ENVIRONMENT WITH THE REACT MODEL

Key Point: In the REACT model below is a plan to begin studying an organization within its environmental context. This model can also be used to begin a team research activity in an organization's HR activities. This model can be used to evaluate a case-studied organization.

Research: *By conducting an HR audit of the organization, to establish the current position and where HR investment is most likely to yield the most productivity benefits.*

Evaluate: *The results from the audit and consider: what most needs doing; when and where investment would be best applied; how the HR initiatives should be delivered; who would benefit most from immediate assistance.*

Action: *People expect to see concrete actions and new initiatives in response to the research and evaluation. Are there any areas where action is required to get new initiatives implemented? Consider whether the initiatives can be delivered internally, or if a business school or consultant may be more able to help produce the outcomes required.*

Control: *Does the organization monitor progress and adapt the new HR initiatives as and where necessary? Even the best-laid plans need fine-tuning. Is the management prepared to respond flexibly to people's needs?*

Time: *Managers should have realistic time-bound objectives so that colleagues can be kept informed of progress. Staff morale can be boosted by recognition, so look for indications of morale. People involved in new initiatives should be praised for improvements and successes throughout the process, not just at the end.*

SUMMARY OF HRM AND ORGANIZATIONAL STRUCTURES

(a) HR in the twenty-first century has continued to become an increasingly integrated discipline.

(b) There has been a paradigm shift in HRM philosophy, away from employee relations, with its tendency to paternalism, towards employee partnership.

(c) An organizational structure which encourages the flow of information is more likely to produce creative inputs and thereby be responsive to changing circumstances. This can also help an organization to become more adaptable within a changing environment.

(d) The matrix approach may be empowering for employees, but it can also cause difficulties for leadership and priorities.

(e) A project-led matrix requires managers to trust that their teams are getting on with their assignments.

(f) 'Mechanistic' describes organizational characteristics tending to be constrained by the inflexibility of their structure. Mechanistic organizations therefore favour adherence to rules and narrowly defined job roles and tasks.

(g) Uncertainty and disturbances created by a new organizational structure can disturb employee trust, commitment, motivation and social cohesiveness to the detriment of organizational performance.

(h) An integrated approach to HR combines human resources with organizational development.

(i) The REACT model is a plan for studying an organization within its environmental context.

REVISION SECTION

1. Explain how a matrix structure is organized. What are the advantages and disadvantages of this system?

2. Evaluate why trust between managers and staff can benefit workplace performance and morale?

3. Apply the REACT model to an organization you have selected for study.

TAKING IT FURTHER

Key texts to look up:

Handy, C. B. (1995) Trust and the Virtual Organization. *Harvard Business Review*. May–June.

Joachim, W. and Egelhoff, W. G. (2012) Network or matrix? How information-processing theory can help MNCs answer this question. Collaborative Communities of Firms. *Information and Organizational Design Series*. (9) pp. 35–57.

Morgan, H. and Jardin, D. (2010) Integrated Talent Management. OD Practitioner: *Journal of the Organization Development Network*. 42(4), pp. 23–29.

Refer to the books and journals in this references section.

REFERENCES

Refer to the books and journals in this references section. Each one can take you to new sources and information.

Argyris, C. (1990) *Integrating the Individual and the Organization*. London: Transaction.

Berends, H., Boersma, K. and Weggeman, M. (2003) The Structuration of Organizational Learning. *Human Relations*. September, 56(9), pp. 1035–1056, Sage Publications.

Blau, P. M. (1955) *The Dynamics of Bureaucracy*. Chicago: University of Chicago Press.

Das, J. P. and Sen, J. (1991) *Planning Competence and Managerial Excellence. Paper presented to the International Association of Cross Cultural Psychology*. 4–7 July: Debrecan, Hungary.

Den Hartog, D. N. and Verburg, R. M. (2004) High Performance Work Systems, Organisational Culture and Firm Effectiveness. *Human Resource Management Journal*. 1 January, 14(1), pp. 55–78.

Eisenstadt, S. N. (ed.) (1968) *Weber on Charisma & Institution Building*. Chicago: University of Chicago Press.

Farnham, D. (ed.) (1997) *Employment Flexibilities in Western European Public Services: An International Symposium*. Review of Public Personnel Administration. Volume xvii, number 3, Columbia (USA), University of Southern Carolina.

Farnham, D. and Horton, S. (eds) (1996) *Managing the New Public Services*. London: Macmillan.

Hall, P. (2000) Feel the Width. *People Management*, 6 January. www.cipd.co.uk/pm/peoplemanagement/b/weblog/archive/2013/01/29/2733a-2000-01.aspx.

Handy, C. B. (1995) Trust and the Virtual Organization. *Harvard Business Review*. May–June.

Higginbottom, K. (2003) *HR Influence on the Increase*. People Management. 23 October. www.cipd.co.uk/pm/peoplemanagement/b/weblog/archive/2013/01/29/9549a-2003-10.aspx.

Joachim, W. and Egelhoff, W. G. (2012) Network or matrix? How information-processing theory can help MNCs answer this question. Collaborative Communities of Firms. *Information and Organizational Design Series*. (9), pp. 35–57.

Kotter, J. P. (2001) What Leaders Really Do. *Harvard Business Review*. 79(11), pp. 85–98.

Morgan, H. and Jardin, D. (2010) Integrated Talent Management. OD Practitioner: *Journal of the Organization Development Network*. 42(4), pp. 23–29.

Nieto, M. L. (2003) The Development of Life Work Balance Initiatives Designed for Managerial Workers. *Business Ethics: A European Review*. 12(3), pp. 213–215.

Nieto, M. L. (2006) *An Introduction to Human Resource Management: An Integrated Approach*. Basingstoke: Palgrave Macmillan.

O'Neill, O. (2002) *Is Trust Failing?* Reith Lecture. BBC Radio 4. 17th April.

Peters, T. J. (1994) *The Tom Peters Seminar: Crazy Times Calls for Crazy Organizations*. London: Macmillan.

Ruona, W. E. A. and Gibson S. K. (2004) The Making of Twenty-first-century HR: An Analysis of the Convergence of HRM, HRD, and OD. *Human Resource Management*. 43(1), pp. 49–66.

Tiller, S. R. (2012) Organizational Structure and Management Systems. *Leadership and Management in Engineering*. January, 12(1), pp. 20–23.

Touraine, A. (1974) *The Post-Industrial Society. Tomorrow's Social History: Classes, Conflicts and Culture in the Programmed Society*. London: Wildwood House.

Watson, T. J. (1994) *In Search of Management: Culture, Chaos and Control in Managerial Work*. London: Routledge.

Zijderveld, A. C. (1972) *The Abstract Society. A Cultural Analysis of Our Time*. London: Penguin Books.

3

Recruitment, Selection, Job Analysis and Employment Law

INTRODUCTION

Anyone who aspires to move into a managerial role will benefit from improving his or her understanding of recruitment and selection. In reality, any management role can benefit from being more effective in recruitment and selection. This chapter provides a practical guide in which you will learn how to be a more effective interviewer or interviewee.

Although managers are not expected to be legal experts, it is relevant to have a background understanding of the legal matters relating to employment. So this chapter includes an interesting contemporary review of legal issues relating to employment by Danielle Wootton LLB (Hons) Law, who also teaches at Birmingham, Exeter and Southampton Universities.

By studying this chapter you will learn about how to conduct a recruitment and selection campaign. The chapter also contains activities to develop your recruitment and selection skills set.

LEARNING OBJECTIVES

The key learning outcomes for the chapter are below:

- The aims of recruitment and the changing role of HRM.
- Recruitment and selection – the legal context.

- Equality Act 2010.
- Police Act 1997.
- The Asylum and Immigration Act 1996.
- The Data Protection Act 1998.
- The contract of employment.
- Evaluating recruitment and selection methodologies.
- Job analysis and design.
- Activity: the recruitment assignment
- New graduate CV.
- Halo and horns effects in the selection process.

THE AIMS OF RECRUITMENT AND THE ROLE OF HRM

The aim of a recruitment and selection process is to match the most suitable person to the chosen job description. However, without some background knowledge and training, the selection process might be less than successful or possibly fail to meet legal requirements.

Key Point: The ability to comprehend recruitment and selection also improves your knowledge and skills in applying for and successfully obtaining a new job. It is for these reasons that recruitment and selection is often offered on both undergraduate and postgraduate-level courses. Because it is so fundamental to management, anyone can visit or revisit this area throughout their working career.

Any experienced manager who has hired the 'wrong' person will confirm how inconvenient and costly poor recruitment performance can be. It is equally possible that good candidates can be missed; people who could have added value to an organization, simply because they were filtered out by inappropriate selection schemes which might have placed an unnecessary premium on one aspect of the job role such as a particular qualification (Nieto 2001).

The purpose of this chapter is therefore to address the area of recruitment and selection in a manner which is both theoretical and practical. The overall method I have advocated is an integrated approach, which by its nature is a flexible system offering the opportunity to design organization and situation-specific recruitment and selection solutions (Nieto 2006).

Modern functional managers (managers with responsibility for a section/team of staff) have become more directly responsible for HR activities. Consequently, the role of the traditional HR/personnel departments has been evolving from one which traditionally focused on operational implementation to a more consultative function.

> **Key Point:** In researching this book I have studied organizations including international businesses and SMEs. In meeting and interviewing managers during the last decade, there appears to have been a movement towards using more external service providers and employing specialist internal HR teams.

For many years it has been recognized that HR initiatives can influence staff performance, productivity and financial performance (Huselid 1995; Fried et al. 2003; Paauwe 2009). Hence, recruitment and selection ensures that the most importance resource, people, is available to meet the organization's workload. The strategic planning of HR should be about reaching the correct staffing levels. This means that there should be sufficient people to maintain a responsive organization which can cope with new opportunities.

RECRUITMENT AND SELECTION – THE LEGAL CONTEXT

The employment environment, both local and international, is regulated by stringent legal requirements. Employment legislation is in constant change, so even well-informed HR persons and managers are not in a position to safely advise their organization upon every legal matter relating to employment.

If a situation arises where the management team requires specific legal advice they should seek professional legal advice. It would be prudent to invite an independent legal advisor to validate recruitment policies and procedures. In the first decades of the twenty-first century there has been a transfer of HR responsibilities from the HR department to line managers. The role of HR has become more facilitative and that includes providing guidance and training on legal matters relating to employment.

For general information visit:

In Direct
Gov.www.direct.gov.uk/en/Employment/index.htm

Advice Now
www.advicenow.org.uk/

Take Legal Advice
www.takelegaladvice.com

The following section on employment law was provided by Danielle Wootton LLB (Hons), MA, PGCE, MCIPD. Danielle works as a consultant and also as a lecturer at the Universities of Exeter, Birmingham, Southampton and Warwick. Her portfolio includes courses and consultancy in how to conduct successful disciplinary procedures, employment law updates, ethical conduct for businesses and strategic legal issues for HR managers.

The status of employment regulation has gained prominence in the last 30 years due to successive governments' legal interventions in the form of Employment Acts, with their curbs on trade-union practices. The regulative employment environment is a constant force of change on organizational perspectives, affecting the employer's right to manage and also the employee's expectations of their own employment legal rights. The employment legal climate has influenced organizations' operational and strategic thinking by demanding that practices and systems assist legal compliance.

This results in making the management of any legal situation particularly daunting for an inexperienced, non-legal, professional manager, as well as being demanding for human resource practitioners and managers keeping up to date with the relevant legal employment knowledge. Most managers have little option but to engage with employment regulation, which manifests through good-practice 'legal' guidance generated by the HR function.

Employment regulation is constantly changing not only due to UK and European government interventions but also from binding judgements that stem from the judicial system known as 'case (judge) made law'. This type of law originates from the courts and employment tribunal system where the Judiciary makes binding precedents in the higher-level courts that become law and legal practice. The legal mechanics of workplace regulation are driven in part by contractual (contract of employment or other forms of contract) or statute law (act of Parliament). There is now a consensus that employment relations in the UK are dominated by employment regulation through the work of the HR function.

There is no specific law relating to recruitment and selection practices in the workplace, making it daunting for HR practitioners, students and legal professionals alike to source employment regulation. Yet, at the very least, managers need to understand the legal consequences for ill-advised or hastily made decisions, and to prevent potential employment litigation or unwelcome publicity by adopting good management practices. The recruitment and selection process is always at the beginning of the employment journey. For both parties it is of paramount importance that the employment relationship starts off with the right contractual and psychological foundation. However, following the correct legal procedures cannot prevent employees feeling aggrieved, consulting legal professionals or the trade union.

Recruitment and selection is complex as the law relating to it is not defined within one legal code, meaning that knowledge of the process and any subsequent legal implications is not always fully understood. When in doubt, it is prudent for managers to seek legal advice from HR management with reference to the individual circumstances of a case.

In areas such as discrimination, it often helps to operate a checklist of activities to assist good legal practice since no employer or employee is exempt from anti-discrimination legislation, now amalgamated into the Single Equality Act (2010). It is against the law to discriminate against anyone because of known characteristics such as sex, age, religion and disability. There are other checks that employers have to undertake stemming from statutory requirements regardless of what employment sector the organization operates in or the number of employees who work in it.

The acts outlined below are not an exhaustive list, just representative examples of statutory interventions affecting management's policies and practices during the recruitment process.

Equality Act 2010 – cited from The ACAS Recruitment and Induction Booklet – October 2010

The Equality Act 2010 (covering disability, sex, race, gender reassignment, marriage and civil partnership, pregnancy and maternity, sexual orientation, religion or belief and age) sets out the legal requirements for employers. Organizations should be aware that the provisions of the Equality Act 2010 not only make it unlawful to discriminate against disabled individuals without justifiable reason but also require employers to make reasonable adjustments to the workplace or working arrangements.

Police Act 1997 – cited from www.ind.homeoffice.gov.uk

The Police Act provides a statutory basis for certain criminal record checks which may be used by employers. These checks can be made via the Criminal Records Bureau, which came into being in 2001. Three types of certificate are available. They are intended to provide information on applicants for jobs which are exceptions to the Rehabilitation of Offenders Act 1974 (for instance, those occupations including working with children or vulnerable adults, and work in medicine, the courts and other sensitive areas). In most cases employers in these areas are required to register with the Criminal Records Agency and to follow a code of practice.

The Asylum and Immigration Act 1996 – cited from www.ind.homeoffice.gov.uk

Under the Asylum and Immigration Act 1996 it is a criminal offence for an employer to employ those who do not have permission to live or to work in the United Kingdom. This applies only in relation to employees who started work for the employer on or after 27 January 1997. For further information visit the Home Office website at www.ind.homeoffice.gov.uk.

The Data Protection Act 1998 – cited from www.acas.org

The Data Protection Act 1998 (and subsequent Codes of Practice on recruitment and selection, employment records, monitoring at work and information on workers' health) need to be noted – if any recruitment records are to be held on computer or in a manual system, the applicant should be advised of this and for what purposes and duration the information is to be held.

THE CONTRACT OF EMPLOYMENT

The Contract of Employment is a legally binding agreement between an employer and employee. It is created when an employee agrees to work for an organization for pay, and can be made up of oral and written agreements (www.acas.org.uk). Originally enacted through the Contract of Employment Act 1963, it is now defined in the Employment Rights Act 1996. It cannot be stressed too much how legally important it is to provide a contract of employment as it governs the terms and obligations strictly related to the position. Depending on the contract given, it opens up flexibility options for the organization, which has led in recent years to the increase in temporary, work, casual, agency work and self-employed work. Organizations need to think about their future staff in terms of whether they have the legitimacy to fire if the work is no longer available and the amount of notice an employee/employer is legitimately expected to give. If the contract is not correctly drafted it can lead to future problems, especially if employers want to terminate the employment of staff.

The type of employment contract or the status of the potential worker has to be established but employers are not restricted in the type of contracts that they issue to the workforce. For instance, the organization or business may only want a temporary worker to cover three months during the busy summer period. In this case the organization will want a contract that can be legally terminated at the end of three months. There are numerous types of contracts as the 'freedom of contract' allows differing levels of duration and status, and gives different levels of legal protection to the worker. There are different regulations that deal with all types of employees, workers or self-employed contracts that can be accessed from the Department of Business, Innovation and Skills

The latter's website is very useful and well worth investigation. They recommend five steps to take when an employer – regardless of sector – takes on a new employee or worker:

- *Decide how much you need to pay someone: you must pay your employee at least the National Minimum Wage (NMW).*
- *Check if someone can legally work for you: you need to check if they have the legal right to work in the UK. You may have to do other employment checks as well.*
- *Get employment insurance: you need employers' liability insurance as soon as you become an employer. It must cover you for at least £5 million and come from an 'authorized insurer' – you can find one online.*
- *Register with HM Revenue & Customs (HMRC) and pay your employee: you need to register as an employer, make any deductions (i.e. PAYE and National Insurance contributions) and give a pay statement to your employee.*
- *Send details of the job (including terms and conditions) in writing to your employee: if you're employing someone for more than a month, you need to give them a written statement of employment within their first 2 months.*

There are some good-practice guidelines that HR management can operate to ensure they provide the right policies and practices to protect the interests of the organization.

- Make sure managers understand the law relating to recruitment and selection.
- Give advice on how to handle recruitment issues effectively, in ways that are not only within the law but also comply with best-practice guidelines.
- Ensure the interviewers understand how law relating to recruitment and selection must be adhered to in the interview and the selection process.

EVALUATING RECRUITMENT AND SELECTION METHODOLOGIES

The recruitment and selection methodology is influenced by the organization's management style and culture (Judge and Cable 1997). For example, an entrepreneurial organization which is seeking rapid expansion may favour a positive, independent personality.

The HR specialist should therefore investigate what is required and then select the most appropriate method/s of recruitment.

By selecting a combination of tools for the particular recruitment assignment, the opportunities for a successful recruitment are likely to improve. To begin with, it is helpful to identify the nature of the vacancy.

Listed below are a set of questions a manager can use.

1. In which area does the vacancy exist?
2. How many more people are required to meet current and planned levels of organizational activity?
3. Is the vacancy a new position/a replacement for someone who has been promoted/temporary cover/full-time/replacement for someone who has moved to another organization?
4. Has a job description/specification been prepared? Is it up-to-date with current requirements? This should include a review of the job requirements and responsibilities.
5. What are the essential and desirable attributes, experience and skills?
6. How are applicants to be found? Advertising internally/externally?
7. Would it be helpful to include external expertise, such as a specialist recruitment consultancy?
8. Does the organization have access to legal advice on recruitment and selection?
9. What is the timescale for the search and selection process?

The following are guidelines on preparing a recruitment plan:

Publishing the vacancy internally: The job should be published internally so those existing employees/workers have an opportunity to apply. Sometimes the most suitable person is already in the organization. S/he may be full-time, part-time, or working as a consultant.

Publishing the vacancy externally: It is important to form a general impression of the kinds of people who could be interested in the vacancy. Select media that the target groups are likely to use and that fit into the agreed budget of expenditure for the particular vacancy. This can include national and local newspapers, the organization's web pages, radio/television, trade and professional journals. It is important to investigate which specific advertising media is most relevant to the vacancy.

Headhunting: As the term implies, specific person/s are sought out and approached. Care should be taken to ensure that other interested persons are not disadvantaged. Professional legal advice should be sought on issues pertaining to equal opportunities.

External consultancy: It may be appropriate and more cost and time-effective to brief a specialist recruitment consultancy to search and select candidates for the final shortlist. There are both general recruitment consultancies and ones that specialize in specific areas such as law, sales and marketing, finance, HR, computing, and engineering.

The curriculum vitae (usually referred to as a CV): The CV offers applicants the opportunity to express their attitudes, knowledge and skills in their own way. This shows the prospective employer how well (or not) the applicant presents themself on paper and explains how their unique set of abilities relates to the advertised vacancy. Overall, the CV is a well-tried and commonly accepted method, which is used in conjunction with other selection tools. However, for unskilled jobs, the CV may be unnecessary and even act as a barrier to entry. If literacy and written communications are not key vacancy criteria then the CV may not be appropriate to the selection method.

Application forms: The alternative to a CV is the application form. If very large numbers of applicants are anticipated then an application form may be a way of managing the HR workload. The application form also has the potential to provide more standardized data in that it dictates what specific information is to be included.

Online application forms: Similar to application forms and using the internet as the means of communication.

Telephone interviews: This method is particularly useful for vetting applicants for job roles, which entail high levels of telephone contact such as some types of market research, customer services and call centre roles. This method enables the recruiter to conduct a lot of interviews in a short space of time.

Work-based tests: It is useful to see if a person can complete a work-like simulation. However, it can also be a time-consuming method and one that is not practical in all situations. Some job roles, such as management, can be difficult to evaluate in a test situation.

Psychometric testing: This method can be a used as a supplement to other selection methodologies. Each candidate is tested and their performance compared to selected norms. The extent to which a test is valid and reliable is dependent on the quality of the test design and the skills of the person who interprets the results. The use of tests can be a useful supplement to other methodologies; however, organizations should not be tempted to become overly reliant upon tests. Some managers may seek to justify selection decisions by the test results, or become predisposed towards candidates who perform well in the tests. According to Maund (2001: 153), there has been a tendency among some organizations and commentators to seek a pseudo-scientific veneer for recruitment and selection.

Team-working skills evaluation: The interaction of humans and their ability to cooperate towards mutually agreed goals requires many interactive team-working skills (Belbin 1993, 2000). The recruiters may consider such tests as one element of a process of selection.

The assessment centre: This approach utilizes a range of selection tools. In addition to any or all of the previously mentioned methods, role-playing, team exercises and social-interaction observations may be included. The advantage of the assessment centre is that by employing a fuller range of methods over a longer period of time, from a day to a weekend and sometimes longer, a broader picture can emerge of each participating applicant. It should however be noted the applicants are still doing exercises in an artificial environment. For example, in team exercises the essential element of good teamwork, mutual cooperation, could be eroded where members know that in reality they are not a team at all but a group of individuals competing for a job! Candidates can have varying reactions to their experiences of assessment centres (Fletcher 1991). The assessment centre can be a useful tool, although it is clearly likely to be relatively expensive and time-consuming.

References: The reference is one of the most commonly used documents in selection. During the time I have worked as a manager, recruitment consultant and lecturer, I have rarely seen a really bad reference. Although most organizations use this selection method, many managers would admit that since the applicant selects the referees they are hardly likely to use someone who dislikes them. Conversely, a less than scrupulous manager might be tempted to give a supportive reference to a mediocre employee they want to get rid of, or a cooler one to an indispensable member of their staff. Furthermore, within British law, both the applicant and the prospective employer may have legal redress against a referee if they can prove that the document was materially untrue. In all cases, remember that the reference is a subjective assessment of past performance in a different situation. The more time that has elapsed between the events that shaped the reference and the present day, the less useful it is as a selection indicator. For example, character references are more useful from someone who is more familiar with a person's recent behaviour and abilities than what that person was like a few years earlier. People change over time, as may the referee's memories of events.

It is important to select the correct media to reach potential applicants. Consider where people seeking work in the selected area usually search.

The selection methodology employed should be tailored to the vacancy. The more highly valued the role, the more it is worth investing time and resources. Select in haste and repent at leisure. It is much easier to employ someone than to dismiss them later. Consider the fitness for purpose of the selected methodology. Practical issues such as the time available to recruit staff and cost also need to be taken into consideration. In the majority of situations, a combination of methods such as a CV, interview and references would suffice. However, more tools may be deemed appropriate in particular organizational situations.

The weight given to a particular element of the selection process also requires consideration. Although the past is relevant, the assumption that it can accurately predict future potential can be problematic. For example, Winston Churchill's school record was poor and would hardly recommend him as a world leader. The entrepreneur and chairman of Virgin, Richard Branson, did not go to university, but that clearly did not prevent him becoming a successful businessman.

JOB ANALYSIS AND DESIGN

In modern organizations, working practices are less static than they were in the past. The famous business consultant and ICI's former chairman Sir John Harvey-Jones (1995: 81) has observed that in his experience the world of business never remains static. If this is the case, then job descriptions also require regular updating because what people do in organizations needs to respond to the changing environment. By the late twentieth century, academics were recognizing that a flexible model of job design was more compatible with the faster rate of change in organizations. For example, McKenna and Beech (1995: 96; Nieto 2006) found that traditional job descriptions were being replaced by more flexible approaches. In the twenty-first century, the orientation of job descriptions has moved towards abilities and skills rather than lists of job responsibilities.

One model that offers a more flexible alternative to the traditional job analysis and design is AKS (Attitudes, Knowledge, Skills). This approach structures the analysis and job design upon the most recent job requirement and necessary personal attributes. So how does the theory work in practice? Below are descriptions of AKS stages.

Key Point: The AKS model is a tripartite system which enables managers to analyse a job for Attitudes, Knowledge and Skill. Each element of the AKS trio has a contribution to make in the selection of the most appropriate person to complete the tasks required by the job role. The weightings attributed to each element of AKS depend upon the job analysis. Avoid qualification inflation (see paragraph below).

The AKS model is a tripartite system which enables managers to analyse job descriptions and translate them into a person specification. During the last decade there has been a tendency to increase the qualification requirements, though mainly through the qualification expectations. This might be described as qualification inflation. Theoretical knowledge and qualifications have their place in the tripartite model of AKS. The value-adding benefit of this approach to job analysis and person specification is that the areas of attitudes and deliverable skills are also evaluated. Hence it delivers a selection process which reflects upon the kinds of attitudes, knowledge and skills relating to the job.

A person's attitude to a job can make all the difference as to whether they do really well or just adequately. However, the reason attitudes are sometimes left out of a recruitment plan may be that they are difficult to quantify. For example, I have found it interesting to ask students which attitudes they think a university lecturer should display. Although the content of observations varies from group to group and year to year, some

Figure 3.1 The AKS Model

items such as a sense of humour and willingness to listen have appeared regularly on their lists. These kinds of attitudes can translate into positive attitudes towards students and interpersonal relationships.

The easiest area of an applicant's attributes to assess is that of knowledge. Given that knowledge is often associated with former experiences and the acquisition of qualifications, it is a relatively simple task to ask applicants to provide evidence of their course grades and work experience. However a display of technical knowledge should not automatically be regarded as evidence, in itself, of the ability to perform a job role successfully. While a person might be well qualified and have succeeded in a similar role elsewhere, it is important to consider whether they will be able to transfer successfully to another organization structure/culture.

Attitudes and knowledge are supported by skills. According to Reid and Barrington (2000: 59) the development of skills is important because if our learning focuses only on attitudes and/or knowledge then our behaviour may not necessarily change. The workplace is an excellent environment in which employees can develop skills by actually doing the job and learning from their experiences. It is for this reason that experiential learning can be a particularly valuable element of university courses. For example, the skills involved in recruitment can be developed by groups of students actively role-playing the recruitment processes.

An organization is people, and it is built upon their commitment, creativity and cooperation with the stakeholders. The stakeholders could be any group which is interested in the work of the organization; for example, customers, local and national government, local community groups, shareholders, cooperative members to name a few. Consequently, employment selection is at the centre on any strategic decision because stakeholders identify the organization by the people associated with it.

ACTIVITY: THE RECRUITMENT ASSIGNMENT

This study is based on real recruitment and selection situations I completed whilst working in consultancy. For the purposes of this study, I have created a short profile for the organization to protect anonymity.

Organizational profile

(a) A successful, city-based consultancy

(b) Highly profitable

(c) Well-educated staff

(d) Accustomed to advising other organizations on staffing matters and performance

(e) Image-conscious management

(f) Prestigious offices

(g) High-profile client portfolio

Profile for the first set of vacancies

(a) Maintain business in established markets

(b) Continue long-standing client relationships

(c) Promote repeat business opportunities

(d) Interpersonal communication skills

(e) Presentation skills

(f) Ability to learn technical details to service client requirements

(g) Retain portfolio of business within an established market sector

Profile for the second new market vacancy

(a) Market services in a new business sector

(b) Make contact and create new client relationships

(c) Interpersonal communication skills

(d) Presentation skills

(e) Promote/increase the organization's profile in a new market sector

(f) Find new business opportunities

(g) Ability to learn the technical details of client's market sector

(h) Build a new, profitable and expanding business portfolio

Read the two job roles above and consider what the differences are in the kinds of attitudes, knowledge and skills a person would require for an existing client base and developing a new market.

Justify why you have selected certain AKS as essential and other as desirable.

In the real situation I was able to recommend several young people (mid-20s) who had many of the personal qualities required. Some of the successful applicants lacked the specific consultancy experience the client had asked for. However, it was decided that the successful candidates could have their consultancy skills developed. It is interesting to note that good presentation skills at interview played a significant role in the appointments. The successful

Attitudes		Knowledge		Skills	
Key areas	Desirable	Key areas	Desirable	Key areas	Desirable
-					
-					
-					
-					
-					

Figure 3.2 First job profile (existing clients)

Attitudes		Knowledge		Skills	
Key areas	Desirable	Key areas	Desirable	Key areas	Desirable
-					
-					
-					
-					
-					
-					

Figure 3.3 Second job profile (new client development)

applicants were also, interestingly, not always those who had the closest match to the client's job specifications, nor did they all have a degree. However, they were all able to fit into the organization's culture and management style.

The actual outcome of the second, new business position was particularly interesting. The person I eventually recommended had no consultancy experience, no relevant technical knowledge and, initially, no interest in changing career! What they *did* have were the right kinds of attitudes and interpersonal skills, knowledge of the market sector and presentational skills to do the job. The key tasks were therefore to:

1. Provide the applicant with sufficient information to decide whether or not to consider making a career change.
2. Brief the client organization of the potential added value this person could bring to their business.
3. Enable both client and applicant to be flexible in their discussions.

The applicant was eventually offered the position on a high salary and generous benefits package. Ironically, it is unlikely that they would have been selected by the client's original brief. Ultimately, it is a matter for each person responsible for recruitment to decide what kinds of attitudes, knowledge and skills are essential or non-essential to the selection process, which leads us to the discussion areas, noted below.

1. How much influence do you believe organizational culture has on selection decisions? Discuss your thoughts as a small group/seminar activity.
2. Consider the relevance to the job roles discussed above and grade the following elements. Give each a mark out of 7 where 7 is essential and 0 represents unnecessary. Use only whole numbers. Hence you have to make a clear decision either way.

   - Ability to work with little supervision
   - A driving licence
   - Communication skills
   - Determination to achieve positive results
   - Effective time management

- Entrepreneurial characteristics
- Intelligence
- Interpersonal skills
- Professional dress style
- Previous experience
- Qualifications
- Score highly in psychometric tests.

The job design and the recruitment and selection strategy deployed depends upon the organizational context; that is to say, recruiters should consider the kind of environment they are working in and the influences exerted by the organization's structure and culture. For example, the characteristics required for an HR manager in a bureaucratic sector may be entirely different from the kind of attitudes, knowledge and skills needed for someone appointed to a new entrepreneurial enterprise, although some of the core areas of knowledge and skills may be similar. Hence job design and recruitment and selection are necessarily situation-specific. An integrated approach to recruitment and selection therefore recognizes the need to offer flexibility, not prescription in the design of recruitment strategies (Nieto 2006).

An integrated approach to recruitment and selection may include:

- the practical involvement of HR staff or specialist external advisors in strategic planning of recruitment and selection policies
- recognition of the organization's culture and, as necessary, a re-evaluation of recruitment and selection policies where they are more a part of 'tradition' than modern practice which meets the organization's current needs.
- input from external advisors including business schools, professional bodies such as the CIPD (Chartered Institute of Personnel Development), and recruitment consultancies
- involvement of experienced professionals who have decided to work part time, such as men/women electing to invest more time with their family, or those who have decided to 'retire' from full-time working but who have many years' experience to offer
- an evaluation of the current job role
- a decision as to the most appropriate selection/recruitment approach.

NEW GRADUATE CV

In a competitive job market, a well-organized CV can really make a difference as to whether someone secures a work placement or a permanent job after graduating. In the United Kingdom, the National Career Service provides, free of change, advice and guidance (at the time of writing in 2013). This service provides impartial advice on CVs, covering letters, interview skills, job-search tips and areas connected with work and training. To view the National Career Service's website, visit nationalcareersservice.direct.gov.uk or telephone 0800 100900.

Each person is unique and there are many different potential employers. Furthermore, organizational sectors may differ in the information they would like to receive. The CV is, however, often the first impression a prospective employer gets of an applicant so it is important for both applicants and employers to understand how to interpret CV information. In a practical sense, the objectives of the applicant and recruiter should be similar, namely to recognize those aspects of attitudes, knowledge and skills which are most relevant to the job vacancy.

Some organizations elect to avoid receiving any CVs by requiring potential applicants to complete an application form, either on paper or in electronic format from their websites. The decision has to be a matter of fitness for purpose. A CV is likely to provide a better insight into the applicant's ability to present information and distinguish what is required to fulfil the job description.

Alternatively, an application form can be computer-scanned for key words, such as honours degree or any other prescribed criteria. In such cases, the recruitment process is predestined by the initial selection criteria and may permit less flexibility. For example, some of the world's leading entrepreneurs would probably have been filtered out by such electronic systems because they lacked conventional qualifications and career profiles. The use of CVs also places the onus upon the applicant to ensure that the information provided is correctly presented.

From the applicant's perspective, the objective of a CV is to generate sufficient interest to prompt an interview invitation. Do remember that first impressions can count for a lot if the employer has a large pile of applications, so the first page is particularly important. Your key information has to be clear and easily accessible.

Example of a CV layout

The section headings below provide a simple format. The new graduate can follow the format when applying for positions either for a work placement or full-time/part-time employment. For information on CVs and applications, view the National Career Service's website: nationalcareersservice. direct.gov.uk.

Page 1
CURRICULUM VITAE
NAME
CONTACT DETAILS
HIGHER EDUCATION
UNIVERSITY
DATES
(FULL-TIME/PART-TIME)
MAIN MODULES STUDIED
DEGREE CLASSIFICATION/S
PRIZES/ SPECIAL RESPONSIBILITIES
LANGUAGES
CAREER AND SKILLS SUMMARY

PAGE 2
WORK EXPERIENCE (start with the most recent and work back)
DATE TO PRESENT
TYPE OF BUSINESS
POSITION/S:
INTERESTS

The first page provides applicants an opportunity to highlight their key skills in relation to the job they have applied for. For example, one of my students was applying to the BBC to work as a journalist. When she brought her CV in I noticed that she has placed her experiences working in South America as a charity aid worker in a general interests section on the second page. Instead, I recommended that she move the information onto the front-page career and skills summary section, and that she highlight what she had learnt from the experience, thereby drawing attention to her ability to take the initiative and work abroad with a small team of people.

The most frequently used method of recruitment is the interview. A few sensible preparations can make this a more productive activity for all those involved (Goltz and Giannantonio 1995).

For managers setting up an interview schedule, consider the following:

1. The room selected should be comfortable. It is not conducive to effective recruitment if the room is too small or poorly ventilated.

2. The telephone should be redirected so that there are no unnecessary interruptions.

3. Avoid asking leading questions, or questions, which already contain the answer: 'What we are looking for is a real team player. How do you feel about working in a team?'

4. Closed questions tend to produce simple yes or no answers.

5. Using open questions, encourage interviewees to expand upon their replies. Open questions are those which begin with: What, Where, How, When, Who, Which, Why.

   For example:

   - *What* do you most like about working at…?
   - *Where* do you see yourself in two years?
   - *How* useful have you found the work placement in preparing you for full-time employment?
   - *When* did you first decide you wanted to become an HR specialist/ marketing/finance/IT manager?
   - *Which* part of your degree course did you find most relevant to your current job?
   - *Why* did you choose this organization for your work placement?

6. The interviewers should prepare a plan of questions they want to ask which relate to the attitudes, knowledge and skills the particular job role requires. The wording of the questions must be fair to all applicants and framed so that they avoid any discrimination concerning disability, ethnic background, gender, race, religion or sexual orientation. Legal advice should be sought through professional associations and in-house/external legal input.

HALO AND HORNS EFFECTS IN THE SELECTION PROCESS

Stereotyping is a psychological process used by humans to assist in the categorization of the complex world of information that surrounds us (Devine 1989; Hilton and Von Hippel 1996; Von Hippel et al. 2001). One of the challenges for people involved in recruitment is the unconscious influence stereotyping can have on their decision making. More commonly described as the 'Halo and horns' syndrome, stereotyping can prevent recruiters evaluating the person before them fairly because they allow a stereotype to condition their choices, irrespective of any new information being presented. In this respect it is helpful to design an AKS for the vacancy and avoid codifying stereotyping into the model. Hence, each essential quality needs to be critically evaluated from the perspective of whether candidates with this characteristic or qualification are more likely to be successful in actually completing the job functions than someone who does not have the qualification or characteristic.

> **Key Point:** Consider the time it takes for you to form an impression of a new person you have just met. When I ask students about how long it takes them to form a judgement, the timeframes they offer are usually measured in seconds. This is because humans use a form of categorization of impressions based on past experiences to make judgements about the people they meet.

Summary of recruitment, selection, job analysis and employment law

(a) The ability to comprehend the recruitment and selection process can also increase your knowledge and skills in applying for and successfully obtaining a new job.

(b) The method I have advocated is an integrated approach, which by its nature is a flexible system, offering the opportunity to design organization and situation-specific recruitment and selection solutions.

(c) The research studied organizations including international businesses and SMEs.

(d) For many years there has been recognition that HR initiatives can influence staff performance, productivity and financial performance.

(e) Employment legislation is in constant change, so even well-informed HR professionals are not in a position to safely advise their organization upon every legal matter relating to employment.

(f) In the first decades of the twenty-first century, there has been a transfer of HR responsibilities from the HR department to line managers.

(g) The contract of employment is a legally binding agreement between an employer and employee which is created when an employee agrees to work for an organization for pay. It can be made up of oral and written agreements (www.acas.org.uk).

(h) Further information is provided by DirectGov (www.direct.gov.uk/en/Employment/index.htm), Advice Now (www.advicenow.org.uk) and Take Legal Advice (www.takelegaladvice.com).

(i) There is no specific law relating to recruitment and selection practices in the workplace, making it daunting for HR practitioners, students and legal professionals alike to source employment regulation. Yet, at the very least, managers need to understand the legal consequences of ill-advised or hastily made decisions by using good-practice policies to avoid potential employment litigation or unwelcome publicity.

(j) The HR specialist should therefore investigate what is required and then select the method/s of recruitment most appropriate to the task.

(k) AKS is a flexible alternative to the traditional job analysis and design. This approach structures the analysis and job design upon the most recent job requirement and required personal attributes.

(l) The job design and the recruitment and selection strategy deployed depend upon the organizational context; that is to say, recruiters should consider the kind of environment they are working in and the influences exerted by the organization's structure and culture.

(m) Stereotyping is a psychological process used by humans to assist in the categorization of the complex world of information that surrounds us.

REVISION SECTION

Either: Select an organization and make up a job vacancy such as Human Resources Associate, Marketing Assistant or IT Assistant. (Choosing a specific job role will make it easier to compile a profile.)

Or: Select a job vacancy from a newspaper or professional journal.

Then: Compile a list of the attitudes, knowledge and skills for the vacancy, which a new graduate might apply for. Create two columns for each area: one for whatever is essential and another for the non-essential but desirable items.

TAKING IT FURTHER

Key texts to look up:

Devine, P. G. (1989) Stereotypes and prejudice: Their automatic and controlled components. *Journal of Personality and Social Psychology*. 56(1), pp. 5–18.

DirectGov: www.direct.gov.uk/en/Employment/index.htm.

Fried, Y., Slowik, L. H., Shperling, Z., Franz, C., Ben-David, H. A., Avital, N. and Yeverechyahu, U. (2003) The Moderating Effect of Job Security on the Relation Between Role Clarity and Job Performance: A Longitudinal Field Study. *Human Relations*. July, 56(7), pp. 787–805.

Refer to the books and journals in this references section.

REFERENCES

Acas Recruitment and Induction Booklet – October 2010.

Acas www.acas.org.uk.

Advice Now www.advicenow.org.uk/.

Belbin, R. M. (1993) *Team Roles at Work*. London: Butterworth-Heinemann.

Belbin, R. M. (2000) *Beyond the Team*. London: Butterworth-Heinemann.

Devine, P. G. (1989) Stereotypes and Prejudice: Their Automatic and Controlled Components. *Journal of Personality and Social Psychology*. 56(1), pp. 5–18.

DirectGov www.direct.gov.uk/en/Employment/index.htm.

Fletcher, C. (1991) Candidates Reactions to Assessment Centres and Their Outcomes: A longitudinal Study. Journal of Occupational Psychology. 64(2), pp. 117–127.

Fried, Y., Slowik, L. H., Shperling, Z., Franz, C., Ben-David, H. A., Avital, N. and Yeverechyahu, U. (2003) The Moderating Effect of Job Security on the Relation Between Role Clarity and Job Performance: A Longitudinal Field Study. *Human Relations*. July, 56(7), pp. 787–805.

Goltz, S. M. and Giannantonio, C. M (1995) Recruiter Friendliness and Attraction to the Job: The Mediating Role of Inferences about the Organization. *Journal of Vocational Behaviour*. 46(1), pp. 109–118.

Harvey-Jones, J. (1995) *All Together Now*. London: Manderin.

Hilton, J. L. and von Hippel, W. (1996) *Stereotypes*. In: Spence, J. T., Darley, J. M. and Foss, D. J. (eds) *Annual Review of Psychology*. (47), pp. 237–271.

Huselid, M. (1995) The Impact of Human Resource Management Practices on Turnover, Productivity, and Corporate Financial Performance. *Academy of Management Journal*. 38(3), pp. 635–670.

Judge, T. A and Cable D. M. (1997) Applicant Personality, Organizational Culture, and Organizational Attraction. *Personnel Psychology*. 50(2), pp. 359–394.

Maund, L. (2001) *Introduction to Human Resource Management: Theory & Practice*. Basingstoke: Palgrave Macmillan.

McKenna, E. and Beech, N. (1995) *The Essence of Human Resource Management*. London: Prentice Hall.

National Careers Service www.nationalcareersservice.direct.gov.uk.

Nieto, M. L. (2001) Who Are the Right People? *HR. Com*, 7 November.

Nieto, M. L. (2006) *An Introduction to Human Resource Management: An Integrated Approach*. Basingstoke: Palgrave Macmillan.

Paauwe, J. (2009) HRM and Performance: Achievements, Methodological Issues and Prospects. *Journal of Managerial Studies*. 46(1), pp. 129–142.

Reid, M. A. and Barrington, H. (2000) *Training Interventions: Promoting learning opportunities*. (6th Edition), London: CIPD.

Take Legal Advice www.takelegaladvice.com.

Von Hippel, W., Hawkins, C. and Schooler, J. W. (2001) Stereotype Distinctiveness: How Counterstereotypic Behavior Shapes the Self-Concept. *Journal of Personality and Social Psychology*. August, 81(2), pp. 193–205.

www.gov.uk/browse/employing-people.

www.ind.homeoffice.gov.uk.

4

Leadership Development and Appraisals

INTRODUCTION

The management of people is about building and encouraging others to become better at whatever it is they are tasked to do within the organization. The appraisal can therefore be a valuable tool in the dialogue between managers and staff on how to develop and improve their work. My experience in designing appraisals and conducting appraisal review meetings in a variety of organizations has been used to inform the content of this chapter.

In this chapter you will learn about the effective and motivational use of appraisal interviews. The content and design of the materials that follows reflects the particularly practical, applied nature of the subject so there is even more emphasis on activities for seminars and personal learning. This experiential approach provides the opportunity to develop your knowledge and skills concerning the interpersonal nature of appraisal interviews. The chapter also encourages you to evaluate the purpose and strategic role of appraisals and guides you towards designing situation-specific appraisal schemes that can add value to organizational performance.

LEARNING OBJECTIVES

The key learning outcomes for the chapter are below:

- Critically review appraisal objectives. Selecting areas for appraisal.

- Appraisal models by: immediate supervisor; self-assessment; peers; customers; subordinates; 360° review; mentor/s; external consultant.
- AKS appraisals framework.
- Design an appraisal system based on Attitudes Knowledge and Skills.
- The Confidence and Competence Model.
- Reviewing your self-perception of confidence and competence.
- Role-play an appraisal interview.
- Leadership Model.
- Attitude Evaluation Model.

CRITICALLY REVIEW APPRAISAL OBJECTIVES: SELECTING AREAS FOR APPRAISAL

An appraisal system can provide the opportunity to find the areas where people can develop their attitudes, knowledge and skills, which in turn can enhance their work-life experience and future employability. When managed collaboratively with staff, the appraisals can provide a springboard for development (Franco and Bourne 2003). Engaging staff through consultation is likely to build a cooperative and sustainable environment for progress. If employees are engaged positively with the appraisal it can build mutual understanding and commitment and be a motivating and beneficial experience (Thorpe and Beasley 2004; Bambacas and Prashant 2009). As with HR management in general, the purpose for which the appraisal is used has a significant influence on how employees respond to the process (Bourne and Neely 2000; Amaratunga and Baldry 2002; Bititci et al. 2005). Appraisals can be designed as a motivating and developmental process; however, if managed incorrectly, appraisals can demotivate employees. If appraisal is linked to rewards such as pay or promotion then the developmental qualities are likely to be subordinated as people contend for the most favourable remuneration package (Halachmi 2002).

Key Point: It is advisable to have a developmental appraisal system which is separate from the annual pay and review process. In such a system, the appraisal could focus on developmental matters rather than endeavouring to agree how much a person will be paid.

Each organization will need to review what its aims and objectives are in constructing an appraisal system. For example, an SME may require a different appraisal system to one used by a multinational company (Yeniyurt 2003; Garengo et al. 2005; Sharma et al. 2005). It is helpful to build the appraisal process in conjunction with staff consultation. Appraisals can differ in approach according to national/cultural environment. Accordingly, local sensitivity to national context is recommended so that the focus of the appraisal fits with the local cultural norms and is thereby more likely to be received positively by the participants. This approach engages the staff in the process, which can thereby be improved by staff input. An appraisal system is also likely to require revisiting as the organizational requirements change over time.

ACTIVITY: EVALUATING APPRAISAL OBJECTIVES

The appraisal interview may be used to evaluate a range of attitudes, knowledge and skills, though the wider the range of objectives set, the more likely it is for the process to become too complex and time-consuming.

For example, a set of appraisal objectives might include some or many of the following areas:

(a) Assess/award a comparative grade for performance.

(b) Analyse training and development needs.

(c) Set performance objectives.

(d) Assess salary rewards.

(e) Approve individual performance-related pay plans.

(f) Encourage and motivate team-working.

(g) Motivate individuals.

(h) Provide a channel for communication.

(i) Coaching and counselling.

(j) Identify potential for career development.

(k) Linking individual performance objectives to those of the organization.

(l) Gather information to assist HR planning.

(m) Listen and assess individual preferences for personal development.

(n) Assess potential for promotion.

Consider the list of possible appraisal aims above and think about which ones may have conflicting aims. For example, if you knew that the appraisal would decide if you received a pay rise, how honest might you be about your weaknesses (areas for personal development)?

In small groups, discuss which items on the list are most helpful for encouraging an honest and constructive discussion about how to develop an employee.

APPRAISAL MODELS

The context of the organization should be considered before the appraisal procedure is designed. It follows that the appraisal design integrates into the wider strategic plans and objectives of the organization. This is in harmony with the organizationally situation-specific philosophy of integrated HR practices (Nieto 2006).

Consult staff about what they would like to achieve from the appraisal process. Establish clear objectives. Too many objectives can result in the appraisals achieving none satisfactorily.

There are many appraisal methods and even more variants. The most appropriate approach will depend upon the purpose/s selected and other local considerations such as time availability, preferences and organizational structure culture. The notion that there may be a 'best practice' somewhere that everyone ought to copy is best avoided.

> **Key Point:** Organizations can learn from each other, but the design and methodology of an appraisal should reflect local situation-specific requirements, interests and needs.

Although organizations can learn from each other, the design and methodology of an appraisal should reflect local situation-specific requirements, interests and needs (Burgoyne 1988; Amaratunga and Baldry 2002; Audit Commission 2002, 2003; Kennerley and Neely 2003).

Appraisal by immediate supervisor

In what is probably the most commonly used appraisal method, the immediate manager conducts the appraisal and passes a report to the next management level and the HR team. The information then provides a springboard for initiating actions based on the appraisal's objectives.

Advantages

It is a simple system and less time-consuming than other methods.

Providing the objectives are agreed with the interviewee prior to the meeting, this system can offer a useful springboard for progressing agreed objectives. The interviewers are all likely to require training by an internal/external HR professional/consultancy/university business school, thereby improving HR knowledge and skills.

Disadvantages

The employee and immediate manager may not share or agree objectives.

The record of the meeting may be predominantly the manager's interpretation of events. Will the interviewee regard this approach as a fair assessment?

Self-assessment appraisal

This approach enables each person to evaluate his or her own performance prior to the appraisal meeting. The interviewee is thereby more able to become an active participant in the appraisal.

Advantages

The interview is based on two perspectives (manager and interviewee) so that both parties bring materials to the meeting to discuss. This creates more opportunity for mutual reflection. The interviewers are likely to require training by an internal/external HR professional/consultancy/ university business school, thereby improving HR knowledge and skills.

Disadvantages

What if the two assessments are very different? What if the employee/ manager and immediate manager cannot agree the outcomes?

Peer appraisal

This approach involves the person's work colleagues providing assessments, based on the appraisal criteria selected. The people we work with generally have an opinion as to our performance.

Advantages

Used non-judgementally, as a team-working developmental tool, it can help colleagues understand each other better and thereby improve effectiveness and cooperation. The interviewers are all likely to require training by an internal/external HR professional/consultancy/university business school, thereby improving HR knowledge and skills.

Disadvantages

Involves more work for colleagues and is therefore quite time-consuming.

Customer appraisal

This approach involves internal/external customers. So, for example, internal departments assessing the performance of the HR team may use it. Alternatively, the customer could be the clients a person works with, or any other stakeholders with whom the interviewee has regular contact.

Advantages

This approach draws from a much larger sample of inputs than those previously discussed. A wider strategic picture of a person in context may emerge. The interviewers are all likely to require training by an internal/external HR professional/consultancy/university business school, thereby improving HR knowledge and skills.

Disadvantages

It is a much more time consuming project than the earlier approaches. What are the achievable outcomes that would justify the time and expenditure? With so many people involved it may be difficult to provide feedback that reflects the depth and breadth of comments received. Who will provide the feedback? How does the interviewer interpret the feedback materials?

Upward appraisal

The employees/workers review their own manager. A person's managerial style/competence can be exposed by the opinions of those who work for him/her. This can be very useful in circumstances where there is high staff-turnover. Is it the job they are leaving or the manager?

Advantages

It can encourage people to feel that their views on how the organization is managed are listened to. The manager can learn about how they are perceived by their team. The interviewers are all likely to require training by an internal/external HR professional/consultancy/university business school, thereby improving HR knowledge and skills.

Disadvantages

The method can suffer from unhelpful/hurtful criticism of the manager. The most 'popular' manager might not necessarily be the most effective. The feedback has to be confidential otherwise employees might fear that negative remarks may have repercussions later. What is the intended outcome to justify the process? Will the manager be more or less motivated after the appraisal?

360° appraisal

Numerous people are involved in the appraisal process from every direction, hence the 360° description. A whole range of diverse inputs may be included from immediate subordinates, colleagues, senior management, customers and other stakeholders.

Advantages

The method may produce a wide-ranging and comprehensive picture of a person in their overall organizational and stakeholder context. The interviewers are all likely to require training by an internal/external HR professional/consultancy/university business school, thereby improving HR knowledge and skills.

Disadvantages

There may be a lack of trust or rivalries between colleagues that may render peer evaluation impractical and even problematic.

It is likely to be a costly and very time-consuming process. Eventually the feedback has to be delivered in a conventional interview. Who will be selected to interpret the material and present it? Can any anticipated outcomes/benefits of a complex 360° appraisal be justified in terms of the time invested?

Appraisal by external assessment centre/consultancy

The organization may decide to outsource part or all of the appraisal procedure to an external provider. External consultancies and university business schools can provide a diverse range of alternative appraisal methods. These can include appraisal by psychological evaluation, role-play, and outward-bound activities. The discipline of situation-specific design should still be applied.

Advantages

The appraisal is taken out-of-house so managers are not distracted from their primary roles whilst conducting appraisals. The external provider should design a programme that is situation-specific.

Disadvantages

The external provider may attempt to sell their 'off the shelf' programme. There is going to be an investment cost in using an external provider, though this needs to be regarded in the context that using internal staff also incurs costs in time and lost opportunity. (People have to stop doing the primary jobs to conduct appraisal interviews.) Nevertheless, a strategic HR decision should be made as to how situation-specific the external provider's service is and the value in terms of outcomes.

Appraisal by mentor

This approach may use an independent third party from within the organization, or expert from outside the organization. This could be a consultant or a manager from an external organization or a university business school.

Advantages

The mentor is usually selected by/with consultation so the interviewee is more likely to feel that the mentor is an 'honest broker' is so much as the person selected is not in their immediate management/peer/departmental/team.

Disadvantages

There is likely to be a consultation investment for the mentor's time/involvement. Some further HR research work may be required prior to the appraisals to establish the objectives with the mentor. The mentor may not be as familiar with the organization's internal structure/culture as someone inside the organization.

SHORT CASES FROM CONSULTANCY AND RESEARCH: WHICH APPRAISALS SYSTEM DO I USE?

For the research below, I used case-study methodology (Yin 2003). The case study is particularly helpful for HR investigations because the work can focus on a specific area within the organization. The following studies focused on employee attitudes regarding appraisal procedures (Eisenhardt 1989; Nieto 2006).

The two short case studies below illustrate some of the problems managers I have interviewed encountered in the design and implementation of appraisals. Essentially, they are both concerned with what an appraisal should be used for in organizations. The names of individuals and organizations have been removed to protect their anonymity in line with ethical guidelines on confidentiality.

Two appraisals

The first attempt

A manager from a major international company told me that his organization had had two completely different appraisal systems in one year. The first was internally designed and focused on identifying each employee's areas of strength and weakness. Interestingly, the manager reported that after the employees' weaknesses were identified there were no prearranged provisions for follow-up on personal development and training. This left some staff feeling demotivated because they had been told of weaknesses in their knowledge and skills base, but not given support to improve their performance. He thought that the appraisal procedure had consequently disaffected employees. It was also reported that some negative criticisms by appraisal interviewers had diminished some employees' confidence and even led to a diminution of competence.

The managers interviewed observed that the appraisal process was a costly investment of employee time and resources. Furthermore, respondents thought that the appraisal procedure was not worthwhile if the outcome was a reduction in performance and poorer management–employee relationships.

The second attempt

An external consultancy firm was brought in to introduce an alternative appraisal method, which the company adopted. This system required every employee to sit a set of tests on areas such as literacy and analytical skills. The consultancy advice, which followed, recommended that employees focus on building upon their areas of strength. Again, no specific follow-up training programme as to how people could develop their 'strengths' was put in place.

There was evidence of contradictory messages with the two appraisals. In the first appraisal method, the company sought out areas of weakness for the employee to address, while the second encouraged people to concentrate on their areas of strength. Employees reported feeling confused about what was expected of them. The managers therefore questioned which of these approaches might be the most beneficial, focusing on weaknesses or focusing on building strengths? The managers also noted that the lack of training support was a key omission.

Discussion questions

1. Why do you think the appraisal procedures were unsuccessful?
2. The managers appeared to have no clear understanding of the appraisal's objectives. Why would this make it more likely to fail?
3. Why is it important to put a follow-up training and development budget/package in place before commencing appraisal interviews?
4. Why do you think appraisal interviewers should receive training?

One of the key issues of appraisal is to recognize the requirement of fitness for purpose, so one size does not fit all (Nieto 2006). The HR team should therefore design appraisal formats in close consultation with members of the operational departments to agree the objectives (Dipboye and de Pontbriand 1981; Axtell and Parker 2003; Franco and Bourne 2003). It is likely to be more productive to engage colleagues in a dialogue whereby they can express their needs and aspirations and then discuss their contributions to the organization's plans.

Key Point: It is better to undersell the importance of appraisals, and overdeliver in staff development, rather than to oversell the appraisals and then underdeliver on improvements, precipitating future disengagement with the appraisal procedure.

Furthermore, appraisals are likely to raise expectations, so plans should be in place to deliver development and training before the appraisals take place.

DESIGN AN APPRAISAL SYSTEM BASED ON ATTITUDES, KNOWLEDGE AND SKILLS (AKS)

The job description is a good place to begin when constructing an appraisal framework. The original AKS for which the person was selected may form the starting point for the appraisal design. However, it is also possible, indeed likely, that the job-role and person have developed so the recruitment criteria may be out of date, even after a few months. The framework is similar to the selection.

AKS APPRAISALS FRAMEWORK

Attitudes		Knowledge		Skills	
Key areas	Desirable	Key areas	Desirable	Key areas	Desirable

To being with, consider the attitudes that a person would need to succeed in the job-role. For example, if a person is working directly with customers then their attitudes to customer service are likely to be in the key area. Additionally, other attitudinal characteristics such as empathy, enthusiasm and trustworthiness may be important when communicating with customers.

Within the tripartite balance of attitudes, knowledge and skills, the most difficult set to change is attitudes. For example, if a person has both the knowledge and skills to do the job, yet lacks the attitudinal motivation or interest, then that person is less likely to do the work particularly well. Conversely, a person who has the attitudinal set of characteristics is more likely to respond positively to training and development.

The knowledge which is required for a particular job-role is an interesting area to review when using an AKS appraisals framework. Where a person is already part of the organization, they can develop their knowledge by taking a course and engaging in CPD (continuous personal development). In terms of building a stable organization with low staff turnover, developing the existing staff through training and development is likely to encourage people to stay. Furthermore, the organization's reputation as an employer improves where careers can be developed and employees can see the benefits of longer-term service. Conversely, if the organization chooses not to invest in the existing staff, then the organizational reputation may suffer, particularly if as a result it has to recruit external people instead of developing and promoting internally.

There is little incentive for people to stay with an organization if either job security or promotion prospects are poor.

In the area of skills, it is possible that over time a person has built the experience and skills to be competent in a job-role, even if they do not have the qualifications (knowledge). It is helpful to retain experienced staff who have demonstrated they have the experience and skills because they provide stability and may serve as mentors to new and less experienced employees.

ACTIVITY: PREPARING AN AKS APPRAISAL FOR A UNIVERSITY LECTURER

Many of the postgraduate/undergraduate students I've worked with particularly enjoy this 'role reversal' exercise. Designing an AKS appraisal form for a lecturer, from a student's perspective. For example, the area of communication skills often scores high with students. The other area that I have found students often select within the context of a business school is a career history either prior to academia or concurrently. Using the AKS appraisals framework above, write an AKS appraisal for a university lecturer.

THE CONFIDENCE AND COMPETENCE MODEL

Our confidence and competence to perform effectively can be influenced by many factors, such as personal circumstances, social, health and life-work balance (Nieto 2003). Each of us comes in to contact with other people and how those interactions work can help or hinder our and their success (Nieto 2006).

In my management and teaching experience, most people respond positively to encouragement. Conversely, people in the workplace usually respond negatively to managers who resort to sarcasm, insults or negative criticism. Indeed, such behaviour should not be accepted in any organization. It follows that providing opportunities for personal development and nurturing improvements in self-worth is good for people, and thereby can also improve organizational performance. A longitudinal study by Axtell and Parker (2003) indicated that membership of an active improvement group and personal development could influence confidence in performing interpersonal tasks.

The appraisal interview is an opportunity to help build on the positive aspects of a person's attitudes, knowledge and skills. The model below is provided to help you evaluate your awareness of confidence and competence (Figure 4.1).

Although vocational business courses provide an excellent foundation for organizational life, they cannot supply someone who has little or no work experience with all the attitudes, knowledge and skills they will need in a lifelong career. Instead, the first-degree business courses may be viewed as the starting point of a lifelong learning process, which can include further formal education, professional development and experiential

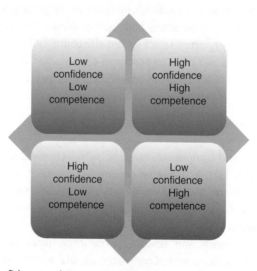

Figure 4.1 Confidence and Competence Model

Source: Nieto (2006).

learning gathered over many years of working in a variety of organizational situations.

Low confidence, low competence

If a person is aware of their limitations (low confidence, low competence), this can be a good starting position for development. For example, if an employee is promoted into a managerial/new position of responsibility too quickly then they may feel overwhelmed by their new job role. Any initial bravado of may soon evaporate in the heat or workplace pressures. In this scenario, the newly promoted employee is likely to display low confidence and low competence. Unless sufficient support is provided, they are likely to make more than the average number of errors and misjudgements, which in turn will dampen their confidence. This may be compared to the proverbial swimming 'instructor' who throws the novice into the deep end of the swimming pool. It such circumstances it really is sink or swim. In other words, to expect a new manager to cope with all the aspects of a new role may be an inefficient approach because they are likely to make mistakes. Without adequate guidance, it is by no means certain that a novice manager can gain the attitudes, knowledge and skills required to become competent.

High confidence, low competence

In this situation, the person may be unaware of their areas requiring development. This could be because they are new to the job-role and unaware of what is required. A job may appear fairly straightforward to an external observer, yet it is only when someone is in post that the reality of the tasks involved all become apparent. However, high confidence, low competence may also occur where employees/managers are unable or unwilling to develop their attitudes, knowledge and skills. For example, high confidence, low competence may be a factor when there is high staff turnover and managers do not recognize that their organizational policies are deterring staff from remaining with the organization. It such circumstances it is worthwhile exploring what it is about the organization that people find difficult to work with by using an external consultant (or HR academic) to research the reasons staff are leaving the organization.

Low confidence, high competence

Examples of low confidence, high competence might be a person who is returning to employment after a career break, or people moving into a new sector, or possibly someone whose knowledge and skills have not been recognized by the organization.

In higher education, I have noticed that some mature students can be found in this category. By providing sufficient encouragement and recognition, such people can perform very well, because they have high competence. Mature returnees may (though certainly not in all cases) require some additional training in the use of new information technologies. The knowledge and skills such employees can bring to an organization are worth the small additional investment in training them to build up confidence.

High confidence, high competence

The high confidence, high competence refers to accomplished managers/professionals who can achieve high standards of performance and who are sufficiently confident to understand the importance of continuous professional development for both themselves and the people they work with.

My research with recruitment consultancies indicated that confidence and competence did not automatically ensure selection to senior organizational positions. This may be because a significant part of career success also relates to cultural behavioural norms and organizational politics. Hence, it is also possible that senior managers may lack the confidence to select the most capable person for a job precisely because those high levels of ability might lead to them to challenge the status quo which top management wishes to preserve. Nevertheless, there are clear advantages in personal professional integrity and self-worth by aiming to be the best that you can be in any given job role. The values portrayed by confident, competent employees are likely to increase employability and are more likely to result in new job opportunities in the future. In an employment environment where no one organization can realistically guarantee long-term employment, the only real security is employability. It is therefore worthwhile investing in personal professional development irrespective of whether it produces immediate progression in your current organization.

REVIEWING YOUR SELF-PERCEPTION OF CONFIDENCE AND COMPETENCE

Activity: confidence and competence

Read the descriptors for the Confidence and Competence Model. Think about a specific work situation you are – or have been – involved in to answer the self-assessment questionnaire. The context of your answers can also be based on a course of study you are currently following. There are no right or wrong answers to the questions. Instead, use them to reflect upon the extent to which you feel confident/competent to undertake the work you are involved in.

If you are working in a team, it may be useful to have a discussion about your results with your colleagues. Please do not be judgemental. The aim is to *encourage* others in developing self-confidence and competence.

Your responses to each item are measured as: (1) strongly disagree; (2) moderately disagree; (3) slightly disagree; (4) neither agree nor disagree; (5) slightly agree; (6) moderately agree; (7) strongly agree.

1. I am always confident that I will be successful in whatever work I do.

1   2   3   4   5   6   7

2. I am very good at the work I am currently involved in.

1   2   3   4   5   6   7

3. If someone is finding their work difficult I am usually able to help them.

1   2   3   4   5   6   7

4. I have received a lot of personal support to help me improve my work performance.

1   2   3   4   5   6   7

5. It is rarely the case that someone finds I have made a significant error in the work I am responsible for.

1   2   3   4   5   6   7

6. I have to check my work several times to correct earlier mistakes.

1   2   3   4   5   6   7

7. I do not think I am naturally very good at the work I am currently required to do.

1   2   3   4   5   6   7

8. I enjoy working on my own more than working with other people.

1   2   3   4   5   6   7

9. I felt more confident doing my previous job/course.

1   2   3   4   5   6   7

10. The work I have been given is too difficult.

1   2   3   4   5   6   7

Activity: role-play an appraisal interview

This exercise provides an experience of appraisal design and the opportunity to critically evaluate the key factors involved in appraisal implementation.

Using the AKS framework, design an appraisal for:

a management student on your course,

or

an HR associate in your organization

or

your own job.

AKS APPRAISAL FRAMEWORK

Attitudes		Knowledge		Skills	
Key areas	Desirable	Key areas	Desirable	Key areas	Desirable

Designing the appraisal can be an individual or team task. However, to get the most from the appraisal interview, form teams of three: the interviewer, the interviewee and an observer.

Afterwards, the observer can give feedback to their team on how effective the appraisal interview was.

Observer's brief:

Make notes on the following:

- How positive was the interviewer?
- Where was the interview conducted? Was the environment conducive to discussion or was it too public? Were there interruptions by outsiders/telephone/passers by?
- Did the interviewer/interviewee agree?
- If there were disagreements how did the interviewer handle the situation?
- Was the overall outcome of the appraisal likely to increase or decrease the interviewee's motivation?

LEADERSHIP MODEL

The meetings I have with Duncan Christie Miller are characterized by a mixture of friendship and sharing ideas. Duncan, leads a consulting and personal leadership consultancy.

The MILK perspective on leadership

Memories

In building postive memories, leaders encourage their teams to draw positive energy from their memories of past successes.

Individualism

Each person has individual and particular attitudes, knowledge and skills which can serve the team. Leaders require different approaches for each person.

Laughter

Work also has to be enjoyable. It is for leaders to create the atmosphere, and some laughter – at an appropriate time – can serve as a release to pressures and workplace tensions.

Kinship

A sense of kinship, of belonging serves an organization more than a transactional pay for work relationship. A sense of belonging also benefits personal wellbeing and stabilizes employee relationships even where the external environment might be in constant change.

We discussed the changing environment and the implications that might have for organizational behaviour. The research I have conducted into how people respond to different contexts also informed that design of the model. I subsequently modified the model for this book.

The model offers a view of where a person may be in their organizational, personal life or both.

ATTITUDE EVALUATION MODEL

The model below can be used to reflect upon your personal attitude to a given situation (Figure 4.2). This could be about your job, a course of study, a training programme or life in general.

- **Positive and inert:** This area give people the time and space to relax, to think and to be creative.
- **Positive and alert:** In this area there is a higher level of activity. Interpersonal relationships contain affection. Kinship indicates that a person feels they are part of the organization. In this area, the surprises which occur in the external environment are met as opportunities to adapt and respond postively.
- **Negative and dull:** This indicates disengagement. Apathy in what happens to the organization. Boredom with the work role and conformity. A weak leader may regard conformity as a sign of their team agreeing with them. In this area, it is more likely to signify that staff wish to retain their jobs by avoiding disagreement with management. So poor decisions may progress unchallenged to the detriment of the organization and its stakeholders.
- **Negative and aroused:** In this area staff are actively hostile to the leadership. It may have begun with fear of redundancies or loss of positional status, and progressed to anger and active resistance.

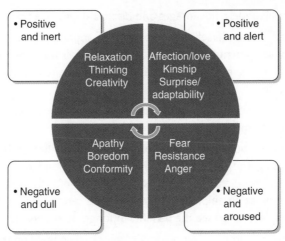

Figure 4.2 Attitude Evaluation Model

SUMMARY: LEADERSHIP DEVELOPMENT AND APPRAISALS

(a) Consultation is likely to build a cooperative and sustainable environment for progress. If employees are engaged positively with the appraisal it can build mutual understanding and commitment and be a motivating and beneficial experience.

(b) If it is linked to rewards such as pay and promotion then the developmental qualities of appraisals are likely to be subordinated as people contend for the most favourable remuneration package.

(c) An SME may require a different appraisal system to the one used by a multinational company.

(d) Appraisal design integrates into the wider strategic plans and objectives of the organization.

(e) Although organizations can learn from each other, the design and methodology of an appraisal should reflect local situation-specific requirements, interests and needs.

(f) Appraisal models: advantages and disadvantages (see text).

(g) It is better to undersell the importance of appraisal and overdeliver in staff development than to oversell the appraisals then underdeliver on improvements, precipitating future disengagement with the appraisal procedure.

(h) The job description is a good place to begin when constructing an appraisal framework.

(i) In terms of building a stable organization with low staff turnover, developing the existing staff through training and development is likely to encourage people to stay. Furthermore, the organization's reputation as an employer improves where careers can be developed and employees can see the benefits of longer-term service.

(j) The appraisal interview is an opportunity to help build on the positive aspects of a person's attitudes, knowledge and skills.

(k) Review the Confidence and Competence Model (Nieto 2006).

(l) Apply the leadership models and reflect upon how you behave in relation to the work/study environments.

REVISION SECTION

Why are good interpersonal skills essential to being an effective leader?

How does consultation with staff enable new initiatives to progress more efficiently?

Evaluate the disadvantages of reorganizing an organization and displacing established staff with new outsiders.

TAKING IT FURTHER

Key texts to look up:

Bambacas, M. and Prashant, B. (2009) Predicting Different Commitment Components: The Relative Effects of How Career Development HRM

Practices Are Perceived. *Journal of Management & Organization*. 5(2), pp. 224–240.

Sharma, M. K., Bhagwat, R. and Dangayach, G. S. (2005) Practice of Performance Measurement: Experience from Indian SME's. *International Journal of Globalisation and Small Business*. 1(2), pp. 183–213.

Thorpe, R. and Beasley, T. (2004) The Characteristics of Performance Management Research, Implications and Challenges. *International Journal of Productivity and Performance Management*. 53(4), pp. 334–344.

Refer to the books and journals in this references section.

REFERENCES

Amaratunga, D. and Baldry, D. (2002) Moving from Performance Measurement to Performance Management. *Facilities*. 20(5–6), pp. 217–223.

Audit Commission (2002) *Targets in the Public Sector*. London: Audit Commission.

Audit Commission (2003) *Acting on Facts: Using Performance Measurement to Improve Local Authority Services*. London: Audit Commission.

Axtell, C. M. and Parker, S. K. (2003) Promoting Role Breadth Self-efficacy through Involvement, Work Redesign, and Training. *Human Relations*. 1 January, 56(1), pp. 113–125.

Bambacas, M. and Prashant, B. (2009) Predicting Different Commitment Components: The Relative Effects of How Career Development HRM Practices Are Perceived. *Journal of Management & Organization*. 15(2), pp. 224–240.

Bititci, U., Mendibil, K., Martinez, V. and Albores, P. (2005) Measuring and Managing Performance in Extended Enterprises. *International Journal of Operations & Production Management*. 25(4), pp. 333–353.

Bourne, M. and Neely, A. (2000) Performance Measurement Interventions Succeed and Fail. *Proceedings of the 2nd International Conference on Performance Measurement, Cambridge UK*, pp. 165–173.

Burgoyne, J. (1988) *Management Development for the Individual and for the Organisation*. Personnel Management: June.

Dipboye, R. L. and de Pontbriand, R. (1981) Correlates of Employee Reactions to Performance Appraisals and Appraisal Systems. *Journal of Applied Psychology*. 66, pp. 248–251.

Eisenhardt, K. M. (1989) Building Theories from Case Study Research. *Academy of Management Review*. 14(4), pp. 532–550.

Franco, M. and Bourne, M. (2003) Business Performance Measurement Systems: A Systematic Review. *Proceedings of the EUROMA POMS Conference, Como* 1, pp. 451–460.

Franco, M. and Bourne, M. (2003) Factors that Play a Role in 'Managing through Measures'. *Management Decision*. 41(8), pp, 698–710.

Garengo, P., Biazzo, S. and Bititci, U. (2005) Performance Measurement Systems in SMEs: A Review for a Research Agenda. *International Journal of Management Reviews*. 7(1), pp. 25–47.

Halachmi, A. (2002) Performance Measurement: A Look at Some Possible Dysfunctions. *Work Study*. 51(5), pp. 230–239.

Kennerley, M. and Neely, A. (2003) Measuring Performance in a Changing Business Environment. *International Journal of Operations & Production Management*. 23(2), pp. 213–229.

Nieto, M. L. (2003) The Development of Life Work Balance Initiatives Designed for Managerial Workers. *Business Ethics: A European Review*. 12(3), pp. 213–215.

Nieto, M. L. (2006) *An Introduction to Human Resource Management: An Integrated Approach*. Basingstoke: Palgrave Macmillan.

Sharma, M. K., Bhagwat, R. and Dangayach, G. S. (2005) Practice of Performance Measurement: Experience from Indian SME's, *International Journal of Globalisation and Small Business*, 1(2), pp. 183–213.

Thorpe, R. and Beasley, T. (2004) The Characteristics of Performance Management Research, Implication and Challenges. *International Journal of Productivity and Performance Management*. 53(4), pp. 334–344.

Yeniyurt, S. (2003) A Literature Review and Integrative Performance Measurement Framework for Multinational Companies. *Marketing Intelligence & Planning*. 21(3), pp. 134–142.

Yin, R. K. (2003) *Case Study Research: Design and Methods* (2nd Edition). Newbury Park: Sage Publications.

5

Performance and Rewards Management

INTRODUCTION

Performance and rewards can motivate and energize us to overcome obstacles, to preserve and achieve more than we expected. Understanding what motivates us and, just as importantly, other people is a key area of management. Rewards are a universal and international language. People around the world respond positively to a caring and supportive employment environment.

The subject of rewards is particularly interesting to all of us. People like being rewarded. For example, a child smiles when they receive a gift. Our colleagues generally respond positively to encouragement. Yet we are all individuals, preferring and making different life choices. So while a young and ambitious City trader may respond to the opportunity to earn large bonuses, the voluntary worker's efforts receive no pay, though they may find their work very rewarding. Therefore, the first step in evaluating rewards is to consider which rewards are appropriate to the situational context. In this chapter you will read about a variety of organizations drawn from consultancy and research work to illustrate different approaches to rewarding people. The rewards strategy, as with other HR policies, has to be an integrated part of the organization's strategic plan (Nieto 2006; Bratton and Gold 2012).

LEARNING OBJECTIVES

The key learning outcomes for the chapter are below:
- Understanding intrinsic and extrinsic rewards.
- The application of benchmarking analysis to reward management interventions and strategies.
- Employee Economic Value Model.
- Critical evaluation of PRP (performance related pay) schemes.
- The purpose and use of flexible reward systems. The 'Cafeteria Model'.

UNDERSTANDING INTRINSIC AND EXTRINSIC MODELS OF REWARD

There are examples of intrinsic and extrinsic rewards in every working environment. For example, in August 2012, the efforts and achievements of Olympic athletes were broadcast from London around the world. The efforts of athletes competing to achieve their dreams of Olympic success were evidence of individual and team commitments to achieve. For the athletes, the reward was to represent their country and for a few athletes, the glory of an Olympic medal. In each case, the athletes were motivated to give their best performance on the day. The intrinsic reward could include the personal satisfaction of achieving the best one could be on the day of competition and the recognition of family, friends, fellow athletes. The extrinsic rewards could include the possibility of an Olympic medal, the opportunities to enhance a sporting career and, for the most successful, the financial rewards of fame and sponsorship and product promotional contracts.

In this chapter you will explore the balance between the external rewards (and how they might motivate you) and intrinsic rewards which can generate the determination and commitments displayed by successful people (Sansone and Harackiewicz, 2000; Levesque et al. 2004). As you read this chapter and explore the activities, you should reflect upon your own behaviour, in your university study groups or workplace to consider what extrinsic and intrinsic rewards mean to you. Indeed, an organization is a form of team, which may succeed or fail depending upon the performance of its staff. It is worth noting here that rewards are positive reinforcements. In general, people respond more favourably to positive reinforcements than negative criticisms.

> **Key Point:** Whether small or large, an organization can only perform as well as the attitudes, knowledge and skills of its people. The team is dependent upon the positive attitudes, knowledge and skills is has available. While knowledge and skills can be developed, attitudes are more difficult to alter.

With an increasingly diversified workforce including workers – who might be employed full time, part time, on contract, consultancy, as mature returners, women returners, home-based – what each person prefers as a rewards package can vary considerably. The rate of change in the working environment also necessitates more continuous personal development so that employees retain employability for their next job move. Therefore training/education can be included in the rewards package because it reflects an investment by the employer in the medium/long-term employability of the worker. However, sometimes employees dislike changes and, unless new developments are underpinned by sound employee rewards strategies, managers may encounter resistance to their change plans. In a competitive market, people who have invested in their employability through education and training are in a better position to find a new job. Employers who reward their people with learning opportunities may both retain and attract more effective staff (Smith in Blyton and Turnbull 1992).

THE APPLICATION OF BENCHMARKING ANALYSIS TO REWARD MANAGEMENT INTERVENTIONS AND STRATEGIES

Externally initiated factors can have a major influence on organizational rewards systems. A simple business model which can be applied to analyse the environment in which an organization operates is PEST (political, economic, social, technical). The PEST Model descriptors below are designed for HR analysis. Students of management can also use this model to study an organization as part of their research work. Indeed, it is often very helpful to critically review external factors before moving onto internal research activities. For example, if the marketplace for employees in a particular sector is competitive then an organization may have to offer a better package of rewards and incentives to attract and retain staff.

The *PEST* analysis provides four areas of investigation, which are as follows:

1. Political
2. Economic
3. Social
4. Technical

Most organizations recognize their market competition and adjust their services, products and offerings accordingly. Similarly, managers can study the employment environment relating to employee availability, training, rewards and working conditions and thereby compare (benchmark) the rewards offered to other similar organizations. For example, if their competitors are providing better working conditions, career development, flexible working hours, then organizations with less employee-friendly policies may encounter difficulties recruiting and retaining staff. PEST analysis can therefore provide an overview of external factors which may influence organizations. It is therefore important to research an organization and its contextual environment and by doing so provide helpful indicators for the HR management to act upon (Neale 1992; Paauwe 2009).

Political

The political background can be interpreted in a broader context to include: local and national government policies. Additionally, international laws, treaties and agreements as well as employee contracts and trade-union agreements need to be addressed by employment policies. The legal elements of employment law are complex and constantly changing in response to legislation, local national and international, so a legally trained professional should oversee them.

Economic

The economic environment can influence profitability so it is relevant to evaluate the market for the organization's goods or services. If a competitor is outperforming other businesses in the same sector, it can be very useful to study what they are doing regarding the recruitment, development and retention of employees.

Social

Social context can be a helpful guide regarding trends, fashions and attitudes to goods or services. For example, the general trend in the western first-world nations is for smaller families than was the case in the middle of the twentieth century. Additionally, more people may want or need to remain in full/part-time employment to supplement their pension incomes. Hence the workforce is getting older so it is more important to train and retrain older workers and also train and develop young entrants.

Technological

Technological changes can change job content and the attitudes, knowledge and skills required. In some cases whole tiers of employees may require retraining. This can necessitate the design of new training initiatives, and recruitment strategies to maintain efficiency and performance. This places particular value on the attitudes of employees to be flexible and adaptable to learn.

Activity: individual or group seminar presentation

This activity can be used as either a summative course assessment or as formative class work.

Select an organization you are interested in.

Begin by conducting a PEST analysis. It is helpful to think about the kind of industry, business or sector your selected organization is in. Start by thinking about whether it is a 'for profit' or 'not for profit' organization. Once the general sector is established, consider the more specific factors that influence its employee rewards (Zimmeck 2002). If the organization you have selected is 'not for profit' (such as a charity, non-governmental organization, school, national health service, aid agency), then the primary motivational drives people may have might not be financial (Rochester 1999). It should become evident that although organizations may be placed in a generic sector, each one will have situation specific requirements relating to its culture (the way they like to do things) and structures (Handy 1993; Hofstede 1994; Patterson et al. 2005).

In reality, the preliminary stages of the process are quite straightforward and the research can produce many interesting insights into an organization's HR requirements. Some HR students may progress to conduct in-depth PEST analysis if this is appropriate to their interests and course requirements. An overview of the external factors which can be studied with PEST (combined with more detailed, organization-specific research) should yield some interesting findings.

Questions

1. What were the key points highlighted by PEST analysis on your chosen organization?
2. How do you think the organization's management team should respond to the PEST findings?
3. Evaluate how effective PEST has been in providing you/your team with an overview of an organization within its sector.

EMPLOYEE ECONOMIC VALUE MODEL

Consider these two simple questions in small groups.

- If you are currently employed, how easy do you think it is to secure a job of an equal or higher level to that of your current position?
- If you are a student, how long do you think it will take to secure the kind of career position you would like to be in after you graduate?

The questions above arose from an MBA executive class I was delivering on employability, which is the subject of this next section of the chapter. The students were mostly mid-career senior managers from a variety of organizational settings in both the private and public sectors. The general consensus of the group was that it would be quite straightforward to secure another comparable position. Indeed, as senior managers with a wide range of professional contacts, the general opinion was that three or four weeks would be sufficient to be offered a comparable or better job than their current one.

Given the confidence expressed by the group, I offered them the opportunity to present their assignments from a 'real world of work' perspective. So, the case study assignment could, if they so decided, be their own employment market investigation. This would include a reflective review comparing their application/s and interviews experience with the theories of employability, recruitment and interviewing. I met the students each week, and by Week 5 it was becoming apparent to them that securing a new job was not as easy as they had first thought. For example: their friends in other organizations did not have a current vacancy; the positions for which they applied did not respond; some students obtained interviews, but were not subsequently offered the position.

In a work environment where job security with just five or six employers in a lifetime of work is unlikely to be the experience of most people, employability is particularly valuable. In contemporary organizations it is therefore the responsibility of the employee to ensure that they have the necessary attitudes, knowledge and skills to obtain a new job. A person's earnings are the minimum payments required to induce someone to do a job. Economic rent is the extra payment a person receives over and above the minimum earnings required (Begg et al. 2011). By applying this economic model to employee relations, it is possible to calculate the difference between what a person earns and their value in the marketplace. In some cases, the person may be undervalued; alternatively a person may not be able to command a comparable salary elsewhere. Clearly the employee, who is able to obtain alternative employment at a similar or higher rate of pay than his or her current job, is in a stronger negotiating position than someone who cannot.

> **Key Point:** Employability is essential to securing continuous employment. Investments in personal development, through learning new skills and obtaining new qualifications are part of a lifelong process of continuous learning.

The employer therefore needs to value the people who have chosen to work in their organization to establish stability for their stakeholders and customers, upon whom the organization's reputation depends. The term *organization* can isolate us from the obvious fact that organizations are no more or less than a set of individuals, each with their own hopes, dreams and aspirations.

Hence, it is not so much the creation of new initiatives and policies which is key to progress, but the interpersonal skills to gain the cooperation and support of the staff.

CRITICAL EVALUATION OF PERFORMANCE RELATED PAY(PRP) SCHEMES

It is the senior executives who select the organization's priorities and the pay and rewards for employees (Delves-Broughton 2002). The choices made about the pay, benefits and rewards influence the decisions people make as to whether to join that organization or indeed look for employment elsewhere. The challenge for organizations is therefore to devise a package of pay, benefits and rewards which encourages people to join the organization and stay as engaged and interested members.

The design of a pay, benefits and rewards system may at first appear fairly straightforward. However, upon further research, that is found to be not necessarily so. To begin with, people are all different. Each person has different interests, motivations and perceptions of what they would like from their jobs. In practice, targeting selected activities for rewards with equity requires careful preparation to avoid difficulties later when the system is implemented (Kessler and Purcell 1992; Kohn 1993; Randle 1997).

People interacting in organizations can produce defensive behaviours and attitudes which emphasize positional advantage and competitive

Key Point: People do not leave organizations; they leave people (Nieto 2006).

People do not leave an organization; they leave people who did not value them, or the policies created by people, which have disaffected them or disregarded their contributions to the work of the organization.

And sometimes they leave because another organization can offer more opportunities and rewards. Either way, it represents a loss of talent, organizational knowledge and experience.

Key Point: The best staff tend to leave first – because they can

When management creates dissatisfaction through reorganizations, it is the more capable people with the best transferable skills who are likely to leave the organization.

So changes in rewards or employment patterns without staff agreement can cost the organization in loss of talented people and experience.

struggles to impress the corporate hierarchy (Thompson and McHugh 2009). Hence, if a performance rewards system is inappropriately designed it may unintentionally produce negative outcomes in staff behaviour. This may surface as discontent, or reduced team-working as people chase individual performance rewards. It may be that rewards systems inadvertently become costly in terms of staff dissatisfaction. Increasing levels of dissatisfaction could also prompt the more capable people to leave the organization. You may ask, 'Why the most capable people?' who could potentially benefit from the extra pay rewards. The reason is simple. If the working environment becomes less convivial, it is the more capable people with the best transferable skills who are likely to be in the best position to leave the organization. Those employees with less transferable skills may have little alternative but to stay with the organization.

This means that those persons tasked with leading the design of the performance rewards system should be cognizant of organizational context: the particular mission, organizational heritage and culture. Accordingly, bringing in new management from a different context to create a rewards system may become problematic. The system may be fine, but might fail to recognize and reward organization-specific differences and needs.

Additionally, employees tend to view their employment holistically so other interventions such as restructuring, redundancies and management changes are also going to influence attitudes and motivation. For example, a longitudinal field study of employees in an organization undergoing major restructuring found a moderating influence of job security and role clarity on employee performance (Fried et al. 2003). When both role clarity and job security were high, job performance increased over a period of time. Conversely, if there is job insecurity and restructuring and uncertainty about who will be in which management role, then the likelihood is that general motivation would diminish.

> **Key Point:** Performance and productivity increase when organizations support a secure working environment.
>
> **Positive Reward Actions:**
>
> 1. Train and develop staff to enable them to step up into management posts when new posts or vacancies arise.
> 2. Promote staff from inside the organization.
> 3. Build staff confidence and commitment through positive feedback and consultation and job security.

These wider issues are relevant here because it is necessary to evaluate a rewards process within the wider context of the organization. If an organization is in the process of restructuring then the possibility of disturbed working patterns and job insecurity is likely to influence employee motivation. Additionally, if the management structure is under review, then the level of ambient uncertainty can have a detrimental influence on motivation, irrespective of what efforts are made to deliver an equitable pay and rewards strategy (Ryan and Deci 2000; Deci and Ryan 2012). In each case, the context of the organization and what else is happening at the same time as a planned rewards system can influence the attitudes staff have to a PRP.

The twenty-first-century environment is such that the rate of change is pronounced. However, with some forethought, it should be possible to create the kind of supportive environment where employees can feel secure and know that their contributions are valued. The case for such an approach is persuasive in terms of the benefits to organizational performance and employee wellbeing (Lepper and Henderlong 2000; Houlfort et al. 2002; Cameron et al. 2005; Cunningham 2010). It is also helpful to consider the extent to which the organization's culture encourages qualities such as autonomy and self-determination, both of which are difficult to quantify in a performance management rewards system, but can be of major significance in determining how a person responds to their tasks (Levesque et al. 2004).

The argument in favour of a PRP scheme is that it can direct the staff's attention and energies towards the areas designated as being important by the senior management team. For example, if profit maximization is set as a key indicator, then the staff can be measured on how much contribution they make to profits. The measures might be direct profits in the case of sales staff. Alternatively, the rewards might be designed for staff whose contribution is in cost savings, which in turn can increase profits. The incentives for cost minimization could also be applied to service departments such as research and design, marketing, accounting, human resources, customer service helplines and so forth.

The extent to which PRP might actually increase performance is open to discussion. Indeed, it is worthwhile considering precisely what the organization collectively understands by 'performance'. As discussed earlier, a variety of factors can influence staff cooperation and motivation, which may not be related to the PRP system. It is for these reasons that there have been critical discussions in academic papers for many years regarding the use of PRP systems (Geery 1992; Kessler and Purcell 1992; Kohn 1993; Marsden and Richardson 1994; Randle 1997). Another issue which is worthy of consideration in evaluating PRP is the influence that focusing on individual performance can have on organizational team-working. In contemporary organizations, successes are more likely to be achieved by a team of people than by an individual. Accordingly, Storey and Sisson in Storey et al. (2005: 178–179) observed that focusing individuals' attention on gaining personal rewards detracts from team-working to the detriment of the organization. What we can surmise from this is that success is less likely to be an individual's performance alone. Instead, it is usually achieved by a team of people. Hence it is difficult to isolate individual contributions from the efforts of the team and the interaction of people in other departments.

When designing a PRP, it is also relevant to consider how much additional pay or rewards a person might accumulate by meeting the planned targets. If the incentives are relatively small then they may do little to alter behaviour, while still generating a significant amount of management administration. Alternatively, if the rewards are large, then the objects of the reward could attract a distorting level of employee preoccupation. For example, the behavior of bank traders in the early part of the twenty-first century was highly incentivized by massive pay bonuses. The traditional banking practice had been for mortgages and loans to be kept inside the originating bank's books. However, by transferring the credit risk to other financial institutions, the traditional banking model was replaced by a complex distribution of debts, so that the original bank could offset the risk of lending to less secure customers, outside the prime market of well-secured borrowers (Brunnermeier 2008). This riskier sub-prime market was necessarily populated by individual mortgagees and businesses which were more likely to default upon their loans if they experienced a financial downturn. While lending to new customers expanded the banks market, it also exposed them to far greater risks (Duffe 2007). More critically for financial stability, it exposed the complex international network of banks and insurance companies which had secured the distributed debt to 'systemic risk in financial systems' if the financial growth rates were to plateau (Eisenberg and Noe 2001: 236–249).

Following an economic downturn in 2008 and 2009, there was a rapid collapse in banking confidence, with some global names failing and others having to be bailed out with huge sums of money injected by governments to maintain the global financial equilibrium. Hence, within a short timespan, there was a worldwide reversal from the free flow of capital to much more cautious lending practices. There followed a systemic liquidity shortage and a banking crisis (Diamond et al. 2005). These events were generically described as the Credit Crunch (Thain 2009).

The large performance-related bonuses which rewarded bankers for expanding their portfolios with new customers are likely to have contributed

to the collapse of several banks. So in this particula,
uted to the collapse of many businesses, either directly
as the crisis unfolded.

Cases from consultancy and research: 'The Virgin Way

The following case study is part of a research project I conduc _d and was
first published in Nieto (2001).

To begin, here are a few questions to consider:

What is business for?

Is it just about making a profit?

Do people matter?

If you were to list the priorities an organization should set itself, what
might those be?

Please list any three of the following in the order you think are important, first, second and third priority.

The Chief Executive; the shareholders; the senior managers; profit;
customers; shareholders; staff; product/services.

The research I conducted was with the Virgin Group. For one part of
the project I visited Virgin's home-based office in London to meet their
corporate affairs director. This was interesting in itself. So instead of a large
office block, the business was being managed from a large house. The
impression I received was that of a homely environment instead of an
impersonal corporation. What emerged from our meeting that day was
an interesting and characteristically unique approach on what to focus on
in a business. In a service-driven environment, the competition can copy
or match anything that a customer is offered. So how can an organization
build its relationship with customers?

The Virgin approach at that time was to focus on building the motivation of its staff team. Hence the priorities were as follows:

1. Staff

2. Customers

3. Profits.

group recognized that their competitors could emulate services. If one airline offers more legroom for passengers the competition could do the same and so on. By concentrating on staff development, Virgin provided the customer with a better service. The customers were happier and therefore used Virgin again which in turn improved the profits.

If I turn the model around, it is easy to understand the point Virgin were making. If an organization chases profits or cost-cutting as a first priority then it will only invest just as much as it needs to in serving the customers. If the staff are placed as the least important factor then their attitudes could be less than positive and enthusiastic. These negative attitudes can filter through to the customers who then are less happy with the service level.

The loss of returning customers in turn reduces the profits. For example, imagine you are a customer in a retail store which may has reduced 'costs' by having fewer staff on the floor, or a restaurant which saves money by employing poorly trained staff. As customers we will quickly notice the deficiencies in service. Similarly, the quality of whatever an organization produces is dependent on the motivation and commitment of its staff.

CASES FROM CONSULTANCY AND RESEARCH: APPLYING A STAFF-FOCUSED APPROACH TO CUSTOMER SERVICE

The restaurant experience: 'we have awards for customer service'

Quality performance is constantly being evaluated. Excellent customer service is what people expect every day. For example, if a customer experiences slow and inefficient service in a restaurant, the fact that the restaurant has previously won an award for customer service is of no relevance to that customer.

The set of questions below asks you to reflect upon your experience of customer service, in a restaurant or with any other service provider, and the impressions which that organization made on you.

1. Have you experienced slow, inefficient customer service?

2. What did you think of the organization?

3. How many people did you tell about your unsatisfactory experiences?

4. Have you experienced good, efficient customer service?

5. How many people did you tell about your positive experiences?

6. How could an organization approach staff rewards to encourage better customer service? Re-read the Virgin Way case study above and discuss the Staff, Customer, Profit approach in relation to the organizations you have discussed in this exercise

The purpose and use of flexible reward systems: the cafeteria system

The term 'cafeteria system' refers to the application of flexible choice to employee benefits. People are individuals and as such have differing needs and requirements. The continuing tendency for people to change organizations more often means that shorter term remuneration, may be of more relevant. Also in the modern workplace worker security is more likely to be found in employability (the knowledge and skills to be able to obtain a new job) than staying in one organization.

Consequently, part of the cafeteria package could be investment in external training and personal career development. Indeed, these changes to working patterns were occurring in the later part of the twentieth century and continue to be significant for staff rewards and retention planning (Parks and Kidder in Cooper and Rousseau 1996; McDermott 1997).

The cafeteria system in practice

The following research was into the application of cafeteria rewards. This is an extract from an interview with the vice president of a large company.

> We have flexibility within our benefits so people can trade up to a different car by putting more money in even if that car is two levels above [the employees' grade entitlement]. However, we would struggle if someone said they didn't want a pension plan or a health plan. So we have considered the cafeteria approach, but there are some core benefits, which we would probably demand that employees take.

In another interview with a successful UK recruitment consultancy with offices throughout the UK, the chief executive advised me that all the benefits were available to individual choice. The way it worked was that each employee was given a total 'spend' according to his or her job role. Within that total spend, employees could then decide what to include in their personal benefits package. For example, the chief executive told me that it was possible for people to select a higher salary if they opted out of the company's pension provision, though he also said that he would counsel staff not to take such a short-term approach. However, the choice was there for people to choose between options, up to their personal package limit.

The content and design of a cafeteria system should be organization-specific so that those involved can discuss and agree the elements to be included.

A cafeteria benefits package can include:

Salary

Pension

Healthcare: personal/family

Personal insurance: accident/death

Car or car allowances

Travel ticket

Subsidized staff lunch/vending machines

Extended holiday entitlement

Extended sick pay allowances

Extended carer time allowance (including partner, elderly parent or children)

Crèche facilities

Flexible working hours

Subsidized travel to work allowance

Free car/bike parking

Concessionary agreements with other companies (discounts on travel, restaurants, clothes, holidays)

Bonuses

Share options

Commission payments

Time off work to study a degree programme

Funding for additional qualifications

Career advice and personal development planning (with internal or external providers)

Examples of non-salary rewards include:

Recognition of good work

Public praise of successful staff

Choice of next project

Overseas assignments

Training and development

Time to attend college courses

Mentoring

Flexible working hours

The above lists are not intended to be exhaustive and each organization should decide what is appropriate to its particular needs (Schrage 2000). The research I conducted with the organizations discussed in this chapter indicated that the key to a successful cafeteria system was the initial set-up and preparation. Most people hope to enjoy their work, and a benefits package that is tailored to their personal needs is more likely to attract and retain employees than a one-size-fits-all approach.

SUMMARY OF PERFORMANCE AND REWARDS MANAGEMENT

(a) Performance and rewards can motivate and energize us to overcome obstacles, preserve, and achieve more than we expected.

(b) An organization, whether small or large, can only perform as well as the attitudes, knowledge and skills of its people.

(c) Intrinsic and extrinsic rewards can be seen in every working environment.

(d) Pay, benefits and rewards need to encourage people to join the organization, stay and remain interested in their work.

(e) Those persons tasked with leading the design of the performance rewards system should be cognizant of organizational context; the particular mission, organizational heritage and culture.

(f) Each person has different interests, motivations, and perceptions of what they would like from their jobs.

(g) Focusing individuals' attention on gaining personal rewards detracts from team-working to the detriment of the organization.

(h) The term 'cafeteria system' refers to the application of flexible choice to employee benefits. People are individuals, and as such have differing needs and requirements at different stages in their lives.

(i) A flexible employee benefits package is more likely to attract and retain employees than a one-size-fits-all approach.

REVISION SECTION

Regardless of whether an organization is small, medium-size or global, why are staff attitudes, knowledge and skills the key to its success?

Explain the differences with examples of intrinsic and extrinsic rewards?

What do you understand by *People do not leave an organization, they leave people*? Why is it important for managers to create policies that:

(a) maintain employee job security and workforce stability?

(b) build positive interpersonal relationships between colleagues?

(c) increase employee motivation through rewards and appraisals?

TAKING IT FURTHER

Key texts to look up:

Deci, E. L. and Ryan, R. M. (2012) *Motivation, Personality, and Development within Embedded Social Contexts: An Overview of Self-Determination Theory*. In: Ryan, R. M. (ed.) *Oxford Handbook of Human Motivation*. Oxford: Oxford University Press. pp. 85–107.

Fried, Y., Slowik, L. H., Shperling, Z., Franz, C., Ben-David, H. A., Avital, N. and Yeverechyahu, U. (2003) The Moderating Effect of Job Security on the Relation Between Role Clarity and Job Performance: A Longitudinal Field Study. *Human Relations*. July, 56(7), pp. 787–805.

Handy, C. B. (1993) *Understanding Organizations* (4th Edition). London: Penguin.

Refer to the books and journals in this references section.

REFERENCES

Begg, D., Vernasca, G., Fischer, S. and Dornbusch, R. (2011) *Economics* (10th Edition). Maidenhead: McGraw-Hill.

Blyton, P. and Turnbull, P. (eds) (1992) *Reassessing Human Resource Management*. London: Sage.

Bratton, J. and Gold, J. (2012) *Human Resource Management: Theory and Practice*. (5th Edition). Basingstoke: Palgrave Macmillan.

Brunnermeier, M. K. (2008) Deciphering the Liquidity and Credit Crunch 2007–2008. *Journal of Economic Perspectives*. 22(1), pp. 77–100.

Cameron, J., Pierce, W. D., Banko, K. M. and Gear, A. (2005) Achievement-based Rewards and Intrinsic Motivation: A Test of Cognitive Mediators. *American Psychological Association*. 97(4), pp. 641–655.

Cooper, C. L. and Rousseau, D.M. (1996) *Trends in Organizational Behavior*, Vol. 1. London: John Wiley & Sons, pp. 47–61.

Cunningham, I. (2010) Drawing from a Bottomless Well? Exploring the Resilience of Value-based Psychological Contracts in Voluntary Organizations. *The International Journal of Human Resource Management*. 21(5), pp. 699–719.

Deci, E. L. and Ryan, R. M. (2012) *Motivation, Personality, and Development within Embedded Social Contexts: An Overview of Self-determination Theory*. In: Ryan, R. M. (ed.) *Oxford Handbook of Human Motivation*. Oxford: Oxford University Press.

Delves- Broughton, P. (2002) Enron Cocktail of Cash, Sex, and fast Living. *News.telegraph.co.uk*. 28 January.

Diamond, D. W. and Ra Jan, R. G. (2005) Liquidity Shortage and Banking Crisis. *Journal of Finance*. 60(2), pp. 615–647.

Duffie, D. (2007) *Innovations in Credit Risk Transfer: Implications for Financial Stability*. Working Paper, Stanford University.

Eisenberg, L. K. and Noe, T. H. (2001) Systemic Risk in Financial Systems. *Management Science*. 47(2), pp. 236–249.

Fried, Y., Slowik, L. H., Shperling, Z., Franz, C., Ben-David, H. A., Avital, N. and Yeverechyahu, U. (2003) The Moderating Effect of Job Security on the Relation Between Role Clarity and Job Performance: A Longitudinal Field Study. *Human Relations*. July, 56(7), pp. 787–805.

Geery, J. F. (1992) Pay Control and Commitment Linking Appraisal and Reward. *Human Resource Management Journal*. 2(4), pp. 36–54.

Handy, C. B. (1993) *Understanding Organizations* (4th Edition). London: Penguin.

Hofstede, G. (1994) *Cultures and Organizations: Software of the Mind*. London: Harper Collins.

Houlfort, N., Koestner, R., Joussemet, M., Nantel-Vivier, A. and Lekes, N. (2002) The Impact of Performance-contingent Rewards on Perceived Autonomy and Competence. *Motivation and Emotion*. 26(4), pp. 279–295.

Kessler, I. and Purcell, J. (1992) Performance Related Pay: Objectives and Applications. *Human Resource Management Journal*. 2(3), pp. 16–33.

Kohn, A. (1993) Why Incentive Plans Cannot Work. *Harvard Business Review*. September–October.

Lepper, M. R. and Henderlong, J. (2000) *Turning 'Play' into 'Work' and 'Work' into 'Play': 25 Years of Research on Intrinsic versus Extrinsic Motivation*. In: Sansone, C. and Harackiewicz, J. M. (eds) *Intrinsic and Extrinsic Motivation: The Search for Optimal Motivation and Performance*. San Diego, CA: Academic Press.

Levesque, C., Stanek, L. R., Zuehlke, A. N. and Ryan, R. M. (2004). Autonomy and Competence in German and American University Students: A Comparative Study based on Self-determination Theory. *Journal of Educational Psychology*. 96(1), pp. 68–84.

Marsden, D. and Richardson, R. (1994) Performing for Pay? The Effects of Merit Pay on Motivation in the Public Sector. *British Journal of Industrial Relations*. 32(2), pp. 243–261.

McDermott, D. G. (1997) Case Studies: Gathering Information for the New Age of Compensation. *Compensation & Benefits Review*. 29(2), pp. 57–63.

Neale, F. (ed.) (1992) *The Handbook of Performance Management*. London: CIPD.

Nieto, M. L. (2001) *Marketing the HR Function*. Oxford: Chandos Press.

Nieto, M. L. (2006) *An Introduction to Human Resource Management: An Integrated Approach*. Basingstoke: Palgrave Macmillan.

Paauwe, J. (2009) HRM and Performance: Achievements, Methodological Issues and Prospects. *Journal of Managerial Studies*. 46(1), pp. 129–142.

Patterson, M. G., West, M. A., Shackleton, V. J., Dawson, J. F., Lawthom, R., Maitlis, S., Robinson, D. L and Wallace, A. M. (2005) Validating the Organizational Climate Measure: Links to Managerial Practices, Productivity and Innovation. *Journal of Organizational Behavior*. June, 26(4), pp. 379–408.

Randle, K. (1997) Rewarding Failure: Operating a Performance-Related Pay System in Pharmaceutical Research. *Personnel review*. 26(3), pp. 187–200.

Thompson, P. and McHugh, D. (2009) *Work Organisations: A critical Approach* (4th Edition). Basingstoke: Palgrave Macmillan.

Rochester, C. (1999) One Size Does Not Fit All: Four Models of Volunteering in Small Voluntary Organisations. *Voluntary Action*. 1(2), pp. 7–20.

Ryan, R. M. and Deci, E. L. (2000) Self-determination Theory and the Facilitation of Intrinsic Motivation, Social Development, and Well-being. *American Psychologist*. 55(1), pp. 68–78.

Sansone, C. and Harackiewicz, J. M. (eds) (2000) *Intrinsic and Extrinsic Motivation: The Search for Optimal Motivation and Performance*. SanDiego, CA: Academic Press.

Schrage, M. (2000) Cafeteria Benefits? Ha! You Deserve a Richer Banquet. 3 April. Fortune.

Storey, J., Salaman, G. and Billsberry, J. (eds) (2005) *Strategic Human Resource Management: Theory and Practice* (2nd Edition). London: Sage.

Thain, C. (2009) A Very Peculiar British Crisis? Institutions Ideas and Responses to the Credit Crunch. *British Politics*. December, 4(4), pp. 434–449.

Zimmeck, M. (2002) *The Right Stuff: Approaches to Volunteer Management*. London: Institute for Volunteering Research.

6

Strategic HRM in a Changing Organizational Environment

INTRODUCTION

The chapter discusses the implications of change on organizations and how HR strategic plans influence employee relations. The first quarter of the twenty-first century has experienced growth and then a recession, which has impacted upon workers across the planet. This is therefore an international management of people issue on a global scale. Transnational organizations need to respond to the local national employment availability and both train people to build capability and retain the talent and experiences of their established workforce.

Understanding the change process has always been important to organizations. Within a rapidly changing business environment, it is even more central to HR strategic planning. In this chapter you will learn how to adapt change modelling for the twenty-first-century environment. You will also have the opportunity to work on change case studies, which are drawn from research and consultancy and thereby build your awareness of change and your knowledge and skills on how to work in a transforming organizational environment.

LEARNING OBJECTIVES

The key learning outcomes for the chapter are below:
• Strategic HR planning for a sustainable organization.

- The old and new psychological contracts. Strategic implications for HR.
- Downsizing and the implications for employee relations.
- Lewin's Change Model.
- Lewin's Change Model adapted for a twenty-first-century context.

STRATEGIC HR PLANNING FOR A SUSTAINABLE ORGANIZATION

During the course of my career in management, consultancy and academia, I have seen change in international businesses, small and medium-size enterprises and public and charitable institutions. These include commercial management, consultancy projects, academic research and in voluntary roles. It is through these experiences, within a diverse range of organizations, that I am encouraged to recommend constructive consultative engagement when proposing organizational changes. This means listening to and working with colleagues to build plans for which they have a sense of ownership because they have been involved in their development. Hence, the HR professional should endeavour to be in a position to advise colleagues on how to build a sustainable organization (Bryson 2011). This kind of proactive approach to HR can also avoid unnecessary difficulties with employees and, sometimes, costly litigation and negative publicity from disaffected staff.

A change programme can only succeed with the proactive support and engagement of the staff. During a change programme which I researched, the chief executive publicly stated that his/her changes would happen irrespective of whether they had to 'change the people or change the people'. In other words, either the staff changed their approach to how they focused their activities or the management would replace them with external appointments. After a formal consultation period, the management advised staff that they no longer met the correct employee profile.

Accordingly, many of the staff left the organization and numerous external appointments were made. The outcome was a negative organizational culture, low trust, low commitment and a major failing in performance. And what became of the chief executive? When the manipulation of statistics to present a positive appearance for the organization's performance was no longer tenable, they left to join another organization as CEO and commenced the same process there. It seems that while competent people learn from experience, others repeat them.

> **Key Point:** The term 'organization' can isolate us from the obvious fact that organizations are no more or less than a set of individuals, each with their own hopes, dreams, and aspirations. If an organization has happy, motivated, secure people, they are more likely to cultivate a positive organizational environment which lends itself to long-term sustainability.

Managers may describe a strategy and set of plans for where they envisage the organization being at some time in the short or long term. Before a strategy can be formed, the organization requires a stable a platform of employee commitment to support it in in operationalizing the new strategy. Conversely, insecure, unhappy, demotivated, employees are more likely to seek short-term gains, which may destabilize the organization's medium to long-term strategic plans. Moreover, an insecure workplace encourages employees to invest time searching for new jobs and to take management actions which are less about long-term strategic sustainability (in the longer term the manager may have left the organization) and more to do with adding something to their CV, to support their current new job search. In practice, this represents reactive short termism, which is the antithesis of strategic planning.

> **Key Point:** Building an organizational strategy which delivers success begins with secure committed employees.

In the contemporary environment, the likelihood of changes to the workplace means that employees also have to take personal responsibility for continually updating their knowledge and skills base. For example, by building a portfolio of transferable knowledge and skills you equip your-self to move from one sector to another or to build a portfolio of projects within an organization (Handy 1994; Nieto 2003). Each person therefore needs to have his or her personal strategic career development plan. This could include: attending short company courses, external accreditations such as the CIPD (Chartered Institute of Personnel Development) and CMI (Chartered Management Institute), and new qualifications such as MBA or a Master's degree. For management professionals, it is also valuable to network with other people, both inside and outside your current sector. It is therefore of significant value to seek membership of professional bodies such as the CIPD and the CMI.

Key Point: Chartered Institute of Personnel Development and Chartered Management Institute.

If you are a prospective student looking for a business degree course, it is worthwhile selecting one where the university has teaching staff who are members of the CIPD and CMI. Such academics are more likely to have industry knowledge/contacts as well as academic qualifications.

Employee commitment is of key importance to managers interested in developing successful organizations. The extent to which employees are committed to their organization is relevant to long-term sustainability. An extensive survey by International Survey Research (which included views from 360,000 employees from the ten largest economies) found a correlation between the extent to which employees expressed com-mitment to their organization and performance. According to Womack (2002) in a three-year study, net profit margins rose by 2.06 per cent in businesses where employees described themselves as committed to their organizations. Conversely, organizations with less committed employees saw net profit margin fall by 1.38 per cent. Other key factors were employees' views of the development opportunities they were offered and whether or not they were empowered to do their work effectively. However, a whole range of other factors could have influenced the rises and falls of under 3 per cent. Correlation does not prove causation. Nevertheless, it is fairly reasonable to propose that a committed workforce is more likely to improve productivity than a disaffected one.

A review of organizational activity may also reveal those procedures which generate little added value while wasting staff time in tedious documentation and bureaucracy. For example, the research conducted with 400 public-sector employees by the Audit Commission in Britain found employees complaining of being overwhelmed by paperwork and bureaucracy and being set too many targets (Womack 2002). Hence, if managers adopt an excessive emphasis on tasks, processes and targets, the outcome may actually demotivate their people and reduce productivity and performance.

THE OLD AND NEW PSYCHOLOGICAL CONTRACTS: STRATEGIC IMPLICATIONS FOR HR

By law, organizations are required to provide written explicit employment contracts. However, the psychological contract is different. It involves unwritten implicit expectations. Employees recognize those activities which are explicitly required from them, and those which are implicitly expected. In return, the employee receives explicit pay and benefits and implicit rewards that they have come to expect through custom and practice (Turnley and Feldman 2000).

Key Point: The psychological contract is represented by those additional unwritten rewards which can nevertheless form a major factor in determining the employee's perception of the organization. The psychological contract focuses on the exchange of perceived promises and commitments which go beyond the written contract.

In a research paper reporting a study based on a survey of 1,306 senior HR managers, Guest and Conway (2002) explored the management of the psychological contract. Three distinct and relevant aspects of organizational communication were identified, concerned with the initial induction of new employees, regular updates on what the organization was doing and longer-term strategic information. The use of communication enabled managers to be (and be seen to be) more transparent in their employee relations so that psychological contracts (organizational promises and commitments) were breached less frequently.

The traditional bureaucracy essentially set out a rulebook approach to employee rights and responsibilities, leaving little room for ambiguity and insecurity of employment tenure. This security, as described by Weber (Eisenstadt 1968: 69) represented a transaction whereby entrance into an office was considered to be an acceptance of an obligation to serve the management in return for a secure existence. Within such an employment environment it was tacitly accepted that providing the employee kept within the bureaucracy's rules they might reasonably expect long-term secure employment. This was a key element of what was latterly described as the old psychological contract. In such circumstances, the strategic HR offering was secure employment for the long term.

It would be a mistake to regard the old psychological contract as a barrier to progress. Indeed, the security of knowing employment is not likely to be snatched away can actually stimulate innovations because employees can take a longer-term perspective on project developments. Conversely, an insecure worker may be less likely to take chances and challenge the status quo if their tenure of employment is precarious.

In many aspects of management, the language in use can indicate changes in the underpinned assumptions and prevailing philosophical approach of the time. For example, the term 'personnel management', which was popular in the mid-twentieth century, might be perceived to be a more person-centred term than 'human resources management' which became common usage in the late twentieth century. The linguistic transition from personnel management to human resources may have reflected a change in management attitudes, indicating that humans are just one more of their organizational resources. Whether these changes of terms are perceived as benign rephrasing, or indicative of a more substantial change in approach, there have certainly been changes in how people have viewed their careers over the last few decades. For example, the contemporary term 'employability' contains an implicit understanding that it is necessary to be in a position to secure a new job. Hence, the change in terms also indicates a strategic realignment, from an offering of the possibility of long-term employment to transferable employability that can enable people to secure work in another organization.

The notion of a secure job for life with just a few employers, during an employee's entire working lifetime, may be described as the old psychological contract. However, such a description has been untrue for many workers in the twentieth century as well as in the first decades of the twenty-first century. Indeed, sociologically, the notion of a secure job was being disrupted throughout the twentieth century by the recessions in the 1930s, 1970s and early 1990s. In this century, following an economic downturn, with multiple company defaults in 2008 and 2009, there was a rapid and catastrophic collapse in banking confidence, with some global names failing and others having to be bailed out with huge sums of money injected by governments to maintain the global financial equilibrium. Hence, within a short span of time, there was a worldwide reversal from the free flow of capital to much more cautious lending practices. The liquidity shortage and a banking crisis have thereby reduced the availability of capital for business, described as the Credit Crunch (Diamond et al. 2005). This has reduced the new investments which organizations can secure, which in turn has shaped the strategic planning for employing staff. Hence it may be argued that the secure bureaucracies described by Weber (Eisenstadt 1968) were not the experience of many employees in either the last or present century.

Furthermore, the globalization of work in both the present and last centuries has eroded the number of industrial jobs in Europe, the US and Japan as manufacturers have moved production plants to lower employment-cost areas of the world (Sisodia 2004; Sussangkarn et al. 2011; Toral 2011; Sitkin and Bowen 2013). These changes in business strategy have thereby altered what employees might understand as their psychological contracts. When combined with the impact of several recessions, the employee–employer relationship has become less predictable. It is therefore probably more useful to think of the unwritten psychological contracts as continually evolving. Furthermore, the term 'psychological contract' – which by its very nature describes something which is fixed, even if it is a short-term contract – is probably not as useful a metaphor in the present century as it was in the mid-twentieth.

The newer twenty-first-century psychological contract encourages a relationship that implicitly recognizes its short to medium-term duration so commitments, by both parties, may be adjusted accordingly. This kind of psychological contract is described in Thompson and McHugh (2002: 162) as a social or psychological contract that is no longer based on large, hierarchical companies providing stable employment, internal labour markets and a career progression. Within the context of the economic uncertainties described earlier in this chapter, this approach appears to be consistent with employability being the new agreement between employer and employee. It thereby follows that people need to continually develop their knowledge and skills to build their personal employability portfolio. Continuous change is discussed later in this chapter.

A research paper by Deery and Walsh, reviewed by Kessler in the CIPD's *People Management* (2002: 54), offered some interesting evidence regarding psychological contracts. Drawing on survey evidence from 200 in-house and 100 outsourced employees working for the same airline on call-centre work but with different employment conditions, Deery and Walsh found that outsourced employees were less loyal and more likely to quit. It was suggested that these differences might be traced to the less secure and more uncertain nature of outsourced employment, as well as to feelings among these employees that they were treated less equitably.

Alternatively, a strategic advantage could be achieved by organizations, which plan to create a working environment where employee relations are at a level where their commitment can contribute to the longer-term success and sustainability. To counterbalance any mistrust that may overshadow such working relationships, Bagshaw (1997) emphasized the value of creating a climate of mutual investment where there is congruence between the goals of employees and employer. However, the research by Nieto (2003) indicated that it may be more difficult to attain corporate congruence in modern diversified organizations

> **Key Point:** An HR approach, which reduces employee security, may thereby also reduce employee commitment and loyalty, the loss of which costs in terms of productivity, performance and high staff turnover.

where the needs, interests and aspirations of workers, – be they full-time, part-time, short-contract, consultancy, to list but a few – are unlikely to be similar. Nevertheless, the strategic aim of creating a climate that builds the trust and commitment of employees may have commercial as well as employee-relations benefits (Kessler 2002).

A person's sense of employment security can influence the way they behave in an organization. The research by Hofstede (1994: 125) found that where insecurity occurs, there can be suppression of deviant ideas and behaviour and resistance to innovation. Hence, people who are on short contacts, or permanent staff who feel in danger of redundancy, are less likely to take creative chances and more likely to acquiesce without enthusiasm tin the directives they are given by managers.

> **Key Point:** Employee compliance does not imply commitment or loyalty to the long-term interests of an organization. Nor does acquiescence produce the kind of new ideas and energy associated with innovation. An organization, in any sector, can only be as good as the people it employs and the motivation, innovation, and commitment to performance which they can collectively produce.

According to Thompson and McHugh (2002: 180), organizations can produce defensive behaviours and attitudes which emphasize positional advantage and competitive struggles to impress the corporate hierarchy between generational, gender and professional groups. The problems associated with poor employee relations are therefore costly in terms of reduced performance and the potential loss of capable people who elect to leave the organization. In political infighting there are likely to be more losers than winners, and even those who triumph are less likely to have retained the respect and personal commitment of their colleagues. The application of sound employee relations is international and as such is a key organizational issue (Fey et al. 2012).

In an interview, a former director of a major retail company told me that at one point the senior management team were so embroiled in political infighting that the company was actually being managed by the middle managers. It is therefore beneficial to organizational wellbeing to construct a strategy for encouraging cooperation instead of internal competition between colleagues. For example, where practical, a team could be rewarded instead of individual employees. A strategic competitive advantage may be achieved by targeting improvements in employee motivation and innovation by giving rewards or bonuses to teams that deliver workable examples of new products or services.

DOWNSIZING AND THE IMPLICATIONS FOR EMPLOYEE RELATIONS

The process of reducing the number of employees is referred to as 'downsizing'. The reduction in staff numbers is likely to impact upon many more employees than just those who are made redundant. To use a simply example, a recommendation to replace a tea person with a vending machine might seem to be a cost-effective change to the office services manager; but to the tea person it might represent unemployment and an act of ingratitude after many years of service; or to other office staff it might offer an unwelcome reduction of employee benefits. It may even transpire that when the redundancy package for the tea person and the complaints from staff are considered, the 'change' to a vending machine is not be such a good idea after all. This should not be taken to mean that changes of service provision should be avoided, but rather to indicate that even a relatively simple change process requires consultation and discussion with all the interested parties.

A change in working patterns and especially job security also has implications for the levels of trust between management and staff. According to Legge (1995: 90), apart from the sacking of individuals (which may actually be a training or motivation issue), HRM provided a new rhetoric to obfuscate mass redundancies with euphemistic language including 'out placing', 'downsizing', 'rightsizing', 'headcount reduction' and even 'workforce re-profiling'. More concerning is that the act of sacking employees for short-term cost reduction was even represented as a positive act. In some cases, the unwanted employees may be paid a sufficiently large redundancy payment to soften the impact of being unemployed. Alternatively, if the job market is buoyant, then people with strong transferable attitudes, knowledge and skills may actually welcome a redundancy package as they have the employability to secure employment elsewhere. Ironically, it is these employees with high levels of transferable skills which the organization is most likely to need in the future. However, even with generous redundancy packages, downsizing is likely to degrade the psychological contract, the sense of commitment and trust among those employees who survive the redundancies.

The term 'downsizing' has come to be recognized as the use of staff redundancies to improve short-term profitability by reducing the payroll costs (Legge 1995: 90). When downsizing is used to remove whole groups of employees, such as junior or middle managers, it is referred to as 'delayering' because whole layers of the organization's structure are removed. The use of downsizing/delayering staff numbers as a means of reducing costs has been criticized by the eminent management commentator Henry Mintzberg. During a radio interview by Day (1996), he predicted that a lot of delayering may turn out to be another form of what happened in years past when organizations got rid of R&D (research and development), thereby saving money in the short term but jeopardizing the organization's future. The organizational value of encouraging people to develop new ideas is also supported by Ballot et al. (2001) in their study of the contribution of human capital, R&D and performance in French and Swedish firms.

The research by Sahdev (2003) into large organizations where downsizing has taken place found evidence to indicate that downsizing can result

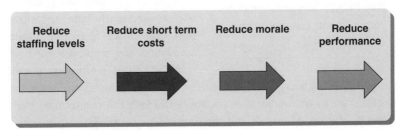

Figure 6.1 Implications of downsizing

in many negative outcomes including the loss of motivation, skills, learning and innovation. This then leads us to the next employee-relations issue: survivor syndrome. The effect on those employees who survive a round of redundancies may be to react by withdrawing their emotional commitment. Newell and Lloyd (Newell et al. 2002: 179) observed that in terms of organizational effectiveness and efficiency, research suggests that job insecurity can lead to employees having lower levels of commitment, being less willing to accept change, feeling more resentful of imposed change and becoming more secretive and competitive. These kinds of behaviours, in response to redundancies, are the antithesis of the cooperative team-working culture needed to sustain an organization in the medium to longer term. In the modern workplace where, often, fewer people are required to cope with larger workloads, the lack of long-term secure employment also places more stress on organizational cohesion. This is because commitment is a two-way street. When staff see their organization routinely expelling its unwanted employees, the survivors are less likely to give their whole unconditional commitment to the service and wellbeing of that organization.

During the 1990s, my work in management consultancy drew me to question the veracity of downsizing and the resultant job insecurity. Commenting on the issue of job insecurity in the *Times*, (Nieto 1992: 23) I observed that the message conveyed to those who survived 'downsizing' programmes was more likely to be negative than to inspire people to greater effort (see Figure 6.1). Hence, less commitment, confidence and creativity would ensue and more self-protection.

> **Key Point:** Downsizing reduces commitment, confidence and creativity.

The reality is that insecure employees are likely to become risk-averse and consequently the organization may suffer from diminished innovation and employee initiative (Hofstede 1994). Although downsizing may provide organizations with a temporary boost to profits (as the largest share of costs comprises employee salaries), this can soon be overtaken by the loss of morale and the competitive survivalist culture which such a short-term management strategy is likely to cultivate. Furthermore, if the prevailing organizational culture becomes less optimistic then some of the better employees are likely to seek jobs elsewhere.

Ironically, it is more likely to be the most capable people with the best CVs who are most likely to be able to find new jobs quickly. These are the very people whose attitudes, knowledge and skills would be most valuable to an organization seeking to bring about successful changes in management practices. The loss of experienced workers can also be detrimental to the organization's stakeholder networks. People work with people and established relationships can be difficult to replace. Consequently, the continuing human capital costs of downsizing can continue long after the displaced employees have gone.

Activity: a study of the long-term impact of downsizing

Choose an organization where a significant downsizing programme has taken place a few years ago. Then look for more recent reports about the organization's financial/ employee-relations performance.

Discuss the significance of whatever you find with regard to the possible implications for future HR policy.

Corporate memory describes the stories and history that underpin the organization's identity. The stories also inform new employees of what fate is likely to await them. In much the same way as certain product brands have a reputation for reliability, so organizations can build a reputation as being a reliable employer. Retaining and developing staff in the contemporary environment can therefore benefit organizational stability and sustainability in a challenging economic environment. Professionally trained HR managers have an important contribution to make in enabling organizations to develop and make the best use of their people (Rodríguez and Ventura 2003).

There are many costs associated with a turnover of staff. For example, in Figure 6.2 the organization is regularly retraining new people and spending time and money recruiting replacement staff. The process is time-consuming and distracts management's attention from the strategic aims of the organization. Obviously, time spent recruiting and retraining new employees takes time away from whatever the organization's primary work might be.

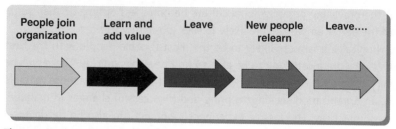

Figure 6.2 The costs of staff turnover

The case study below is of a real company. For reasons of confidentiality, the name and titles have been removed.

Cases from consultancy and research: changing the culture at New Co

The senior management at New Co (fictitious name) believed that in order to respond to new market opportunities, the structure and culture of the organization would have to be changed. However, the transition towards the new business plan was moving slower than they had hoped. Top management therefore took the decision to restructure the organization within two years. The aim of the change programme was to shift the company from a bureaucratic hierarchy into a dynamic sales-orientated organization.

According to the senior managers, the bureaucratic nature of the company tended to be slow in responding to market forces and this was something the directors were keen to change. One of the problems they identified was poor internal communication so they decided to employ more technology and fewer people. As a result, the number of management layers would have to be radically downsized. In other words, many of the current middle managers would be made redundant.

The middle managers and team leaders were therefore required to attend an assessment designed to differentiate between those whose knowledge and skills were useful to the 'restructured' organization and those who were considered no longer suitable. For example, one of the methods for assessing whether a manager might keep their job was to ask them to produce an outline of their current duties and explain why this was important to the future success of the company. Naturally, this created considerable stress and mistrust among staff who felt they were having to justify their existence within the organization, even though many had been with the company for a long time. Those managers who were found to be of no further value were offered voluntary redundancy. Alternatively, managers who decided not to leave could be reassigned, but not necessarily in the same part of the company or location, or at the same grade as their present job. This created both problems in motivation where people were sometimes demoted and practical difficulties with relocation-related upheaval.

The changes were a shock to people who had joined a relatively stable organization with recognized career paths, but who now found themselves in the invidious position of having to apply for new jobs within the company. The reorganization plan produced considerable consternation, as many of the people involved were apprehensive about what all the changes might mean for their future careers.

The senior management had decided that if their staff reduction targets were not reached, then compulsory redundancies could be introduced. However, rumours about this possibility abounded and some of the whispered conversations around the coffee machines greatly exaggerated the number of people who might be forced to leave the company.

As part of the restructuring process, the central personnel department was also downsized and the majority of the survivors were required to move to provincial offices. This effectively removed any central-office HR planning. Within 12 months the change programme was in difficulties and the organization was full of uncertainty and distrust. The levels of staff anxiety and stress were also high. The HR staff who remained were inundated with applications for new jobs. However, the reorganization of this department and the move from a central to a divisional role made the implementation of strategic planning virtually impossible and most of the applications were left unattended. This added to the tensions and frustrations felt by the staff, and effectively brought the culture change programme to a standstill. The company was simultaneously experiencing a talent drain as many of the best staff, which the company had wanted to retain, resigned and joined competitor companies.

Given the many difficulties being experienced by employees, the voluntary redundancy option proved to be much more attractive than the directors had imagined. In fact, applications to leave exceeded their target by a large margin. Senior management found themselves in the difficult situation of having to reject some of the applications for redundancy. At the same time, some of their best, most talented and entrepreneurial staff also resigned, either to join the organization's competitors or set up their own businesses. These were the very people the company wanted to keep if the transition into a more dynamic organization were going to have any chance of succeeding.

The two-year restructuring plan failed, raised costs and reduced productivity and customer satisfaction ratings.

Questions for discussion

1. Critically evaluate the senior management's decision to downsize the HR department and move most of the remaining staff to divisional offices.

2. During the two-year period of restructuring, the company declared increased profits. Consider how this was possible given the low morale of staff and the problems surrounding the restructuring process.

3. Evaluate why some of the best and most able staff left rather than stay to lead the reorganized company.

LEWIN'S CHANGE MODEL

In the world of work, each person has their own aspirations and responsibilities, so change, any change in their work situation, can potentially enhance or threaten pre-existing expectations. Even an apparently positive change can be perceived as threatening if it conflicts with what employees believe to be in their best interests. Human beings are social in nature so any disturbance to interpersonal routines and behaviours is likely to elicit a reaction.

The management of a change programme may be scheduled and project-managed. However, the employee reactions to any given change to their working patterns are less predictable. The model designed by Kurt Lewin (1951), postulated that there would be forces in favour of change and forces against (Figure 6.3). The change programme managers may elect to overcome resistance by insisting upon the implementation of their plans. However, such a strategy is likely to increase resentment and resistance. At best, enforced change programmes produce reluctant compliance, which is far removed from the kind of committed cooperation which is more likely to occur if employees' ideas have been included through active consultations.

Lewin (1951) also provided a three-stage model for implementing a change process. In the first stage, which he described as 'unfreezing', it is necessary to move the organization away from its current posture. Once employees recognize and accept the need for change, the second stage – 'changing' – can begin. If, as is often the case, the changes disturb

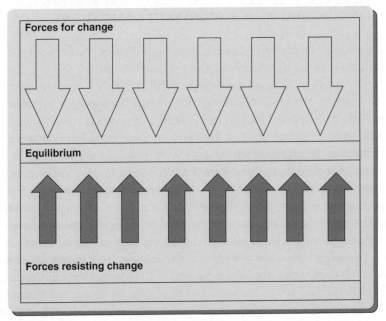

Figure 6.3 Kurt Lewin's model of forces for and against change

established working patterns, then a protracted period of consultation may be anticipated. It also helps if there are some identifiable interim benefits (easy wins) during the change process to stimulate positive support by colleagues. The change process itself has to be carefully managed with some positive incentives built into the process to encourage participation and progress. In Lewin's Model, this is followed by a third stage where the change is established into the organization and 're-freezing' takes place.

Lewin's three-stage change model (1951)

Stage 1: Unfreezing

Stage 2: Changing

Stage 3: Re-freezing

LEWIN'S CHANGE MODEL ADAPTED FOR A TWENTY-FIRST-CENTURY CONTEXT: UNFREEZING, CHANGING AND 'SLUSH' (CONSTANT ADAPTATION)

The elegant simplicity of Lewin's Model (1951) requires further critical evaluation of its application in the twenty-first century (Schein 1996; Burnes 2004). It is, however, a credit to the model's robustness that it continues to provide a foundation for change management. According to Elrod and Tippett (2002), Lewin's Model compares favourably with a wide range of change models. Furthermore, their study found that most approaches to organizational change were strikingly similar to it. It is therefore more a matter of refining Lewin's Model for new circumstances than constructing a completely new change model. What is evident in the twenty-first century, which differs from the previous century, is the rate of change in the business environment; for example, changes in computer technology, software and associated products such as mobile devices. As an example of the rapid growth in communication, the former US president Bill Clinton described the expansion of the Internet for a BBC lecture in 2001 (Clinton 2001). The rapid rate of change, he noted, had increased the number of websites from 50 in the mid-1990s to over 350 million (and growing rapidly) just a few years later.

It follows that the refreezing aspect of the Lewin Change Model requires a reappraisal and indeed alteration to serve the twenty-first century's rapid rate of change. The metaphor of re-freezing represents a new state of rigidity and stability. By the late twentieth century, it was evident that change was becoming almost continuous. If an organization were to resettle into a frozen state then the products and services it produced would remain unchanged from the period of refreezing. However, any consumer of products and services knows that there is constant change to whatever is on offer. Long gone are the days when, as it is alleged, the famous motor car producer of the early Model T Ford, Henry Ford, advised customers that they could have any colour car they wanted as long as it was black.

While the mid-twentieth-century Weberian bureaucracies may have been able to re-freeze after change, the modern analogy might be something more like 'slush'. Where changes in technology, employees, tasks and structure are more frequent, the notion of re-freezing may not be an appropriate metaphor for modern change progression (Nieto 2006).

Key Point: The Slush Model (Nieto 2006) metaphor represents an organization which is flexible and adaptable as an alternative to a re-frozen organization. It also encourages an attitude of continuous development, whereby the organization should resist becoming frozen in the first place.

Retaining and retraining employees ensures stability in an adaptive change environment.

A flexible and adaptable attitude to progress should not, however, be misinterpreted as the unfortunately common organizational tendency to address issues of weaknesses in the strategic development of new products or services by reorganizing their staff. A quotation that has been around for some time, commenting on the futility of unnecessary staff reorganizations, is cited below. Although some commentators have probably incorrectly attributed the words to the Ancient Roman period of history, the earliest manuscript or printed source for the anonymous observation was a magazine article in the mid-twentieth century. In any case, it presents the futility or unnecessary staff reorganizations succinctly. The Slush Model addresses the modern requirement for organizations to regularly review and adapt what they offer their consumers/stakeholders. It does not advocate, as an alternative to new products and services, the restructuring of people into new job roles/titles and or redundancies. As discussed earlier in this chapter, such restructuring interventions have inherent associated tendencies to lower staff morale, productivity and service quality (Hofstede 1994; Legge 1995; Turnley and Feldman 2000; Sahdev 2003; Nieto 2006).

> We trained hard, but it seemed that every time we were beginning to form up into teams, we would be reorganized. I was to learn later in life that we tend to meet any new situation by reorganizing; and a wonderful method it can be for creating the illusion of progress while producing confusion, inefficiency, and demoralization.

Activity: individual or group seminar presentations

In the next exercise, try to honestly explore how much change you are willing to accept. Try the exercise below to reflect upon your willingness to make changes in the way you work.

1. You are a member of a project team which is working effectively. The manager asks if you would like to change teams to gain experience in a different situation. How do you think you would respond? Agree to the change, comply unwillingly, or decline?

2. If you are at university, think about an assignment team which is working effectively. How would you respond if the seminar tutor asked you to move from one assignment group to a new one?

3. The module that you selected for your final year was to be taught by a lecturer you have known since you began your course. The lecturer has been very encouraging and awarded you some first-class grades. Just before the semester begins, you hear that the lecturer has left the university to go to a senior role at another university. A new lecturer will be teaching your course. What is your reaction to the change?

SUMMARY: STRATEGIC HRM IN A CHANGING ORGANIZATIONAL ENVIRONMENT

(a) Listening and working with colleagues builds plans for which they have a sense of ownership, because they have been involved in the development.

(b) If an organization has happy, motivated, secure people, then they are more likely to cultivate a positive organizational environment which lends itself to long-term sustainability. As a strategy, this approach prepares a platform of employee commitment to support the organization's sustainability. Conversely, unhappy, demotivated, insecure employees are more likely to seek short-term gains which may or may not secure their current job. This is more likely to destabilize the organization's strategic plan.

(c) Each person needs to have their personal, strategic, career-development plan. This could include: attending short company courses, external accreditations such as the CIPD and CMI, and new qualifications such as an MBA or a Master's degree.

(d) Profit margins rose in businesses where employees described themselves as committed to their organizations. Conversely, organizations with less committed employees saw net profit margin fall. Other key factors were employees' views of the development opportunities they were offered and whether or not they were empowered to do their work effectively.

(e) The psychological contract focuses on the exchange of perceived promises and commitments.

(f) The security of knowing employment is not likely to be snatched away can stimulate innovations because employees can take a longer-term perspective on project developments.

(g) The term 'personnel management', which was popular in the mid-twentieth century, might be perceived to be a more person-centred term than 'human resources management'.

(h) The contemporary term 'employability' contains an implicit understanding that it is necessary to be in a position to secure a new job.

Hence, the change in terms also indicates a strategic realignment from the possibility of long-term employment to transferable employability.

(i) The notion of a secure job was being disrupted throughout the twentieth century by the recessions in the 1930s, 1970s, and early 1990s. In this century, the same has happened following an economic downturn in the first two decades.

(j) The term 'psychological contract' – which by its very nature describes something which is fixed – is probably not as useful a metaphor for employee relations as it was in the mid-twentieth century.

(k) Differences in commitment might be traced to the less secure and more uncertain nature of outsourced employment, as well as to feelings among these employees that they were treated less equitably.

(l) Even with generous redundancy packages, downsizing is likely to degrade the sense of commitment and trust among those employees who survive the redundancies.

(m) When staff see their organization routinely expelling its unwanted employees, the survivors are less likely to give their whole unconditional commitment to the service and wellbeing of that organization.

(n) Downsizing may produce less commitment, confidence and creativity and more self-protection.

(o) The time spent recruiting and retraining new employees takes time away from whatever the organization's primary work might be.

(p) Human beings are social in nature, so any disturbance to interpersonal routines and behaviours is likely to elicit a reaction.

(q) The re-freezing aspect of the Lewin Model (1951) requires a reappraisal and indeed alteration to serve the twenty-first century. While the mid-twentieth-century bureaucracies may have been able to re-freeze after change, the modern analogy might be more like 'slush'.

(r) The Slush Model (Nieto 2006) offers a metaphor for semi-formed structure which is also flexible and adaptable as an alternative to a re-frozen organization. It also encourages an attitude of continuous development, whereby the organization should resist becoming frozen in the first place.

(s) The Slush Model addresses the modern requirement for organizations to regularly review and adapt what they offer their consumers/stakeholders. The model does not advocate, as an alternative to new products and services, the restructuring of people into new job roles/titles and/or redundancies.

REVISION SECTION

1. In practice, the majority of organizational structures can serve well enough, providing employees are secure, consulted and involved with the objectives of the organization. Why do organizational restructures often fail?

2. Demonstrate your understanding of a psychological contract by explaining how it is different to an employment contract and why it is important to employee relations with managers?

3. Why is employment stability and retention particularly relevant in an international market for employees?

TAKING IT FURTHER

Key texts to look up:

Bryson, J. M. (2011) *Strategic Planning for Public and Non-profit Organizations: A Guide to Strengthening and Sustaining Organizational Achievement* (4th Edition). New York: John Wiley & Sons.

Eisenstadt, S. N (ed.) (1968) *Max Weber on Charisma & Institution Building*. Chicago: University of Chicago Press.

Guest, D. E. and Conway, N. (2002) Communicating the Psychological Contract: An Employer Perspective. *Human Resource Management Journal*. 1 April, 12(2), pp. 22–38.

Toral, P. (2011) *Multinational Enterprises in Latin America since the 1990s*. New York: Palgrave Macmillan.

Refer to the books and journals in this references section.

REFERENCES

Bagshaw, M. (1997) Employability – Creating a Contract of Mutual Investment. *Industrial and Commercial Training*. 29(6), pp. 183–185.

Ballot, G., Fakhfakh, F. and Taymaz, E. (2001) Firms' Human Capital, R&D and Performance: A Study on French and Swedish Firms. *Labour Economics*. 8(4), pp. 443–462.

Bryson, J. M. (2011) *Strategic Planning for Public and Nonprofit Organizations: A Guide to Strengthening and Sustaining Organizational Achievement* (4th Edition). New York: John Wiley & Sons.

Burnes, B. (2004) Kurt Lewin and the Planned Approach to Change: A Re-appraisal. *Journal of Management Studies*. 41(6), pp. 977–1002.

Clinton, B. (2001) *The Struggle for the Soul of the 21st Century*. The Dimbleby Lecture. *BBC*. 14 December.

Day, P. (1996) Attacking the Organisation. *BBC Radio 4*. 8, 15, 22, 29, May.

Diamond, D. W. and Rajan, R. G. (2005) *Liquidity Shortage and Banking Crisis*. *Journal of Finance*. 60(2), pp. 615–647.

Eisenstadt, S. N (ed.) (1968) *Max Weber on Charisma & Institution Building*. Chicago: University of Chicago Press.

Elrod, P. D. II and Tippett, D. D. (2002) The 'Death Valley' of change. *Journal of Organizational Change Management*. (15)3, pp. 273–291.

Fey, C. F., Kasperskaya, N., Kuznetsova, I., Sverdlov, D. and Shvakman, I. (2010) How to Retain Employees. *Harvard Business Review Russia*. September, pp. 61–70.

Guest, D. E. and Conway, N. (2002) *Communicating the Psychological Contract: An Employer Perspective*. *Human Resource Management Journal*. 1 April, 12(2), pp. 22–38.

Handy, C. (1994) *The Empty Raincoat*. London: Hutchinson.

Hofstede, G. (1994) *Cultures and Organizations: Software of the Mind*. London: Harper Collins.

Kessler, I. (ed.) (2002) Deery, S. and J. Walsh Contracting out and Market-mediated Employment Arrangements: Outsourcing Call Centre Work. *People Management*. 7 February. Wimbledon: CIPD.

Legge, K. (1995) *Human Resource Management: Rhetorics and Realities*. London: Macmillan.

Lewin, K. (1951) *Field Theory in Social Science*. New York: Harper & Row.

Newell, S., Scarbrough, H., Swan, J., Robertson, M., and Galliers, R. D. (2002, January). The importance of process knowledge for cross project learning: Evidence from a UK hospital. In System Sciences, 2002. HICSS. Proceedings of the 35th Annual Hawaii International Conference on (pp. 1019–1028), IEEE.

Nieto, M. L. (2006) *An Introduction to Human Resource Management: An Integrated Approach*. Basingstoke: Palgrave Macmillan.

Nieto, M. L. (1992) Macho Talk at BET. *The Times*. 16 June.

Nieto, M. L. (2003) The Development of Life Work Balance Initiatives Designed for Managerial Workers. *Business Ethics: A European Review*. 12(3), July, pp. 229–232.

Rodríguez J. M. and Ventura, J. (2003) Human Resource Management Systems and Organizational Performance: An Analysis of the Spanish Manufacturing Industry. *International Journal of Human Resource Management*. 14(7), pp. 1206–1226.

Sahdev, K. (2003) Survivors' Reactions to Downsizing: The Importance of Contextual Factors. *Human Resource Management Journal*, 1 November, 13(4). pp. 56–74.

Thompson, P. and McHugh, D. (2002) *Work Organisations* (3rd Edition). Basingstoke: Palgrave Macmillan.

Womack, S. (2002) British Workers 'Have Low Levels of Commitment to Employers'. *The Daily Telegraph*, 3 September.

Schein, E. H. (1996) Kurt Lewin's Change Theory in the Field and in the Classroom: Notes towards a Model of Management Learning. *Systems Practice*. 9(1), pp. 27–47.

Sisodia, R. (2004) India's John Smiths Speak Perfect English. Now They Have a Month to Become British. *The Independent*, Sunday, 12 May.

Sitkin, A. and Bowen, N. (2013) *International Business: Challenges and Choices* (2nd Edition). Oxford: Oxford University Press.

Sussangkarn, C., Park, Y. and Kang, S. (2011) *Foreign Direct Investments in Asia*. London: Routledge.

Toral, P. (2011) *Multinational Enterprises in Latin America since the 1990s*. New York: Palgrave Macmillan.

Turnley, W. H. and Feldman, D. C. (2000) Re-examining the Effects of Psychological Contract Violations: Unmet Expectations and Job Dissatisfaction as Mediators. *Journal of Organizational Behavior*. 21(1), pp. 25–42.

7

HRM in a Global Environment

INTRODUCTION

In the other chapters of this book, you have learned about why the way we manage people is central to organizational success. The same attitudes, knowledge and skills are equally relevant to international HR, together with an additional AKS set which is necessary to manage people in an international context. Within a global economy, managers need to have the interpersonal attributes, knowledge and skills to work across national boundaries. For example, to develop both regional sensitivity and global awareness (Bennett 1986). International business management therefore requires people to be 'locally sensitive and globally aware' (Nieto 2006: 261). Hence, managers need to develop the attitudes, knowledge and skills to be able to work across national boundaries, whether for a multinational company (MNC) or a family business.

To learn and develop these skills, it is valuable to work in multinational teams where you can apply the theories in this book to practical activities. The activities in this chapter have been designed through working with international students on postgraduate and undergraduate programmes, to build the attitudes, knowledge and skills that are required in our global business environment.

I am also pleased to have a section in this chapter by Dr Nicholas Bowen on the influence of globalization on organizational behaviour and reputations. Nick has international standing as an author on international business and has been a member of the Editorial Advisory Board of the *Euro Asia Journal of Management* since 2008.

As the twenty-first century leaves behind its twentieth-century origins, a new globalization is emerging that embraces local differences. A globalization where the local customs and preferences are retained as part of, instead of superseded by, the dominant producers of products, services and brands icon of the time.

LEARNING OBJECTIVES

The key learning outcomes for the chapter are below:

- Appreciate the opportunities and limitations of HR initiatives across national/cultural boundaries.
- HRM which is locally sensitive and globally aware.
- Critically evaluate the contemporary debate on the influence of globalization on organizational behaviour and reputations (by Dr Nicholas Bowen).
- The implications of 'culture shock'. Evaluate the influence of cultural diversity in international staff deployments.
- Develop 'cultural sensitivity'. Understand and apply the attitudes, knowledge and skills which enhance success in global organizational management.
- Learn to design an international induction programme.

APPRECIATE THE OPPORTUNITIES AND LIMITATIONS OF HR INITIATIVES ACROSS NATIONAL/CULTURAL BOUNDARIES

In a globalized environment where customers have many more choices of supplier, it is becoming much more important for organizations to recognize that their behaviour towards stakeholders, both local and global, can hold the key to long-term success. Organizations therefore need to include training people to work more successfully across the diversity of global cultures as a key element of their international strategic plans.

It is particularly relevant for organizations to be aware of the preferences for management approaches and styles in other nations. This will be discussed later in this chapter within the section entitled: 'Critically evaluate the contemporary debate on the influence of globalization on organizational behaviour and reputations', contributed by Dr Nicholas Bowen.

> **Key Point:** 'Cultural sensitivity' enables managers to work in a multinational context. As a student, select programmes which recruit students from many different nationalities and thereby learn by studying in teams which reflect the global reality of twenty-first century organizational work across national borders.

The term 'globalization' is generally used to describe the rapidly increasing movement of trade and people around the globe (Albrow 1996). For the twenty-first century, the fluid movement of employees and the work itself, around the globe, means that the manager needs to be the cultural equivalent of multilingual. Hence, a manager will need the attitudes, knowledge and skills which have been described as 'cultural sensitivity' (Nieto 2006: 262). This approach includes tolerance of diversity and flexibility in working with teams of people who may come from a varied mix of international cultural influences.

It is reasonable to anticipate that there will be significant differences in working patterns across national boundaries. Each nation has its individual cultures and traditions, which require a situation sensitive approach (Mensah 2009; Ng 2012; Panibratov 2012). Furthermore, MNCs should avoid cultural arrogance; the implied belief that there is one best practice which can be imposed upon everyone else irrespective of national culture differences.

The model below explains three stages in the procedural approaches to organizational management in an international context. In Stage 1, the business is primarily in one national locality and thereby operates within the cultural norms of that location, though it may export some goods or services abroad. In Stage 2, the organization has facilities in other parts of the world, but imposes the home nation procedures upon its other centres.

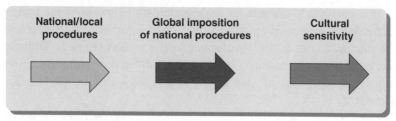

| National/local procedures | Global imposition of national procedures | Cultural sensitivity |

Figure 7.1 Global Sensitivity Model

Source: Nieto (2006: 263).

In Stage 3 the organization is culturally sensitive and adapts its organizational approaches sympathetically to the host nation environments.

HRM: LOCALLY SENSITIVE AND GLOBALLY AWARE

Our growing global interdependence is a significant factor in determining organizational success or failure, so it is all the more important for local managers to appreciate international influences. Modern organizations therefore operate within complex political and often competitive global environments (Albrow 1996; Findlay and O'Rourke 2009; Baylis et al. 2010). Consequently, it is valuable to develop both global and local awareness for people working across international boundaries.

The research work of Hofstede (1984, 1994) emphasized the importance of organizational culture in employee behaviour. Also, according to Hofstede's research, if people are insecure their tendency will be towards less risk taking and the prevailing organizational culture will move towards uncertainty avoidance (Hofstede 1994). Consequently, people in uncertainty-avoiding organizational cultures will shun ambiguous situations. In such cultures, employees will seek more structure and certainly to rebalance the uncertainty in a quest to make their organizational lives more predictable (Hofstede 1994: 116). When these behaviours are set within a global context where change is rapid, a culture of insecurity and caution is unlikely to provide the innovation, new services or products which can generate competitive advantage.

However, national cultures are also being influenced as information travels across national boundaries. In the interconnected world of the twenty-first century, people across the globe have access to instant information via the Internet. This growth of intercommunication has and continues to be expediential. As an example of the rapid growth in communication, the former US President Bill Clinton (2001) described the expansion of the Internet for a BBC lecture: '[T]he information technology revolution: when I became President in 1993, there were only fifty sites on the worldwide web – unbelievable – fifty. When I left office, the number was three hundred and fifty million and rising'. When people have easy access to other cultures, their awareness of different lifestyles and choices is thereby increased. The exposure to different ways of living may either reinforce there local cultural values or bring them into question. Our global interconnectivity therefore requires 'cultural sensitivity' which, as Nieto (2006: 261) has observed, respects diversity and is tolerant of different customs in lifestyles and workplace behaviour.

The challenges of creating effective teams are all present in transnational corporations, with the addition of diverse national cultures to be included into the team dynamic. Inadequate preparations can have high costs in employee dissatisfaction and even legal disputes (Kopp 1994). The efficacy of developing sound interpersonal human relations is also part of any healthy workplace environment and requires particular attention when working with a variety of nation states and across different time zones.

In the twenty-first century, globalization often takes the form of off-shore outsourcing (Bhagwati and Blinder 2009). The movement of work has happened throughout the world's history (Bernstein 2009), with nations trading by ships or by building industrial plant in low-cost areas of the globe. However, by the late twentieth century, the use of Internet technology has meant that many additional administrative roles can be outsourced abroad. One of the common growth areas is the call centre where customer calls regarding a wide range of services from airline ticketing to credit card enquiries can be out-sourced offshore to a lower-cost employment area of the world. Hence, in India, the development of software technology parks has produced growth from a small niche sector in the 1990s to the formation of a significant part of the country's economy in the twenty-first century (Elmuti and Kathawala 2000; Crabb 2003).

Consequently, many first world jobs are now being completed in lower-pay areas in the second and third worlds. This provides new work opportunities in the second and third worlds and increases profits for those businesses which then sell those services and products back into the first world.

> **Key Point:** In an international job market, expect to see people from many different nationalities moving to jobs which offer the best employee environment.

The introduction of appropriate training and development initiatives and the use of experienced employees to oversee outsourced workers are more likely to ensure connectivity with the home-country head office. International, cultural-awareness, development training benefits the performance of off-shore outsourced enterprises (Sisodia 2004; Sussangkarn et al. 2011; Toral 2011; Yesudian-Storfiell 2012). The development of offshore outsourcing also underlines the value of cultural sensitivity, where managers in the home country are in communication with colleagues from a diversity of nations and cultures. If an organization decides to outsource offshore then HR has an important role to play in ensuring that service quality is not sacrificed to cost expediency.

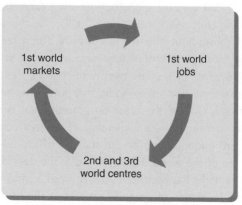

Figure 7.2 Model: movement of jobs through out-sourcing

Activity: the toy factory

The 'toy factory' is a seminar activity which I developed for the international business course at Regent's University London.

The scenario requires students to form groups representing the following stakeholder sets:

- toy factory senior management group
- employee representatives
- the Government of the prospective new factory location
- the UK Government.

Once the sets are formed, the student sets each prepare their positions in regard to the proposed factory relocation.

The seminar tutor can also include newsflashes as the negotiations progress.

Newsflashes:

- The company's sales of toys have declined due to a new entrant manufacturer who is advertising 'locally produced toys'.
- The home country's trading area (e.g. the European Community) imposes an importation tax on non-essential products from outside its trading community area.
- Employees in the proposed country of relocation are asking for a comparable wage to the home country's workers.

Discussion questions

- Discuss the advantages and disadvantages of relocating the toy factory to a lower-wage area of the globe.
- What do you think the training issues are for the home-country management team who are working with an offshore manufacturing site?
- What are the advantages and possible challenges of working in multicultural teams?

- How much incentive do you think the home-country government may offer to retain the factory and preserve local jobs?

CRITICALLY EVALUATE THE CONTEMPORARY DEBATE ON THE INFLUENCE OF GLOBALIZATION ON ORGANIZATIONAL BEHAVIOUR AND REPUTATIONS

Reputations are a major part of brand image, and reputation can be influenced by employee attitudes as much as – if not more than – by expensive marketing campaigns. Furthermore, in the global age, what an organization does in one part of the world can be communicated across the globe in seconds by the Internet. The results of research by Park et al. (2003) indicated that employee attitudes, knowledge and skill are a key factor in producing success within MNCs.

> **Key Point:** Organizational reputation is like a brand. Building good employee relations also creates a positive organizational reputation around the globe.

This following section was prepared by Dr Nicholas Bowen, principal lecturer in international business, Regent's College president, Chartered Institute of Linguists.

Whether one thinks that modern globalization is principally cultural, economic, financial, social, political, technological (whether related to information and communications technology, or more industrial technology), or any combination of these, it is apparent that more people in the world are more connected to each other than in previous eras. This interconnectedness operates across many aspects of work and employment at all levels.

The exceptions to globalization and interconnectedness are related to parts of the world where there are trends towards economic protectionism, financial nationalism, ethnic and religious fundamentalism, and resistance to the perceived 'western-ness' or American-ness of globalization. Quite naturally, there are pockets of insistence on the traditions and resistance to global homogenization. Most of us identify ourselves primarily with family, town, region and nation before we can move towards a wider identity. For example, even within one of the most interconnected parts of the world – the European Union – primary identifications and allegiances are to 'regions' within countries (such as Catalonia, Bavaria and Wales) and to the nation-states themselves (such as Poland, Ireland and Portugal), rather than to the 27 countries as a whole.

The increasing interconnectedness of the world through the various trends and developments within modern globalization means that there is a greater 'evenness' in the treatment of middle-range managers, senior executives and CEOs/presidents. Whereas there used to be a high use of expatriate managers and specialists (even in the relatively recent past of the 1980s and 1990s), the early years of the twenty-first century have seen much greater employment of local people within the management of companies. This applies to the majority of multinational organizations as well as to the larger 'national' companies. The improvements in local, regional and national education and training have provided the world's workforce with a more diverse and more international pool of talent. The consequence of this is that expatriation tends to be more in the nature of what has been called 'international commuter' or 'frequent-flyer' (Marilyn Fenwick. cited in Harzing and Van Ruysseveldt [2004]). This type of expatriation is limited to weekly or bi-weekly business trips with occasional temporary relocation or regular international trips without any periods of relocation. The older practice of managers and specialist employees being relocated from their country of origin typically for periods of 2–3 years (extendable if required) has been largely abandoned in favour of shorter international assignments. The two prime benefits of the new practice are that: (a) more international managers are exposed to cultural differences; and (b) more responsibility is given to national-origin managers.

As was noted in 2010 by Mary Durham, vice-president of finance and human resources, OnPath Technologies Inc., her recent experience and perception of expatriate jobs is that there are fewer of them these days. Expatriation tends to focus on shorter jobs and projects that give people the experience of going abroad without the more permanent moves that used to prevail. International assignments are very useful for understanding international differences and for observing other people's adaptation to different cultures (Sitkin and Bowen 2010: 366). From Durham's perspective, there is a virtue to using international assignments, however short they may be, as part of the training, education and development of many types of employee. It is as important and relevant for a specialist – such as an auditor, engineer, research chemist, or facilities analyst – as it is for managers on the general career promotion ladder within the company.

From the mid-twentieth century to the first quarter of the twenty-first century (1960s–2010s), there has been a significant trend towards the 'nationalization' of employment practices, organizational structures and career paths. In industrial sectors such as oil and gas, steel and shipbuilding, for example, the proportions of local people employed at managerial level have risen significantly on a worldwide basis.

One of the consequences of the globalization of organizational structure and employment relations is that management of workforces requires considerable cultural sensitivity. For managers and other employees working outside their own country, it is essential that challenges of language, culture, behaviour and attitude are understood, confronted and overcome. In many cases, such challenges can be faced and surmounted by the proper design and implementation of cross-cultural training (CCT) programmes.

There are some good examples of the impact of cultural requirements on management within major corporations. For example, with large Japanese companies operating globally from a European base, there is the challenge of matching the cultural range of their departmental general managers to the balance between resorting to instructions and supervision from the home headquarters and taking local responsibility for their decisions. The linkage between national cultures and corporate cultures highlights the crucial point at which managers (and other employees) face the most critical challenges within MNCs. The differences in approaches to work, attitudes to time keeping, team-working patterns and other forms of workplace behaviour combine with some of the stereotypical characteristics associated with particular nations (see the export of national culture model in this chapter). The struggle between national and corporate cultures is fascinating but challenging for global managers, especially for those operating within the field of international HRM.

THE IMPLICATIONS OF 'CULTURE SHOCK': EVALUATE THE INFLUENCE OF CULTURAL DIVERSITY ON INTERNATIONAL STAFF DEPLOYMENTS

As can be seen from the section above by Nick Bowen, working internationally can sometimes be challenging because there are likely to be national cultures and norms to which a person from outside that country is unaccustomed. The experience of being in an environment which is different to a person's home cultural norms and environment is described as 'culture shock' (Ward et al. 2001). One of the factors influencing the success or failure of employees sent to international assignments is therefore the expatriate's ability to function successfully in the new culture (Munton and Forster 1990; Lawson and Angle 1994).

The research by Black et al. (1991) found that up to 40% of American employees who relocated to foreign assignments elected to return sooner than originally planned. The work performance of as many as one in two expatriates was also found to be a disappointment (Bonache 2005). This kind of poor performance is an indicator that more could and should be done to prepare employees for international assignments (Black and Mendenhall 1990; Black et al. 1992). Research by Bennett (1986) postulated a progression from low competence in intercultural sensitivity towards international sensitivity. It thereby follows that employees are more likely to settle into a new location and job role if they receive training and support before they commence the placement or assignment.

While it is common to have an induction programme for people starting a new job, it is not always the case for an international assignment. However, training is even more important if a person is relocating to a different part of the world where they also need to change their home and social arrangements, too (Trompenaars and Woolliams 2003). It follows that in addition to the factors which a manager could expect to receive in an induction

Key Point: Develop awareness of the potential impact of culture shock whereby an otherwise capable professional may find the many new situations and different procedures and expectations difficult to cope with (Adler 1981).

plan, there are additional aspects of learning required when moving to a country with a different culture and different ways of working.

The pre-departure training should include developing intercultural sensitivity to help easier adaptation to a different environment. This kind of initiative can reduce potential problems for the expatriate and the organization they are joining.

Short cases from consultancy and research: home thoughts from abroad

This is a section of a letter from a scientist on an international assignment. The exact locations and names have been removed to preserve the anonymity of the people described.

On the way to the camp [...] there are large swathes of forest which have been bulldozed to make way for palm oil plantations. This is seen as very good by the [...]. In order to address this issue, the forest needs to provide the population with a living – and being as dense as it is, there are not that many large animals. It is a real challenge and it is easy for us Europeans [to] wring our hands and feel that this is criminal, but what else do these people do to survive?

We came across some loggers in the wood on the little walk we took along the tracks. They were very friendly and all speak English (with a strong accent which my ears are not attuned to yet). We had to laugh as we were having a chat with some of the miners. They were chatting in a language I did not understand at all, only to be told that this was English. We all had a good laugh as I had not got a single word.

We got rained out yesterday afternoon – ABSOLUTELY SOAKED. It was oppressively hot when we left – like a sauna which had been turned up too high. The worst is the humidity – you sweat the minute you get up. That didn't last as the heavens opened up a little while later. Warm rain. The driver had patiently waited for us and eventually a soggy team of 6 got in the Land Cruiser with muddy boots for the journey home. I asked him how old he was and he said 40 (he looked more like 60). The guys in the truck all roared with laughter (to the driver's discomfort) as I was told that this was his work age (they are terrified of being pensioned off). There is a real age and a work age.

As we drove back we crossed a river near the village with the topless women still washing clothes in the driving rain. Naked kids splash about in the water and they all shout a word – which the driver tells me is 'white man'. There are not many whites here, and apart from the exploration team, we must be a real novelty to them. They all want to touch me and laugh, smile and wave as we pass with the truck window open.

Questions

The letter illustrates some interesting cultural differences between the European writer and the hosts.

1. Discuss the different attitudes to destroying the dense forest. Why do you think the writer said 'us Europeans [to] wring our hands?' Explain what you understand as being the different perspectives on forestry from the perspective of the local people and the Europeans?

2. Communication difficulties. Although the local people speak English, the team cannot understand them. How could the team have been better prepared?

3. The age of retirement. Why do you think the locals claim that they have a 'work age' and 'a real age'?

4. The 'weather'. How could the team have been better prepared prior to leaving for their international assignment?

DEVELOP 'CULTURAL SENSITIVITY'. UNDERSTAND AND APPLY THE ATTITUDES, KNOWLEDGE AND SKILLS, WHICH ENHANCE SUCCESS IN GLOBAL ORGANIZATIONAL MANAGEMENT

Attitudes

Attitudes include preconceptions and personal prejudices, both positive and negative, regarding the country/region which staff are being posted to and the assignment they will be required to complete. These attitudes predispose a person to certain perceptions of other cultures and the situations they will be entering. The cultural-attitudes awareness programme can include:

- *An evaluation* of the applicant's ability to adapt to the new environment as part of the selection procedure.
- *Discussion* and support regarding any concerns and apprehensions about the new opportunities and challenges that they may meet in their new assignment.
- *Development* of improved self-awareness through discussions/self-assessment questionnaires to assist in the preparation to depart to a new national assignment.
- *The initial programme* of assessment should be used to tailor the subsequent training in knowledge and skills, which can provide positive reinforcement for attitudinal development.

Knowledge

Prior to departure on a new assignment, HR can provide staff with a tailored programme designed to meet both the personal and professional training needs required for success in the location they are going to. In practice, this requires supported research and planning by the employee to prepare them for their new assignment. The research can include:

- *Discussion and support:* regarding any concerns and apprehensions about family relocation and personal matters such as accommodation and health-care provision and schooling, social networks.

- *Agreed plans:* should be agreed and practical matters such as short-term accommodation arranged so that staff have a suitable place to live upon arrival.
- *School places:* if required, should be organized prior to departure. It is important to acknowledge that the expatriate is more likely to succeed if their immediate family also feels comfortable in their new environment.
- *Accommodation:* Where would be a good longer-term place to live? If the expatriate is taking family with them, they would probably like information on the local property market.
- *Partner employment:* Are there good job opportunities for the staff member's partner? Can the necessary visas and or work permits be provided?
- *Living conditions:* Appropriate information for factors such as climate and the kind of working/living conditions the expatriate can expect to experience. Will the new location be cold, hot, wet? Can the staff member expect to work in an air-conditioned office or not?
- *Transport:* How reliable is the local public transport?
- *Cultural values:* Learn about local customs and traditions. Encourage tolerance in areas such as religious faiths, work routines and dress codes.
- *Communication:* What is the main language used for business purposes? Are local people likely to speak the expatriate's language or is a short language course necessary? Are there any specific matters regarding business etiquette and protocol? For example, in some European countries (such as Switzerland and Germany), precise punctuality is regarded as important whereas in areas such as South America people are generally more relaxed about precise time keeping. Is the host's organizational management culture formal or informal in terms of address?

Skills

Theory into practice

There are considerable differences between knowledge and skills. For example, a theoretical understanding of cultural diversity is quite different from moving to and working in a different country. The development of cultural skills therefore empowers a person to put what they know into practical action. To facilitate cultural skills improvement, HR can provide a scheme of training. The skills training programme can include:

- *Learning materials*: Using learning exercises, video and interactive on-line materials and relevant textbook learning materials. This programme may be designed within the in-house HR group or sourced via an external provider, such as a consultant or university business school.

- *Role-playing:* This can be a very useful source of interactive learning, especially if there are several people being posted to an overseas assignment together.

- *Interactive seminars:* If a group of people are to be sent on assignment together then interactive seminars – including regional research activities and team building – can be a very useful experiential learning tool.

- *Orientation trips:* If it is practical, a short orientation visit to the area of placement can provide useful firsthand experiences for employees who are relocating for an extended period of time. It will also provide them with the opportunity to personally experience what living in their new country might be like, prior to taking on their full job-role responsibilities.

Post-arrival induction activity programme

It is helpful to smooth the new expatriate's arrival to their new assignment by providing an orientation programme for their work/personal life, preferably in the first week of arrival.

- *Orientation activities:* Including a tour of the local area. Information on accommodation, local facilities, banking, medical, social, sports clubs, transport.

- *Working practices:* Local working hours, rest breaks. Information on organizational structure and culture ('the way we do things here').

- *Introductions:* It is helpful to have a local manager arrange meetings with new colleagues and key people.

- *Mentoring:* It is useful to provide the new expatriates with a mentor who they can turn to for on-going support and advice. The mentoring schedule may be organized to the convenience of both, although regular monthly/bimonthly meetings are likely to be appropriate.

Coming home: the re-entry programme

Although HR provision is more than likely to be given to expatriates, it is less common for people returning home from overseas assignments. Yet employees returning from overseas assignments may experience reverse culture shock and require a support programme (Gregersen and Black 1996; Stroh et al. 1998). This may be all the more poignant because they are unlikely to be expecting assimilation difficulties returning to their home country. Nevertheless, it is sensible to recognize that someone who has adapted to a whole new environment may find the return home initially disorientating.

Key Point: Develop awareness of the potential impact of reverse culture shock. Employees returning to their home country can find the changes which occurred after they left a challenge. Particularly, if there are different procedures and expectations which are difficult to cope with.

Furthermore, the world that the employee departed from is also likely to have moved on during the time they have been abroad. For example, old and trusted colleagues may have changed roles or left the organization. Conversely, new people may have joined the organization, bringing changes in management style and practice. The home organization is likely to have put in place alternative arrangements regarding the expatriate's former job-role so this may have either changed or may no longer exist in its former configuration. Consequently, the old familiar working environment may have been reorganized or replaced altogether. Indeed, their department or work group could have moved location so that the expatriate's old office may not even still exist. It is, on reflection not at all surprising that people can experience a reverse culture shock when so much of what they thought they were returning to may have changed.

Reorientation plan

Pre-return: Arrange for meetings with home company representatives a few months before returning home from the assignment. Update the returning employee on current/new developments.

Re-orientation: Provide a re-entry pack to include relevant news and information such as the current housing market, and economic environment.

Working practices: Compile a briefing paper on any relevant changes to working practices. This is particularly relevant to senior managers who may find that their junior home-based colleagues are now more up-to-date on current policies than they are.

Introductions: Upon return, introduce the returnee to new colleagues and encourage people to include them in the usual social and information interactions.

Mentoring: Organize a home mentor for the returnee.

DESIGNING AN INTERNATIONAL INDUCTION PROGRAMME AND PRESENTATIONS

The activity encourages interactive research including academic literature, the Internet and the preparation of a training programme supported by a presentation. The activity can be completed by either an individual student or a team. There are advantages to designing the activity as a team exercise as this more closely replicates real working situations. There are also benefits in selecting team members from a range of nationalities so the experience of completing the assignment also provides experiential learning, working with international diversity.

The activity may be delivered as either a group/individual presentation or group/individual briefing paper. I have been involved in team-teaching and examining this kind of exercise with postgraduate international business students who have enjoyed working in teams and thinking about foreign assignments and presentations.

Design an international induction programme for a manager (who is/ will be working in *one* of the following areas:

- Sales/marketing, finance, general administration or production management.

  You may select their assignment to be with any *one* of the following:

    MNC

    voluntary organization

    governmental department.

- The organization selected *must* be real. This creates a realistic HR scenario.
- The organization selected may not, necessarily, currently have a presence in the country to which the employee is relocating.
- Remember to include information on the country to which the employee is being placed including main language spoken, local customs, working conditions, practices, religion and climatic environment.

Recommended programme scheme

It is helpful to include the following headings:

    Pre departure planning

    Arrival induction

    Continuing support

    Returning to home country

    Pre-return

    Post-return

SUMMARY: HRM IN A GLOBAL ENVIRONMENT

(a) Perhaps the essential difference that will emerge as the twenty-first century leaves behind its twentieth-century origins is a new globalization; one that is inclusive of local differences.

(b) The term 'globalization' is generally used to describe the rapidly increasing movement of trade and people around the globe.

(c) Organizations need to train people to work more successfully across the diversity of global cultures as a key element of their international strategic plans.

(d) A global manager needs the set of attitudes, knowledge and skills which have been described as 'cultural sensitivity' (Nieto 2006).

(e) If people are insecure, their tendency will be towards less risk taking and the prevailing organizational culture will move towards uncertainty avoidance (Hofstede 1994).

(f) Reputations are a major part of brand image, and reputation can be influenced as much (perhaps more) by employee attitudes as by expensive marketing campaigns.

(g) International assignments are very useful for understanding international differences and for observing other people's adaptation to different cultures.

(h) Training programme scheme:

    Pre-departure planning

    Arrival induction

    Continuing support

    Returning to home country

    Pre-return

    Post-return

REVISION SECTION

Discuss why a global manager needs the attitudes, knowledge and skills which have been described as 'cultural sensitivity' (Nieto 2006).

How is globalization creating a competitive market for workers?

TAKING IT FURTHER

Key texts to look up:

Bhagwati, J. and Blinder, A. (2009) *Offshoring of American Jobs.* Cambridge, MA: MIT Press.

Hofstede, G. (1994) *Cultures and Organizations: Software of the Mind*. London: Harper Collins.

Ng, M. (2012) *Foreign Direct Investment in China: Theories and Practices*. London: Routledge.

Sitkin, A. and Bowen, N. (2013) *International Business: Challenges and Choices* (2nd Edition). Oxford: Oxford University Press.

Trompenaars, F. and Woolliams, P. (2003) *Business across Cultures*. Chichester: Capstone.

Yesudian-Storfiell, S. (2012) *Innovation in India: The Future of Offshoring*. Basingstoke: Palgrave Macmillan.

Refer to the books and journals in this references section.

REFERENCES

Adler, N. (1981) Re-entry: Managing Cross-cultural Transitions. *Group and Organizational Studies*. 6(3), pp. 341–356.

Albrow, M. (1996) *The Global Age*. Cambridge: Polity Press.

Baylis, J., Smith, S. and Owens, P. (eds) (2010) *The Globalization of World Politics: An Introduction to International Relations*. Oxford: Oxford University Press.

Bennett, M. (1986) A Developmental Approach to Training for Inter-cultural Sensitivity. *International Journal of Intercultural Relations*. 10(2), pp. 179–195.

Bernstein, W. (2009) *A Splendid Exchange: How Trade Shaped the World*. London: Atlantic Books.

Bhagwati, J. and Blinder, A. (2009) *Offshoring of American Jobs*. Cambridge, MA: MIT Press.

Black, J. S., Gregersen, H. B. and Mendenhall, M. (1992) *Global Assignments: Successfully Expatriating and Repatriating International Managers*. San Francisco, CA: Josey-Bass.

Black, J. S. and Mendenhall, M. (1990) Cross-cultural Training Effectiveness: A Review and a Theoretical Framework for Future Research. *Academy of Management Review*, 15(1), pp. 113–136.

Black, J. S., Mendenhall, M. and Oddou, G. R. (1991) Towards a Comprehensive Model of International Adjustment: An Integration of Multiple Theoretical Perspectives. *Academy of Management Review*. 16(2), pp. 291–317.

Bonache, J. (2005) Job satisfaction among Expatriates, Repatriates and Domestic Employees: The Perceived Impact of International Assignments on Work-related Variables. *Personnel Review*. 34(1), pp. 110–124.

Clinton, B. (2001) *The Struggle for the Soul of the 21st Century*. The Dimbleby Lecture. *BBC*. 14 December.

Crabb, S. (2003) East India Companies. *People Management*. 20 February. www.cipd.co.uk/pm/peoplemanagement/b/weblog/archive/2013/01/29/8476a-2003-01.aspx.

Elmuti, D. and Kathawala, Y. (2000) The Effects of Global Outsourcing Strategies on Participants Attitudes and Organizational Effectiveness. *International Journal of Manpower*. 21(2), pp. 114–130.

Findlay, R. and O'Rourke, K. (2009) *Power and Plenty: Trade, War, and the World Economy in the Second Millennium*. Princeton University Press.

Gregersen, H. B. and Black, J. S. (1996) Multiple Commitments Upon Repatriation: The Japanese Experience. *Journal of Management*. 22(2), pp. 209–229.

Harzing, A-W. and Van Ruysseveldt, J. (eds) (2004) *International Human Resource Management* (2nd Edition). London: Sage.

Hofstede, G. (1984) *Culture's Consequences. International Differences in Work Related Values*. London: Sage.

Hofstede, G. (1994) *Cultures and Organizations: Software of the Mind*. London: Harper Collins.

Kopp, R. (1994) International Human Resource Policies and Practices in Japanese, European and United States Multinationals. *Human Resource Management*. Winter, 33(4), pp. 581–599.

Lawson, M. B. and Angle, H. (1994) When Organizational Relocation Means Family Relocation: An Emerging Issue for Strategic Human Resource Management. *Human Resource Management*. 33(1), pp. 33–54.

Mensah, J. (2009) *Neoliberalism and Globalization in Africa: Contestations on the Embattled Continent: Contestations from the Embattled Continent*. New York: Palgrave Macmillan.

Munton, A. G. and Forster, N. (1990) Job Relocation: Stress and the Role of the Family. *Work and Stress*. 4(1), pp. 75–81.

Ng, M. (2012) *Foreign Direct Investment in China: Theories and Practices*. London: Routledge.

Nieto, M. L. (2006) *An Introduction to Human Resource Management: An Integrated Approach*. Basingstoke: Palgrave Macmillan.

Panibratov, A. (2012) *Russian Multinationals: From Regional Supremacy to Global Lead*. London: Routledge.

Park, H. J., Mitsuhashi, H., Fey, C. F. and Björkman, I. (2003) The Effect of Human Resource Management Practices on Japanese MNC Subsidiary Performance: A Partial Mediating Model. *International Journal of Human Resource Management*. December, 14(8), pp. 1391–1406.

Sisodia, R. (2004) India's John Smiths Speak Perfect English. Now They Have a Month to Become British, *The Independent*, Sunday, 12 May.

Sitkin, A. and Bowen, N. (2013) *International Business: Challenges and Choices*. (2nd Edition). Oxford: Oxford University Press.

Stroh, L. K., Gregersen, H. B. and Black, J. S. (1998) Closing the Gap: Expectations Versus Reality Among Repatriates. *Journal of World Business*. Summer, 33(2), pp. 111–124.

Sussangkarn, C., Park, Y. and Kang, S. (2011) *Foreign Direct Investments in Asia*. London: Routledge.

Toral, P. (2011) *Multinational Enterprises in Latin America since the 1990s*. New York: Palgrave Macmillan.

Trompenaars, F. and Woolliams, P. (2003) *Business across Cultures*. Chichester: Capstone.

Ward, C., Bochner, S. and Furnham, A. (2001) *Psychology Culture Shock*. London: Routledge.

Yesudian-Storfiell, S. (2012) *Innovation in India: The Future of Offshoring*. Basingstoke: Palgrave Macmillan.

8

Employee Relations and the Changing Workforce

INTRODUCTION

People are an organization's most valuable asset.

This is what most organizational mission statements usually state or imply. But how true is this assertion in practice? In this chapter you will explore the interrelationships between organizations and people, and the expectations people may form about work. Employee relations therefore comprise more than a list of policy documents and legislative requirements. Indeed, employee relations are intertwined with personal and organizational expectations, often unwritten forms of custom and practice. Positive employee relations help organizations to achieve their aims and objectives. In this chapter your will evaluate practical interventions which can encourage better dialogue between colleagues and thereby nurture more constructive employee relations and organizational performance.

> **Key Point:** Organizations are a group of people and succeed or fail on how well motivated and engaged people are to work together.

LEARNING OBJECTIVES

The key learning outcomes for the chapter are below:

- Managing employee relations with a diversified workforce.
- The Socio-Technical Model: tasks, people, technology, structure.

- Assessing how diversity has implications on HRM policies and practices.
- Examining the implications of demographic age-profile trends.

MANAGING EMPLOYEE RELATIONS WITH A DIVERSIFIED WORKFORCE

Changing the way people do their jobs can have a major impact on employee relations. Remember the word *change* is value-neutral. Changes in organizational structures can be either positive or negative. Historically, many of the employment disputes where large numbers of people went on strike were often as much to do with changes in working patterns as they were to do with pay and conditions. The contemporary HR specialist should recognize that changes to working patterns need to be introduced with care and consultation. According to Friday and Friday (2003), managing diversity begins by valuing diversity and then incorporating policies into the organization in a strategically planned process.

The student of business should be aware that it is necessary to be empathetic to the broader needs of the organization, rather than to just one job-role, whether that is HR, information technology, finance, marketing, law or production operations. This approach was recognized by Wind and Main (1998), who observed that there are no business issues that are resolved in just one professional discipline. The challenges we meet in the workplace are more usually cross-functional. Managers who have benefited from HR training and specialist degree courses (which should be anyone in a people management post) will appreciate the central importance of people cooperating and working harmoniously on cross-functional projects.

In practice, this can also mean introducing external experts to facilitate elements of HR development programmes and or enrolling staff on the appropriate Master's programmes or short professional courses run by universities. The advantage of attending a course externally is that the employee is exposed to a diverse range of other people, from different sectors and organizational cultures. The learning experience is further enhanced if the courses include team-working assignments directed at real organizational issues. This kind of exposure to experiential and theoretical approaches can become the genesis for new innovative management. It also encourages the business schools to work closely with organizations, thereby developing a symbiotic relationship benefiting everyone involved.

> **Key Point:** The primary AKS for anyone who has responsibility for managing people is in HR. Managers need to be able to motivate, encourage and build their teams' confidence so that they can then achieve agreed objectives.

Managing diversity: every manager has responsibility to encourage tolerance and understanding of diversity. There has been a considerable body of academic research into this area since the later years of the twentieth century (Hall and Parker 1993; Kopp 1994; Farnham 1997; Nieto 2003; Nieto 2006; Lautsch and Kossek 2011). Overall, the research indicates that the needs, ambitions and aspirations of a diverse workforce are unlikely to respond to a one-size-fits-all HR strategy. For example, a child-friendly policy could serve the needs of those men/women who have young children (Kossek 2005). However, a different benefits package could be more appropriate for people who do not have children.

Hence, if an employee can have an afternoon off work for childcare, workers who do not have children should also be able to have time for other activities. Again, a temporarily part-time student employee is likely to have different needs to those of a full-time one. How can organizations gain the best performance from people with widely differing needs and interests? A flexible pay and benefits packages can be designed to fit around the person, rather than the person having to fit the package. HR strategies also need to be aware of equal opportunities, meeting statutory requirements, so consultation and legal advice is recommended. In an international context this is particularly important because different countries have regulations about minimum statutory rights for employees. However, the advantage of a flexible approach can be a more balanced offering to meet individual needs and circumstances (Maxwell 2004).

In the 1990s, Handy (1995: 42) predicted that the office of the future would be more like a clubhouse for meeting people. Indeed, the developments in computers and communication technology have increased the opportunities for greater employment flexibility (Kossek et al. 2012). However, the evidence of the morning rush hour, in cites around the globe, is that there is some way to go before electronic communication replaces personal meetings and the workplace (Lautsch and Kossek 2011). One of the advantages of modern technology is that is does create opportunities for a greater diversity of employment: full-time, part-time, disabled, flexible hours, childcare, elderly relative care. Adaptable and flexible working arrangements are likely to be agreed by individual organizations in consultation with their employees (Kossek 2006).

Employee relations in the voluntary sector are different from those in the private and public ones in that many of its key workers are unpaid volunteers. With the absence of extrinsic rewards such as pay, the intrinsic rewards, the psychological fulfilment, become even more prominent. The first question to consider concerns why people volunteer. What do they hope to give and or gain from the experience? In researching this book, I have met many people who have volunteered. Volunteers often say that they are 'working for a good cause' and 'giving something back to society'. Additionally, when I was working with Voluntary Action Management Master's degree students in the University of Surrey, Roehampton (now Roehampton University), their case studies revealed other motives such as: a desire to meet people, to form friendships with co-workers; and to build self-esteem.

This is interesting because such intrinsic motivators are not exclusive to the voluntary sector and people in paid employment could readily identify with those motivations. Indeed, other public and private-sector employees usually express similar motivations (Cnaan Ram 1996; Harris and Rochester 2001). It may be the case that the for-profit sector can learn from the voluntary

> **Key Point:** Intrinsic motivations, such as a desire to meet people, to form friendships with co-workers and to build self-esteem are common to voluntary, not-for-profit and profit sectors.

sector regarding intrinsic rewards and employee relations where people are working because they want to and not just for the financial reward.

THE SOCIO-TECHNICAL MODEL: TASKS, PEOPLE, TECHNOLOGY, STRUCTURE

In the Socio-Technical Model, Trist (1981) provides us with a helpful way of understanding the interdependency of key organizational activities and interventions influencing change. This is relevant to our understanding of HR because the Socio-Technical Model focuses our attention on the influence changes in an organization's activities can have on employees. For example, changes to technology will alter the nature of how tasks are conducted, which in turn influences

Key Point: Changing one area (task or technology, or people or structure) influences all the others. For example, a change in technology changes the way tasks are delivered, which means the people will need to be consulted and then trained. The organizational structure will require adaptation to incorporate the new system.

the way people work and the organizational structure (see Figure 8.1). In the previous paragraph the changes in technology were related to how and where employees conduct their work. It is therefore helpful to review the kinds of

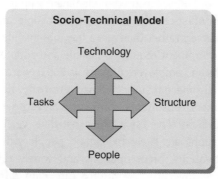

Figure 8.1 Socio-Technical Model

planned changes in an organization and to what extent the appropriate HR initiatives can be put in place to prepare staff to manage the new technology, tasks or structures. For example, if an organization has introduced new technology, but neglected to invest sufficiently in staff training, then it is less likely to be used to its optimum. This may sound obvious, however, people become accustomed to doing their work in a certain way. New technology, new software means they have to change the way they work and that can be stressful. If the employees were not consulted about the new developments, they may question the value and benefits of the new intervention.

ACTIVITY: APPLYING THE SOCIO-TECHNICAL MODEL TO AN ORGANIZATION

1. Select an organization to study where a change in tasks, technology, people or structure has occurred/is about to occur.
2. Apply the Socio-Technical Model to highlight areas that are/could change in the near future.
3. Discuss what HR managers can do to help workers adapt to the changes.

ASSESS HOW DIVERSITY HAS IMPLICATIONS ON HRM POLICIES AND PRACTICES

The old paradigm of HR was focused predominantly upon full-time employees. In the twenty-first-century environment, people are likely to have several different careers rather than just a few jobs in a lifetime. Hence, the contemporary environment requires a flexible and adaptable approach by both organizations and employees (Agarwala 2003; Nieto 2003).

This includes full-time, part-time, women returners, lately retired returners, portfolio workers, consultants, contractors and students working their way through university. This list is not exhaustive, yet it highlights that modern organizations are likely to contain people with a broad range of personal motivations, preoccupations and widely differing concerns and preferences. A diversified workforce can bring different ideas and approaches to an organization (Caulkin 2001).

Activity: the Shackleton expedition

In 1914, an explorer named Shackleton led an expedition bound for the Ross Sea, which is part of the Southern Ocean. The weather that year was particularly poor and his ship became stuck in ice and was crushed. Shackleton then led his party across the ice floes, hauling small boats. When the ice melted, Shackleton got his team to row the boats to safety on Elephant Island. In such difficult conditions, it is less than surprising that some of the team expressed different views as to the best course of action. Shackleton listened to advice, but was firm in focusing the team on the common goal of survival.

Elephant Island was too isolated for the explorers to be found quickly, so it was agreed that a small group would leave its relative safety to find help. Shackleton selected a team of six crew to sail to the nearest inhabited island. They travelled 800 miles in a 22ft rowing boat, and successfully navigated their way to the tiny island of South Georgia. The team then had to cross the island's mountains to alert rescuers. After they had reached safety, Shackleton accompanied another rescue team back to the group who had been set ashore on Elephant Island.

It is worth noting that the men on the expedition were not selected from a special, elite army regiment of exceptionally physically fit soldiers, but comprised ordinary sailors and explorers. This shows that a lot can be achieved with ordinary people, something which is true in organizations, too.

Writing about the expedition's relevance to modern organizations, Kinnes (2001) has observed that the adventurer's leadership skills are now studied in business schools. In the film by Channel 4, broadcast on 2 and 3 January 2002, Shackleton is shown leading a team of men in atrocious conditions. In fact all 28 men survived the expedition. Their survival was arguably, in large measure, due to Shackleton's effective leadership.

The party of explorers faced real dangers to life yet there are significant parallels to organizations. To survive in a difficult and rapidly changing organizational environment, leaders need to be able to adapt their plans, bring out the best in their people, yet remain focused on the longer-term objectives so that the organization survives and goes on to greater successes. The most successful teams are therefore not necessarily the ones with all the most able people, but rather those that can work effectively together.

I have provided an imaginary list of 'excuses' which Shackleton's team members might have offered, and applied them to contemporary work situations.

> *'The task is too difficult ...'* (Unfortunately, we do not always get the easiest circumstances, so people have to work together and produce new solutions to resolve difficulties.)

> *'Some of the team members aren't as "able" as I am ...'* (Shackleton did not have the luxury of 'expelling' weaker team members. Also, the members of the expedition could not complain to the HR manager or appeal to a tribunal about Shackleton's leadership style.)

> *'The staff do not get on well ...'* (When the task is important, personal issues should take second place; it can sometimes help to explore what people have in common interest, rather than dwell on their differences.)

In the Shackleton case study, the advantage to the individual members was obvious: if they worked effectively together they would survive. The counter-argument is that people may become even more dogmatic about what they believe to be right when the teamwork represents something of high personal value. If the team of explorers had not worked together, it is very unlikely that any of them would have survived. Augments about planning inadequacies would hardly have been relevant.

Six points we can learn from Shackleton's leadership

1. Express a positive belief in what you and your colleagues can achieve.

2. Take time to talk to and encourage small groups and individuals. Support people who are experiencing difficulties.

3. Encourage members who have become disillusioned with the project's aims or even lost hope that it is achievable.

4. Listen to alternative suggestions. Adapt plans to incorporate good ideas.

5. Take firm action, where necessary, to keep the project progressing.

6. Respond to unfavourable changes in the 'environment' by initiating changes.

Discussion questions

1. What do you most like about working with other people?

2. What do you least like about teamwork?

3. Make a list of the attitudes, knowledge and skills which you think are most useful to successfully working in teams.

4. List the attitudes, knowledge and skills you believe you can bring to a team project.

5. Make a note of at least one area which, after personal reflection or discussion with someone who knows you well, you need to develop in order to improve your performance in a team-working situation.

The work of Max Weber articulated some of the complex interactions between managers and staff. Translated by Henderson and Parsons in (1947: 325), Weber observed that materialistic interests and calculations alone could not provide a stable employee/management relationships in organizations. While the workplace has changed, there are still contemporary learning outcomes to be drawn from Weber's work. An employee–employer relationship which is built on mutual trust can enable each side to benefit from some flexibility to mutual advantage. For example, employees may be more willing to work additional hours or make an extra effort to support a manager who has responded favourably to their individual needs. Establishing a reciprocal relationship of respect may require some adjustments by both employees and employers. The contractual clauses requiring staff to work additional hours as and when the employer may require can be counter-balanced by similar working-time flexibility for the employees. According to Watson (1994: 171), workplace relationships should be founded upon trust and reciprocity. And Thompson and McHugh (2002: 276) argued for a key measure of managerial competence to be the ability to infuse motivation and commitment in others.

> **Key Point:** A key measure of managerial competence is the ability to infuse others with motivation and commitment. People do not care what you know until they know that you care about them.

The implications for organizations of motivating a diversified workforce are challenging and sometimes difficult to reconcile with external pressures to reduce costs. It is, then, arguably even more important for employers to provide professional development so that instead of a long-term employment guarantee, people can attain employability, equipping them to find another job should the need arise. These kinds of proactive HR initiatives may also contribute towards encouraging improved motivational levels.

EXAMINE THE IMPLICATIONS OF THE DEMOGRAPHIC AGE PROFILE

In many first-world countries, the largest age group of people in the modern workplace is contained in what is described as the 'baby boomers' (Bingham 2012). This group represents the generations of people born after the Second World War (1939–1945) and during the 1950s, 1960s and 1970s. After that time, there was a fall in the number of children born in the affluent economies, and this is reflected in the twenty-first century's workforce age profile. In response to the ageing workforce, governments are rethinking their policies towards the age of retirement. For example, in the US and UK, age discrimination is illegal. It is indefensible for organizations to discriminate on the basis of a person's age, whether younger or older. The changing age demographic creates opportunities relating to the contractual retirement age, the pensionable retirement age and the abolition of the mandatory retirement age (Sargeant 2004). While everyone should have the right to be treated without discrimination in finding gainful employment, the counter-balance is the availability of protected pension reserves, personal, corporate and state-funded, that enable people to retire to a comfortable lifestyle following a lifetime of work.

Key Point: Investing by employing and training younger people and retaining the experience of older workers is beneficial to organizational diversity. It is also beneficial to national economic wellbeing by building employability and engaging people in productive paid employment and not on state benefits.

In a paper by Snape and Redman (2003), the influence of employee attitudes towards perceived age discrimination was evaluated. The research was based on public-sector workers and found that age discrimination occurred towards people who were considered either too young or too old. Employees who felt they had been discriminated against for being too old were also more inclined to retire earlier than they might otherwise have chosen. The research also indicated that ageist discrimination had negative influences on general employee morale, irrespective of their ages. Evidently, employees understand that they are likely to be treated in a similar manner as they grow older too. Furthermore, younger employees have little incentive to remain with an organization if they are not mentored and developed by their more experienced colleagues. At the more mature age range of the demographic, those people who decide to work into their later years can bring organizations the knowledge and skills accrued through many years of experience (Patrickson and Ranzijn 2005). At the younger range of the age spectrum, with high youth unemployment during the first part of the twenty-first century, the forward-thinking organization should be encouraging and training people in the 18–30-year old age groups, so that they have a talent pool as older workers eventually retire or take part-time roles.

In common with other areas of discrimination, ageism can be the result of negative attitudes and misperceptions. Hence, negative characteristics may be erroneously ascribed to a person simply because they are over 70 years of age. Instead, it is more equitable to evaluate individuals by their attitudes, knowledge and skills rather than their chronological age. Attributes such as flexibility, energy and enthusiasm that are sometimes ascribed to younger people are as likely to be found in mature workers. Indeed, older workers may be eager to continue in work, both for financial reasons (inadequate pensions provision) and for the social and the intellectual stimulation of being part of an organization. Conversely, the younger graduate should not be discriminated against for not having any experience. A student who has completed a good-quality business management programme will have a solid base of knowledge and achieved skills via researching organizations and delivering reports and presentations. Consequently, the forward-thinking organization can include a strategy which incorporates training and development programmes for new employees, of whatever age, to enhance their knowledge, skills and employability (Chew et al. 2005; Nieto 2006).

Governments have traditionally encouraged people from other parts of the world into the workforce. For centuries, industrial nations such as the US, Australia and the UK have adopted people from other nations (Cadbury 2003). In Europe, this has been accelerated by the inclusion of more nations into the European Union, whereby skilled workers can move more easily from one nation to another for employment opportunities. This movement of people increases the diversification of the workforce and the rich variety of cultures and perspectives that they bring to organizations.

> **Key Point:** In a national economy, costs cannot be removed, they can only be redistributed. Accordingly, if young people are not trained to obtain jobs and older workers are forced to retire prematurely, then the state has to cover the costs by paying unemployment benefits. And organizations lose the talents of new incomers and experienced workers.

Governments also have a duty of care to provide their home citizens with opportunities to find long-term secure employment through careers guidance, training and access to higher-level qualifications. For the UK, further information, advice and guidance can be found for careers on the National Career Service's website: nationalcareersservice.direct.gov.uk.

SUMMARY: EMPLOYEE RELATIONS AND THE CHANGING WORKFORCE

(a) People, are an organization's most valuable asset. Retain talent by developing staff and promoting internally to build a sustainable organization.

(b) Managers should recognize that changes to working patterns need to be introduced with care and staff consultation.

(c) Managing diversity begins by valuing diversity and then incorporating policies into the organization in a strategically planned process.

(d) The challenges in the workplace are usually cross-functional. HR people can facilitate interdisciplinary cooperation across their organizations, bringing people together to cooperate on cross-functional projects.

(e) Student learning experiences are enhanced if courses include team-working assignments directed at real organizational issues. This kind of exposure to experiential and theoretical approaches can become the genesis for new innovative management. It also encourages the business schools to work closely with organizations: a symbiotic relationship benefiting everyone involved.

(f) Managers have a responsibility to encourage tolerance and understanding of diversity.

(g) Overall, the research evidence indicates that the needs, ambitions and aspirations of a diverse workforce are unlikely to respond to one-size-fits-all HR policies on working hours and benefits.

(h) For voluntary workers, the absence of extrinsic rewards, such as pay, means that the intrinsic rewards, such as psychological fulfilment, become even more prominent.

(i) The for-profit sector can learn from the voluntary sector regarding intrinsic worker motivations and employee relations where people are working because they want to and not for the financial reward.

(j) The Socio-Technical Model focuses our attention on the influence changes in an organization's activities can have on employees. A change in one area affects all the others.

(k) Changes to the way people conduct their work can be stressful. Introduce change with consultation and be willing to listen and adapt the change plan.

(l) In many countries, where people having several careers rather than just a few jobs in a lifetime, the contemporary environment requires a flexible and adaptable approach by both organizations and employers.

(m) The modern workforce includes full-time, part-time, women returners, recently retired returners, portfolio workers, consultants, contractors and students working their way through university.

(n) A diversified workforce can bring different ideas and approaches to an organization and thereby improve effectiveness.

(o) Establishing a reciprocal relationship of respect requires some adjustments by both employees and employers. The contractual clauses requiring staff to work additional hours as and when the employer may require should be counter-balanced by similar working-time flexibility for the employees.

(p) With professional development, people can attain employability.

(q) People are complex and emotional and do not always respond the way rationale theories as set out in the textbooks anticipate. This is a reason for the proposition that management experience is invaluable in informing both theory and practice.

(r) In many first-world countries, the largest age group of people in the modern workplace is contained in what is described as the 'baby boomers'. This group represents the generations of people born after the Second World War (1939–1945) and during 1950s, 1960s and 1970s. It is therefore essential to the economic wellbeing of nation states to ensure that this demographic of people is retained in the workforce.

(s) Age discrimination can happen to both young inexperienced people and mature ones. Ageist discrimination has negative influences on general employee morale, irrespective of their ages.

(t) Governments have a duty of care to provide their home citizens with opportunities to find long-term secure employment through careers guidance, training and access to higher-level qualifications.

REVISION SECTION

'People, are an organization's most valuable asset'. Discuss why it is beneficial to organizational success and sustainability to retain talent by developing staff and promoting internally?

'In a national economy, costs cannot be removed, they can only be redistributed. If young people are not trained to obtain jobs and older workers are forced to retire prematurely, then the state bears the costs *by paying unemployment benefits. And organizations lose the talents of new incomers and experienced workers.'* What should governments do to ensure that younger people receive training and employment and mature workers are retained in the workplace?

Explain why it is that in the twenty-first century it is even more important than before for people to receive professional development people and maintain employability?

TAKING IT FURTHER

Key texts to look up:

Chew, J., Girardi, A. and Entrekin, L. (2005) Retaining Core Staff: The Impact of Human Resource Practices on Organizational Commitment. *Journal of Comparative International Management*. 8(2), pp. 23–42.

Kossek, E., Kaillaith, T. and Kaillaith P. (2012) Achieving Employee Wellbeing in a Changing Work Environment: An Expert Commentary on Current Scholarship. *International Journal of Manpower*. 33(7), pp. 738–753.

Nieto, M. L. (2003) The Development of Life Work Balance Initiatives Designed for Managerial Workers. *Business Ethics: A European Review*. 12(3), pp. 213–215.

Refer to the books and journals in this references section.

REFERENCES

Agarwala, T. (2003) Innovative Human Resource Practices and Organizational Commitment: An Empirical Investigation. *International Journal of Human Resource Management*. 14(2), pp. 175–197.

Bingham, J. (2012) Record Numbers Reach Retirement Age as Baby Boomers Turn 65, *The Telegraph*, 25 September.

Cadbury, D. (2003) *Seven Wonders of the Industrial World*. London: Forth Estate.

Caulkin, S. (2001) The Time is Now. *People Management*. 30 August. CIPD.

Channel 4, *Shackleton*. Broadcast on 2 and 3 January 2002.

Chew, J., Girardi, A. and Entrekin, L. (2005) Retaining Core Staff: The Impact of Human Resource Practices on Organizational Commitment. *Journal of Comparative International Management*. 8(2), pp. 23–42.

Cnaan Ram, A. (1996) Defining Who is a Volunteer: Conceptual and Empirical Considerations. *Non-Profit and Voluntary Sector Quarterly*. 25(3), pp. 364–383.

Farnham, D. (ed.) (1997) Employment Flexibilities in Western European Public Services: An International Symposium. *Review of Public Personnel Administration*. xvii(3), Columbia (USA), University of Southern Carolina.

Friday, E. and Friday, S.S. (2003) Managing Diversity Using a Strategic Planned Change Approach. *The Journal of Management Development*. 22(10), pp. 863–880.

Hall, D. T. and Parker, V. A. (1993) The Role of Workplace Flexibility in Managing Diversity. *Organizational Dynamics*. 22(1), pp. 5–18.

Handy, C. B. (1995) Trust and the Virtual Organization. *Harvard Business Review*. May–June.

Harris, M. and Rochester, C. (eds) (2001) *Voluntary Organisations & Social Policy in Britain: Perspectives on Change & Choice*. Basingstoke: Palgrave.

Henderson, A. M. and Parsons, T. (1947) *Max Weber: The Theory of Social & Economic Organization*. New York: Oxford University Press.

Kinnes, S. Shackleton (2001) *The Sunday Times*, 30 December.

Kopp, R. (1994) International Human Resource Policies and Practices in Japanese, European and United States Multinationals. *Human Resource Management*. 33(4), pp. 581–599.

Kossek, E. E. (2005) *Workplace Policies and Practices to Support Work and Families*. In: Bianchi, S., Casper, L. and King, R. (eds) Work, Family, Health, and Well-Being. Washington DC: Lawrence Erlbaum Associates, pp. 97–116.

Kossek, E. E. (2006) *Work and Family in America: Growing Tensions Between Employment Policy and a Transformed Workforce*. A thirty year perspective. (Commissioned chapter by SHRM Foundation and University of California Center for Organizational Effectiveness for the 30th anniversary of the State of Work in America). In: Lawler, E. and

O'Toole, J. (eds) *America at Work: Choices and Challenges*. New York: Palgrave Macmillan. pp. 53–72.

Kossek, E., Kaillaith, T. and Kaillaith P. (2012) Achieving Employee Wellbeing in a Changing Work Environment: An Expert Commentary on Current Scholarship. *International Journal of Manpower*. 33(7), pp. 738–753.

Lautsch, B. and Kossek, E. (2011) Managing a Blended Workforce: Supervising Telecommuters and Non-Telecommuters-Organizational Dynamics. *Organizational Dynamics*. 40(1), pp. 10–17.

Maxwell, G. A. (2004) Taking the Initiative in Managing Diversity at BBC Scotland. *Employee Relations*, 16 January, 26(2), pp. 182–202.

National Career Service's website: nationalcareersservice.direct.gov.uk.

Nieto, M. L. (2003) The Development of Life Work Balance Initiatives Designed for Managerial Workers. *Business Ethics: A European Review*. 12(3), pp. 213–215.

Nieto, M. L. (2006) *An Introduction to Human Resource Management: An Integrated Approach*. Basingstoke: Palgrave Macmillan.

Patrickson, M. and Ranzijn, R. (2005) Workforce Ageing: The Challenges for 21st Century Management. *International Journal of Organisational Behaviour*, 10(4), pp. 729–739.

Sargeant, M. (2004) Mandatory Retirement Age and Age Discrimination. *Employee Relations*. 26(2), pp. 151–166.

Snape, E. and Redman, T. (2003) An Evaluation of a Three-component Model of Occupational Commitment: Dimensionality and Consequences among United Kingdom Human Resource Management Specialists. *Journal of Applied Psychology*. 88(1), pp. 152–159.

Thompson, P. and Mchugh, D. (2002) *Work Organisations* (3rd Edition). Basingstoke: Palgrave Macmillan.

Trist, E. (1981) *The Evolution of Socio-Technical Systems*. Ontario Ministry of Labour. Ontario Quality of Working Life Centre.

Watson, T. J. (1994) *In Search of Management: Culture, Chaos and Control in Managerial Work*. London: Routledge.

Wind, J. Y. and Main, J. (1998) *Driving Change: How the Best Companies are Preparing for the 21st Century*. London: Kogan Page.

9

Communicating in Organizations

INTRODUCTION

The management of people is about achieving agreed plans with and through the efforts of your team. Hence, good communications and interpersonal skills are a key element of management. Indeed, it is possible that a well-constructed strategy might fail if it does not have the support of your team, while an adequate strategy which is supported by the majority of the organization is more likely to be improved, progress and succeed.

This chapter is about how effective communication influences the way organizations function, and how that communication can be improved. The section containing a model by Duncan Christie Miller is really useful in this area, and comes from a consultant with a wide range of experience from global and national organizations within both the private and public sectors.

As an undergraduate or postgraduate, you will be keen to gain excellent grades on your business course and get on in your career/ future career. While it is fair to say that good communications cannot deliver poor materials, poor personal communication skills can weaken the influence of good-quality materials. In this chapter you will learn how to design effective written and presentational communications for your university Master's or undergraduate degree and beyond into your chosen career.

LEARNING OBJECTIVES

The key learning outcomes for the chapter are below:

- Understand the importance of how HR initiatives are presented in organizations.
- Develop effective written business communications.
- Organize and manage more productive meetings.
- Apply the REACT system to facilitating meetings.
- Conduct an effective business presentation.
- The INTRO presentation system.
- Recognize the importance of interpersonal communications in organizational performance. The GIFT Model.

UNDERSTAND THE IMPORTANCE OF HOW HR INITIATIVES ARE COMMUNICATED IN ORGANIZATIONS

Over the years, professional organizations such as the Chartered Institute of Personnel Development (CIPD) and the Chartered Management Institute (CMI), academics and writers have provided guidance on how to improve communications inside organizations (Stanton 2009). However, it is how people choose to interact that shapes the tone and form of organizational communications. For example, in studying communication within organizations, Blundel and Ippolito (2008) found that the issues and challenges regarding communications were similar, whether the organization was in the private, public or not-for-profit sector. This indicates that improving communications in organizations is more likely to be addressed by developing individual communication skills than through issuing a series of policy documents.

It is therefore worth emphasizing that one of the key roles of HR-trained professionals is to communicate the importance of investment in employees to their management colleagues (Currie and Procter 2003). The role of

HR professionals in proactively persuading management colleagues of the value of people development has been promoted by the CIPD for many years. For example, according to Alberg (2002), the CIPD has done its best to give HR professionals the information required to support the case for people development. The reason I raise this here, with a reference to an article published in the CIPD's *People Management* magazine some years ago, is to emphasize that addressing communication skills is a continuous process of people development within organizations.

Furthermore, improving communications is a matter for everyone, not just senior managers or the HR specialists; each person has a part to play in the way communications are conducted within their organization (Argyle 1995; Covey 1999; Stanton 2009).

A study by Tzafrir et al. (2004) into the relationship between human resource HRM practices and employees' trust in their managers, based on a sample of 230 respondents, found a significant and positive influence of empowerment and organizational communication. While this is broadly what might be expected, the study offers a reminder to HR people and line managers that involving staff in the decision-making process and communicating plans builds important trust between management and staff.

> **Key Point:** Trust between management and staff is central to organizational success. Trust is built over years and can be lost with one poorly considered change programme.

If colleagues trust each other, their organization is more likely to produce cooperative exchanges (O'Neill 2002). Conversely, distrust in human exchanges may produce strategies which might become mutually disadvantageous to individuals and their organizations (Axelrod 1984, 1997).

Following the discussion on communication and trust, it is interesting to consider how a person's mind-set influences the communication approach. Furthermore, the way ideas are communicated can either promote or detract from the possible success of a strategic plan. For example, the personal priorities of a manager are likely to influence the way in which they communicate to people in the organization. To begin with, think about your priorities. What is at the top of your communications list? Is it your own needs, your agenda, your plans and proposals? Even if the proposals could be generally beneficial, they may not reach their full implementation potential if other people are disinclined to listen. A study by Jones and Stubbe (2004) on the use of workplace language brought together the sociolinguistic analyses of workplace discourse with organizational research. The study indicated that a reflective approach to how people communicate with their colleagues might reveal issues which could be hindering the organization.

To being to understand this, reflect upon how you would communicate a new plan to other people. When you offer a new initiative or proposal, do you consider the advantages to the other people involved first, or is it your own position, career, security or organization that has first priority? A person-centred approach considers the benefits to the audience to which the communication is being addressed and is more likely to gain support. A self-centred approach presents proposals which place the interests of the recipients as a lower priority.

It is interesting to listen to other people speaking or to read the documents they send to colleagues and think about the implicit priorities in their verbal and written communications. For example, if a speaker's focus of importance usually begins with there own interests, it can communicate less empathy towards the recipients of their communications. Hence, '*I want* to have the appraisals completed by January because *I am* being monitored by *my boss to pass a quality audit,* so *we must* get them done as soon as possible and *you have to* submit your evaluations to me by Friday because that fits *my* agenda' sounds very self-centred.

An alternative approach could be: 'Are there any issues about your work *that you would like* to raise with me? If so *we can get together* as soon as is *convenient for both of us* to discuss them. Is there anything *I can do to assist you*?' This approach places the other person's needs first.

Communications beginning with 'I want', 'I need', 'I think' may imply that you are the centre of things and that the recipients of your communications are, implicitly, the servants to your needs. In the first example, it is evident that the manager is much more concerned with fulfilling an appraisal process than listening to the employee's needs. This kind of enforced quality assurance can disaffect staff and may have negative outcomes. The indication that the manager is under pressure to complete the appraisal process may be due to internal or external forces to meet targets regarding employee monitoring. Nevertheless, it is the second approach that is more likely to produce more positive responses from employees because the manager centres the request on the employee's needs rather than a demand to meet his or her own needs.

> **Key Point:** There are three useful words when developing a new policy: consultation, consultation and consultation. By listening to what other people think and are interested in first, it is more likely that a new initiative will receive a more favourable reception from colleagues.

For example, instead of stating what you think should be done, ask open questions such as: What is *your* vision for the organization's future? How do *you* see the situation? What can *we* do to improve the HR provision to the departments? How can the personal development plans be tailored to the needs of *your people*?

Effective communications are particularly relevant because modern HR managers may be required to sell the HR portfolio of services to colleagues in other functions within the business. Indeed, department heads might have the right to elect to buy in from external providers, for services such as recruitment search or training (Nieto 2002). Hence, functional managers can use their budgetary discretion to select the services which are most appropriate to their requirements. For example, in the public sector, within UK schools, the principal and governors can choose whether or not to buy in the services of their local authority's HR team. In the private sector, an HR department could be organized as a separate cost centre where they have to secure work within their organization on a competitive basis with external providers.

The role of HR people has therefore changed with the movement to outsourcing service functions so that organizations – both public and private – can concentrate on their core activities. This approach places more responsibility for internal HR activity on the department managers, thereby creating a more integrated human resources role for managers (Kessler et al. 2002; Nieto 2006).

DEVELOP EFFECTIVE WRITTEN BUSINESS COMMUNICATIONS

The style, content and structure of written communications should be designed to serve the needs and interests of the reader (Stanton 2009). As discussed in the previous section, effective communication is about meeting the particular audience's needs. A senior manager with a commercial bank told me that he asks all potential new graduate trainees a simple question: 'How would you set out a management report?' He then said that he considered the best answer to be 'Who is the report for?' This is because the prospective audience should influence the content, style and range of what the report contains. For example, a report outlining the need for a new training initiative could highlight the cost-saving implications for the finance director, the improvements in staff skills to the project managers, and the personal development benefits to the trainees (Aragón-Sánchez et al.: 2003).

Many universities require students to prepare a report including primary and secondary research on an organization as part of their assessment procedure. Each university or college will have set particular guidelines and students should always refer and comply with whatever regulations apply to their course. In the model below is a structure which you can use to write a report.

- *Executive summary*: The purpose of this section is to briefly outline the report. Ideally divide this into three paragraphs setting out:
  - *What the report sets out to investigate.*
  - *Briefly – the methodology used*
  - *The main conclusions.*

The executive summary is the first item the reader is likely to review. Take care to write something that will encourage the reader to think the report will be interesting. A report does not get a second chance to make a good first impression.

- *Contents page:* This provides a simple guide to the contents of the report.

- *Acknowledgements:* It is polite to acknowledge organizations, individuals and academic staff for their contributions and advice in the preparation of the report.

- *Introduction:* Outline of the organization. Area of study and research methodology.

- *The literature review:* It is helpful to select headings or themes that link to the primary research. If you use the same subsections for the three key sections – literature review, findings and analysis – it encourages focus.

- *Findings:* These comprise primary research results, such as information from interviews, observation studies or questionnaires. Note that assignment word restrictions may require a critical assessment of what to include in this section.

- *Analysis and discussion***:** This includes references to literature and compares and contrasts the practices found in the primary research with theory, models and case studies discussed in the literature review.

- *Conclusions:* A summary of the main results. No new material should be introduced in this section.

- *Recommendations:* These should be specific to the organization, time-bound and achievable with the organization's resources and culture.

- *References:* Cited from published works rather than generic lecture notes. References should just include those texts directly used and referred to in the report. The section should not be just a long booklist.

- *Appendices:* These provide additional background, such as examples of interview schedules, questionnaires (blank copies only) and other relevant material if available, such as mission statements, letters to organizations.

It can be helpful to type each of the above headings into a file so that future materials can be correctly allocated as and when required. For example, you may find an interesting reference and type it into the literature section in readiness to use later.

The report structure can, of course, be modified to meet situation-specific requirements. For example, when I was commissioned to prepare an HR study report for a charity, their brief was to analyse the organization's current HR status. My initial background study indicated that some of the management committee required convincing of the value-adding benefits of HR. The report they received therefore had less of an introductory overview and the selected references to literature were focused to support their situation-specific requirements. In common with most reports, the executive summary and recommendations were key elements. Hence, the report was tailored to the needs to the client.

If it is consistent with the learning outcomes of your degree validation, it can be helpful to adopt what might be described as a 'practical academic' approach, wherein the research benefits from the rigours of academic discipline, but is designed to produce some practical outcomes for the organization(s) which take part in the work. Hence a report that is both practical and academic.

ORGANIZE AND MANAGE MORE PRODUCTIVE MEETINGS

Apply the REACT system to facilitating meetings

A meeting may be organized for any number of reasons: political, social, compliance requirements and, sometimes, a genuine exchange of ideas. Adopting a structured model to guide the meetings process can assist efficiency and reduce time being dissipated as colleagues drift onto either non-agenda items or use up too much time on individual items.

The REACT facilitated meetings guide

To facilitate meetings successfully, the facilitator needs to be able to REACT to the needs of the participants.

Research – Issues that are important to the participants. What do the people coming to the meeting want to discuss? Circulate a request for agenda items in advance of the meeting.

Empathy – Make every effort to understand colleagues' viewpoints. Listen to the opinions and ideas expressed.

Actively – Encourage the participation of quieter and less confident people. Their silence does not necessarily indicate either agreement with the general flow of discussion or that they have nothing to contribute; it may just be shyness about taking part in the discussion.

Control – Stay calm, endeavour to ensure fairness for all opinion groups. Try not to let the most vocal dominate the discussion.

Time – Agree a time to *begin* and *end* the meeting. Provide regular breaks for tea/coffee and toilet breaks. It is helpful to regularly get up and move away from the meeting to refresh and reflect.

Do not allow the meeting to overrun. This creates a more professional atmosphere and encourages focus. Colleagues usually have other important activities scheduled.

CONDUCT AN EFFECTIVE BUSINESS PRESENTATION

The presentation is often used as part of the employment selection process, which is one of the reasons many university business schools encourage students to improve this key transferable skill (Littleford et al.: 2004).

Presentations are more than the delivery of information. If all you want to do is give out information it would be easier, though much less effective, to send an email or put the material on a website.

> **Key Point:** The skill of presenting is in generating interest, not downloading information onto an audience.

The skill of presenting is in generating interest, not downloading information onto an audience. Why? The attention and retention levels of an audience can vary considerably according to how interested they are in what they are hearing and seeing. If the audience feels involved, engaged, they become active listeners rather than just passive observers. Dull presentations produce bored observers who are likely to remember little of the presentation content. It is not whether the presenter has delivered materials, but whether the audience has understood the presentation. Remember to design your presentations around the needs and interests of the particular audience.

The research conducted by Albert Mehrabian (cited in Egan 2009: 102, 132) on how we receive messages found that:

Verbal (words only) accounted for	7%
Vocal (tone of voice) accounted for	38%
Non verbal (expression) accounted for	55%

> **Key Point:** Non-verbal communication accounts for over half of how what we say is perceived.

While the exact division of percentages may vary in experimentation, the underlying message is that humans gather more information from non-verbal communication than words alone (Morris 1994, 1978, 2002; Hunt and Baruch 2003; Mehrabian 2009). For example, anyone who has received a hollow greeting from a store assistant whose boss has demanded they 'greet' every customer can recognize the difference between genuine friendliness and a forced smile.

It is therefore useful to remember to make eye contact with the audience (Honey 2001; Morris 2002). Do not be tempted to just read notes from a file or screen (this can cause the presenter to turn away from the audience). Try to learn the materials you are presenting so that you can concentrate on communicating rather than reading them.

The following questions can help to establish the content of the presentation.

Who for? Who is going to be in the audience? Business colleagues, clients, academics? Remember it is important to design a message that is relevant to the particular audience.

Achieve what? What do you want to achieve by making this presentation? Persuade others to support your viewpoint? Increase awareness of HR issues? Gain funding? Obtain a job promotion? Get a top assessment grade?

Why should they listen? Why are people attending this meeting/ seminar/presentation? Why are they coming to listen to *you*? How will it benefit the audience?

Expectations: What do they expect from you? Are they hoping to hear an in-depth detailed analysis, or an overview of the subject matter? It is always helpful to put yourself in the place of the audience when thinking about how to design your presentation.

Special interests: what is the audience most interested to hear about?

Vocabulary: The use of appropriate language is important. So, for example, while the directors of an international company may respond favourably to a presentation about strategic planning and auditing HR performance, these terms may not be as well received by a group of charity fieldworkers who have just returned from working in a famine zone. Always consider the interests and the terms that are appropriate to your audience.

Provide relevant examples: Are you examples up-to-date? Regularly updating materials will make your presentations interesting for both you and the audience.

The following items provide a simple guide to collecting information, which can make presentations more interesting:

1. Topical news reports
2. Relevant publications and journals
3. Recent research papers
4. Your own research
5. Textbooks
6. Company financial reports
7. Quotations from literature
8. Anecdotes and stories
9. Interviews with staff/managers
10. Interviews with clients/users.

If there is a lot of general background information, it is more useful to hand this to the audience in the form of an information pack after the pre-sentational session. However, the professional presenter should be aware that most managers do not have time to read a long briefing document so it is *still* more effective to discuss an outline of the most important issues during the presentation.

THE INTRO PRESENTATION SYSTEM

When teaching both undergraduate and post-experiential students, many of them have told me that the most difficult part of a presentation is getting started. So to help you get a good start, have a look at the INTRO system below.

In-terest: Aim to gain the audience's **interest** from the outset. How this is achieved depends on the audience. Refer to your earlier work on who the audience are and what their expectations are likely to be. You never get a second chance to make a good first impression.

Plan the introductory statements carefully. So, the first slide should set out who you are and the subject area(s) you are going to discuss. The second slide sets out the specific content headings. This is also an opportunity to briefly highlight why the presentation's contents are of interest to the audience.

T-ime: It is not only polite but also practical to give the audience some indication of the duration of the presentation. Agree a time for the presentation and keep to that schedule. This makes the presenter look professional and encourages the audience to be more attentive, in the knowledge that what they are about to hear is likely to be concise and relevant. Include a period for questions and answers in the total allocated time.

R-ange: The range of the material depends on how much time you have to present and the purpose of the presentation. If you have selected one area within a large topic, explain to the audience why it was chosen rather than the other elements of that subject area.

If your allocated time is brief, then at the end of the presentation guide the audience to where they can source further information. For example, provide a list of the full academic references you have used in the presentation.

For academic presentations, it is also useful to include references in each slides so that the audience knows where you have gathered the information.

O-bjectives: Think about your objectives. What do you want to achieve by making the presentation? A presentation is about more that communicating information. If it were just information, then a briefing paper would suffice. A presentation brings key areas to the audience's attention and enables interaction and follow-up discussion.

Finally, practise the presentation. Once the presentation materials are complete then you/your team need to ensure it runs smoothly by practicing. This is particularly important for team presentations because it takes practice to coordinate the group of speakers.

Prepare a presentation

You/your team are invited to design a twenty-minute presentation, including a short question-and-answer session. The topics can be selected from the following questions, which are based on the chapters in this book. Select a topic you/your team are interested in and re-read the relevant chapter(s) for guidance.

1. Can integrated HR be described as a paradigm shift in HR, or is it more an evolution of pervious models?
2. Why is the organizational context important to HR planning?
3. Why do teams work? How do teams fail?
4. Why do psychological contracts matter?
5. Can life and work be balanced in modern organizations?
6. Does the right person always get the job? Discuss this in relation to AKS.
7. Appraisals. Evaluate how they can be made more motivational.
8. Can investing in employee development make a difference to organizational performance?
9. Different people have different requirements. How can HR help to address the opportunities/challenges of a diversified workforce?

10. Rewards: Is it just about money?

11. If HR is situation-specific, how does this influence the design of policy for international organizations?

RECOGNIZING THE IMPORTANCE OF INTERPERSONAL COMMUNICATIONS IN ORGANIZATIONAL PERFORMANCE

This section was provided by Duncan Christie Miller. After a first career in the Royal Marines and Special Forces, Duncan established CM Ltd in 1986, having previously been part of the initial management team of Textainer – a global containers leasing company.

Duncan is also a visiting lecturer with the University of Warwick and runs specialist workshops at Wellington College.

Before we start answering the questions posed in the title, let us look at what happens when interpersonal communications inside an organization are poor. There is an immediate and dramatic loss of morale, internal factions develop, personal aims take over from corporate objectives, and there is a huge amount of wasted time, energy, and effort.

The measurement of the success or failure of interpersonal communications is done through regular and sensitive audits of performance and morale.

Feedback

Let us look firstly at the concept of feedback and how it can be introduced into an organization. Feedback is often misconstrued and sometimes purposefully misused as criticism. There will of course be occasions when feedback does contain negative comments, recommendations for improvement or suggestions for changes in a person's attitude or behaviour. If feedback is to be a significant part of the company's core values, it needs to be taught as a personal and management skill. It is for line managers to ensure that everybody understands both the value of feedback and the methods of giving and receiving it. Using the annual assessment procedure is not good enough.

Feedback can be taught using the acronym **GIFT.** This stands for:

Giving: Treat feedback as a gift or a present. This means that it is carefully considered and properly delivered, with the recipient acknowledging its value by thanking the giver for taking the time and trouble to express what may be difficult and personal issues.

Individually: Feedback is best done individually, but in a very well-structured and harmonious team it can be done inside the group. This relies on the group understanding the individual nature of the feedback and not using the discussion between the two individuals to become a collective and uncontrolled expression of sentiment.

Fairness: It is important to provide fair and accurate comments. This is a prime requisite of any feedback. Therefore it needs to be given as soon as possible after an incident and needs to be based on an accurate assessment of the situation in which it occurred. There is no value in giving feedback about an incident which occurred more than a week ago. Accuracy depends on the giver of the feedback being able to refer to specific incidents and using them to highlight the points which are to be made. It may be thought that these incidents are on the whole negative, where correction is required. However, in practice, once feedback is an established and accepted part of the team's behaviour, it will be found that the majority of it is positive and will often include a request for that behaviour to be repeated or improved upon in the future. Even when the comments are referring to an incident, which is potentially negative, a positive outcome can be enjoyed as the assumption is made that such an incident will not be repeated in the future. Therefore, all feedback can be seen as positive.

The time and place of both giving and receiving feedback is vitally important. There is little value in wanting to discuss a particular incident if the potential recipient is putting on his or her coat to depart at 5 o'clock on a Friday afternoon. Therefore, the time, place and theatre of the feedback needs careful consideration. Time should always be allowed for discussion and indeed for reciprocal feedback.

The Coffee Shop

Organizations which enjoy positive and vibrant interpersonal communications often have a quasi-social centre which can usefully be referred to as The Coffee Shop. This may indeed be a restaurant or canteen. Or it could be an informal meeting place including unusual locations such as a photocopying office. We know that when staff are given the opportunity casually to encounter each other, interpersonal communications develop; ideas are shared and enjoyed so that managers can deftly use this as an informal arena for testing ideas.

Responsibility for communications

All boards and partnerships should have a designated officer responsible for communications – both internal and external. This ensures that the *what* and the *how* of communications are given due emphasis by a responsible person, and that communications are not all left to chance. If left to chance, rumour and gossip will take precedence over fact and genuine information.

Morale

There are three major components of this very personal subject: spiritual, intellectual and material.

The *spiritual* side has nothing to do with religion but refers to our unique ability as humans to feel very strongly about the value and authenticity of what we are trying to achieve. We want to be motivated by the importance of the objective, the fact that it is vital. As an individual I need to feel that I am incorporated into the body politic as an important albeit perhaps small part of the whole. Therefore, communication to me needs to encompass my own spiritual needs – being relevant and emotional without being mawkish or frenetic.

Intellectually, each and every individual needs to think that his or her contribution is both valuable and appropriate. We are able to make impressive deductions from what we are told and what we see and what we experience – intellectually we need to rationalize and to rationalize correctly that what we are being tasked to do is both appropriate and realistic.

The *material* aspect to morale is double-edged. By material we mean the provision of resources, which allow us to do our job to the best of our ability. People at all levels need to be convinced that they have the best possible, the best available and the best funded resources – even if they know that they are not the optimum which could be provided under the most benign circumstances. The cry of 'give us the tools and will finish the job' is entirely valid, with the tools being convincing within their own integrity.

Listening

It is essential that managers and staff develop the art of listening. As one becomes more senior in an organization, listening becomes far more important than talking. To listen well is an art, to listen badly an offence. The following will help you become a magnificent listener:

Giving encouragement and reassuring the other party that what they are saying is both interesting and valuable is a major component of active, positive listening.

Listen to the content and do not be seduced either positively or negatively by the delivery. Many people have excellent things to say and often say them badly. Therefore, being critical of delivery will prevent you from hearing what they're saying. Alternatively, some people have brilliant delivery and very little of value to say.

Ask sequential questions. We humans are very good at telling stories. Therefore helping the deliverer by asking 'What happened next?' is a very valid method of giving encouragement and getting the best out of the conversation.

Summarize frequently and ensure that by doing so you and the other party confirm that what has been said has actually been understood. This is a very useful technique employed by chairpersons at meetings.

Really listen. Listening is extremely hard work, is tiring and demands sustained concentration. It is too easy to pretend to listen and allow your mind to wander. Therefore look at the other party, give them verbal signals that you are engaged with them, and do not be frightened of asking for clarification if you do not understand.

Try never to interrupt. It is very tempting to finish other people sentences for them and to suppose that you are a mind reader. Most people say what they mean at the end of their sentence, so preventing them from getting there ensures that you will have missed most of what they are actually trying to communicate. All of us to some extent suffer from having a speech defect and it is tempting under such circumstances to interrupt and to intervene. Don't.

Making notes, however brief, will enhance your listening. However, the making of the notes must not prevent you from listening. If you are unable to make notes during the discussion then do so as soon as possible after the conversation ends. And lastly adopt a demeanour and body language which allow the other party to feel that you are fully engaged with them. At the very least smile.

SUMMARY: COMMUNICATING IN ORGANIZATIONS

(a) A key role of HR-trained professionals is to communicate the importance of investment in employees to their management colleagues.

(b) Each person has a part to play in the way communications are conducted within their organization.

(c) If colleagues trust each other, their organizations' behaviour is more likely to produce cooperative exchanges.

(d) Distrust in human exchanges can be disadvantageous to individuals and their organizations.

(e) Consultation of staff is central to constructing new plans.

(f) The facilitated meetings guide REACT reduces time being dissipated on either non-agenda items or using too much time on individual items.

(g) The presentation is often used as part of the employment selection process.

(h) Humans gather more information from non-verbal communication than words alone.

(i) Design presentations which are relevant and interesting to the particular audience.

(j) Feedback can be taught using the acronym GIFT.

REVISION SECTION

Evaluate why trust between managers and staff is central to organizational performance.

Discuss the benefits of staff consultations in developing organizational plans.

TAKING IT FURTHER

Key texts to look up:

Covey, S. (1999) *The Seven Habits of Highly Successful People*. London: Simon & Schuster.

Jones, D. and Stubbe, M. (2004) Communication and the Reflective Practitioner: A Shared Perspective from Sociolinguistics and Organisational Communication. *International Journal of Applied Linguistics*. 14(2), pp. 185–211.

Morris, D. (2002) *People Watching. Guide to Body Language*. London: Vintage.

Stanton, N. (2009) *Mastering Communications* (5th Edition). Basingstoke: Palgrave Macmillan.

Refer to the books and journals in this references section.

REFERENCES

Alberg, R. (2002) Counting with Numbers. *People Management*. 10 January. CIPD.

Aragón-Sánchez, A., Barba-Aragón, I. and Sanz-Valle, R. (2003) Effects of Training on Business Results. *International Journal of Human Resource Management*. August, 14(6), pp. 956–980.

Argyle, M. (1995) *The Psychology of Interpersonal Behaviour*. London: Penguin.

Axelrod, R. (1984) *The Evolution of Cooperation*. New York: Basic Books.

Axelrod, R. (1997) *The Complexity of Cooperation: Agent-Based Models of Competition and Collaboration*. Princeton, NJ: Princeton University Press.

Blundel, R. and Ippolito, K. (2008) *Effective Organisational Communication: Perspectives, Principles and Practices*. Harlow: Financial Times Prentice Hall.

Covey, S. (1999) *The Seven Habits of Highly Successful People*. London: Simon & Schuster.

Currie, G. and Procter, S. (2003) The Interaction of Human Resource Policies and Practices with the Implementation of Team Working: Evidence from the UK Public Sector. *International Journal of Human Resource Management*. June, 14(4), pp. 581–599.

Egan, G. (2009) *The Skilled Helper: A Problem Management and Opportunity Development Approach to Helping*. Belmont: Brooks Cole, Cengage Learning.

Honey, P. (2001) *Improve your People Skills*. Wimbledon: CIPD.

Hunt, J. W. and Baruch, Y. (2003) Developing Top Managers: The Impact of Interpersonal Skills Training. *The Journal of Management Development*. 27 August, 22(8), pp. 729–752.

Jones, D. and Stubbe, M. (2004) Communication and the Reflective Practitioner: A Shared Perspective from Sociolinguistics and Organisational Communication. *International Journal of Applied Linguistics*, 14(2), pp. 185–211.

Kessler, I. (ed.) (2002) Deery, S. and Walsh, J. Contracting Out and Market-Mediated Employment Arrangements: Outsourcing Call Centre Work. *People Management*. 7 February. Wimbledon: CIPD.

Littleford, D., Halstead, J. and Mulraine C. (2004) *Career Skills: Opening Doors into the Job Market*. Basingstoke: Palgrave Macmillan.

Mehrabian, A. (2009) *Non Verbal Communication*. New Jersey: Transaction.

Morris, D. (1994) *Bodytalk: A World Guide to Gestures*. London: Jonathan Cape.

Morris, D. (1978) *Manwatching*. London: Harper Collins.

Morris, D. (2002) *People Watching: Guide to Body Language*. London: Vintage.

Nieto, M. L. (2002) *Marketing the HR Function* (New edition). Industrial Society, Learning & Development. Spiro Press. London.

Nieto, M. L. (2006) *An Introduction to Human Resource Management: An Integrated Approach*. Basingstoke: Palgrave Macmillan.

O'Neill, O. (2002) *Is Trust Failing?* Reith Lecture. *BBC Radio 4*. 17 April.

Marsen, S. (2007) *Professional Writing* (2nd Edition). Basingstoke: Palgrave Macmillan.

Stanton, N. (2009) *Mastering Communications* (5th Edition). Basingstoke: Palgrave Macmillan.

Tzafrir, S. S., Harel, G. H., Baruch Y. and Dolan, S. L. (2004) The Consequences of Emerging HRM Practices for Employees' Trust in Their Managers, *Personnel Review*, 33(6), pp. 628–647.

10

Employability, Continuous Personal Development and Team Building

INTRODUCTION

Employability and continuous personal development represents a commitment to becoming the best you can be. Employability includes a positive attitude to learning. It is for this reason, among others, that this book emphasizes the Attitudes, Knowledge and Skills (AKS) approach to personal development. Employability is an outcome of continuous personal development and includes transferable AKS, which can enable us to serve in many different types of organization. For example, during a lifetime of working, a person may work in several sectors and in different job roles.

In this chapter, you will learn about employability, attitudes to learning and what you can do to be more successful in teams. Students who are conducting teamwork projects may find it helpful to study this chapter early on in the course.

This chapter also contains a section on e-learning by Dr Bradley Saunders, who leads the e-learning delivery for Derby Business School at the University of Derby.

LEARNING OBJECTIVES

The key learning outcomes for the chapter are below:

- To understand employability and continuous personal development and what they mean for employee learning.

- To evaluate when to use e-learning as part of training and development strategy.
- To appreciate the benefits of teamwork in achieving organizational objectives.
- To evaluate issues in team development and performance.

WHAT EMPLOYABILITY AND CONTINUOUS PERSONAL DEVELOPMENT MEAN FOR EMPLOYEE LEARNING

For training development plans to remain relevant to current requirements, it is necessary to regularly re-evaluate them, so that employees have the knowledge and skills base to enable the organization to adapt to changing circumstances (Kleiner et al. 2012). In organizations that use multidisciplinary teams to manage projects, employees can benefit from training and development in areas such as team-working and project management to embed participation and involvement into their workplace culture (Cox et al. 2006). There is, for the most part, consensus about the importance of training as a means of helping organizations in the development of sustainable performance, based on their human resources (Bartel 1994; Barrett and O'Connell 2001; Aragón-Sánchez et al. 2003; Thang and Buyens 2008; Thang et al. 2008).

If people are asked to complete a review of their training and development requirements, then their expectations of being supported are likely to be heightened. Similarly, this applies to performance reviews whereby if people are expected to take on new tasks and processes then the HR team should have prepared a schedule of supportive training. This approach assists formation of training plans by which people can build their skills and knowledge to address performance gaps and optimize resources (Mabey and Finch-Lees 2008: 22).

The more flexible psychological contract emphasizes employability over employment security. Essentially, it is the responsibility of the employee to ensure that they have the necessary AKS to obtain a new job. However, in such circumstances, some employees may respond by focusing on their

Key Point: The flexible psychological contract emphasizes employability over employment security. Essentially, it is the responsibility of the employee to ensure that they have the necessary attitudes, knowledge and skills to obtain a new job.

Key Point: The organizational cost of insecure employment is that some employees may respond by focusing on their own best interests before those of their current employer. In practice, they may seek short-term performance gains which enhance a CV over long-term sustainability.

own best interests before those of their places of work. This does not imply that an employee will not work conscientiously, but it may be more difficult to sustain long-term commitment where the employer does not reciprocate such loyalty. According to the research by Clarke and Patrickson (2008), the changes in career patterns mean that people do not stay with one employer for many years. There is also more emphasis on each person continually investing in his or her employability as a means of securing future employment. However, Clarke and Patrickson (2008) also observed that there is still an expectation by employees that employers should provide job-specific training and development. Employers may need to reconsider providing more job security to ensure that they retain talent. For evidently, the more employable person may seek alternative employment opportunities if they do not feel secure in their current workplace.

Activity: reflecting on my attitudes to work

Consider the following short questions about you attitudes to work:

What motivates you to go to work?

How would you describe your attitude to work?

How much time do you invest in thinking about how to improve the work environment for the people you work with?

What time do you invest in meeting people outside your immediate working environment? For example, attending professional groups such as the CIPD or CMI?

How important is work to you as part of your life–work balance?

After you have answered the above questions, think about how your attitudes can influence your employability.

In the modern work environment, the best security an employee has is their ability to get another job, hence to ensure that they are employable (Bagshaw 1997). According to Begg et al. (2000: 189), earnings are the minimum payments required to induce someone to do a job. Economic rent is the extra payment a person receives over and above the minimum earnings required. By applying this economic model to employee relations, it is possible to calculate the difference between what a person earns and their value in the marketplace. In some cases, the person may be under-valued by their current employer; alternatively a person may not be able to command a comparable salary elsewhere. Clearly, the employee who is able to obtain alternative employment at a similar or higher rate of pay than their current job is in a stronger negotiating position than one who cannot. Employability is essential to securing continuous employment, so investments in personal development are very worthwhile. When an employee leaves to take another position with more pay and greater responsibilities, it is helpful to question whether their former line manager had underestimated the employee's potential. This is important because the organization has lost talent and will incur consideration costs in recruitment, selecting and induction for an alternative new employee.

WHEN TO USE E-LEARNING AS PART OF TRAINING AND DEVELOPMENT STRATEGY

The following section is by Dr Bradley Saunders, who leads the e-learning delivery for the Derby Business School at Derby University.

A key question for managers is whether training and investment in people really work. There is some evidence that productivity increases in companies which place an increased emphasis on employee development. However, this is arguably because human behaviours such as self-worth, motivation, commitment and enthusiasm make a positive contribution to workplace performance. It follows that what makes the real difference in increasing productivity is not the provision of more and more training, but rather the ability to anticipate employees' developmental needs and to provide training which harnesses these positive qualities.

Therefore, the mere provision of technology to enhance the learning experience does not automatically ensure increased productivity. At the core of the organization's training methodology should be a clear awareness of purpose. Thus, the implementation of e-learning should be done not as an end in itself but as a way of making an organization's training more closely connected to the needs of its employees and more likely to motivate them to complete the training and put what they learn to good use.

What is e-learning?

It is important to define what we mean by e-learning, since no universal definition exists. Given the prevalence of the Internet in our everyday lives, there is clearly a large emphasis placed on learning delivered over the Internet or by means of a company intranet. However, this 'online learning' is merely one type of the broader term 'e-learning' – 'learning that is delivered, enabled or mediated using electronic technology for the explicit purpose of training, learning or development in organizations' (CIPD 2012). Importantly, this definition does not include the word 'Internet', nor does it rule out the inclusion of non-networked technology such as CD-ROMs, DVDs or USB memory sticks.

It is common to think of e-learning as largely a twenty-first-century phenomenon – indeed the term was coined in October 1999. However, we could consider our definition to include even early computer-based programmes such as Plato (Programmed Logic for Automated Teaching Operations), which was developed at the University of Illinois in the 1960s and marketed commercially in the 1970s and 1980s. Clearly, however, the technical advances in computer technology over the last few decades (such as enhanced graphics and use of multimedia) have enabled authors of learning material to significantly enhance the way in which people learn.

Types of e-learning

Several broad categories of e-learning can be identified:

Courses, which can be Internet-based or contained on CD-ROMs and DVDs, aim to deliver formal training in a topic to learners. Some involve input from tutors, who guide and encourage learners through the course. Others are more self-contained and the learner is expected to progress at his or her own pace and without formal support. An example of the former might be an online top-up degree in accountancy, consisting of a number of tutor-guided course modules culminating in an online examination, approved by an official accountancy body. An HR example of the latter would be a DVD on how to conduct performance appraisals, featuring text and video input and self-tests. The key feature of *courses* is that they can be seen as formal e-learning vehicles, which are intended to meet specific learning goals. The learner starts, continues, and (hopefully) completes these courses.

Resources are less formal and can be seen as self-standing items which help people to do their jobs. Rather than something that people start and work through, *resources* enable learning to take place when it is needed. We are all familiar with the Frequently Asked Questions (FAQ) list. Such a resource is not one which most people read from start to finish in one go! Rather, it is accessed as and when a question arises. Similarly, a help file accompanying a computer programme such as Word allows users to gain knowledge related to a task at hand. When we think of e-learning, we need to consider not just formal learning such as that offered by *courses* but also the informal learning provided by *resources*. Since a lot of knowledge resides in the heads of workers, companies are well advised to set up good resources within their knowledge management system. Technology, with its advanced search function, can be an excellent way to capture knowledge and procedures which may otherwise be lost when knowledgeable workers move on to another organization. *Resources* often take the form of examples of good practice, such as videos and other user-generated content (Towards Maturity 2012).

Social media incorporates the use of 'Web 2.0' technology. In contrast with what might be termed 'Web 1.0', this use of Internet and Intranet technology focuses on interaction and collaboration between users rather than on a one-way consumption of online content (CIPD 2012). Tools such as Twitter and Yammer enable professionals to discuss technical issues, and the ensuing discussion can be accessed to provide a resource on a specific topic. The use of 'hashtags' within Twitter enables users to search for a specific topic easily and quickly and to interact with the authors of these messages if required. Social-media technology allows practitioners to set up and take part in communities of practice which enable them to benefit from the experience of others in similar roles elsewhere. Wikis – knowledge bases built up by a group of users collaboratively – can be developed as a result of social interaction and serve as a useful resource for others.

The use of *Virtual Learning Environments*, incorporating tools such as online meeting software, video conferencing platforms, virtual classrooms and webinars, is growing (Towards Maturity 2012). Such tools can greatly facilitate learning by enabling practitioners to meet without travelling, and are popular with more than a fifth of organizations (CIPD 2011).

Blended Learning refers to the mixture of e-learning and more traditional learning. For example, learners may interact online but attend weekly lectures. There is a widespread feeling among organizations that e-learning should not be seen as divorced from traditional learning. According to CIPD (2011), 93% of organizations believe e-learning is enhanced by combining it with other types of learning in a blended learning approach.

Benefits of e-learning

The major benefits of e-learning are: a reduction in training costs; flexibility of access; greater reach (a classroom holds 20 people whereas an online course can cope with an unlimited number of people); the provision of 'just-in-time' resources which can be accessed at any time; uniformity of delivery of training; and the ability to log and track learning – which is especially useful when delivering 'compliance' training such as health and safety courses (CIPD 2012; Towards Maturity 2012).

The future of e-learning

The future of e-learning in organizations looks bright, with recent surveys showing a clear growth in use. A major driver in this uptake may be that organizations perceive e-learning to be a less costly way to deliver training. A majority of organizations rely on e-learning to deliver compulsory 'compliance' training programmes, induction, on-boarding and technology programmes (CIPD 2011).

What of the other types of learning that need to take place in organizations? Research shows that many employees who undertake formal e-learning courses find it a lonely frustrating experience and drop out. For example, CIPD (2011) reports that over a quarter of organizations state that under 10% of employees enrolled on e-learning courses actually complete them. Towards Maturity (2012) reports that the benefits of social media may also not be fully appreciated, with many employers reluctant to allow employees to access third-party social media sites such as Twitter and Linkedin while at work.

Clearly, the mere application of technology is not enough to guarantee that effective learning takes place. Rather, learning, whatever media it uses to get its message across, should be carefully designed with the needs of the learner in mind. According to Towards Maturity (2012: 41) it is important to ensure that e-learning engages users' interests, and encourages them to think rather than just work their way through the e-learning programme.

TEAMWORK BENEFITS IN ACHIEVING ORGANIZATIONAL OBJECTIVES

Prospective employers frequently request specific information requiring evidence of team-working on course-work assignments and the student's performance and experiences of team-working. The specialist HR student also needs to understand team-working so that when they enter the workforce they are able to advise colleagues on how to achieve the best from people in teams and, equally important, how to avoid potential pit-falls. Over the years, I have worked with many teams of staff and students in several universities. In the majority of cases, team-based projects are successful and those involved enjoy the experience. However, while writers and lecturers can point the way towards more effective team-working, it would be an oversimplification to advance the view that all that is required to become proficient in team-working is a few HR textbooks and a set of lectures.

> **Key Point:** Team-working requires the acquisition and practice of a set of interpersonal AKS. Hence, the development of values such as tolerance of diversity, compromise and the counter-balancing pleasant assertiveness are practical skills which are encouraged by well-managed teamwork projects.

People learn and develop through the action of team-work participation (Revans 1982). Although theory is useful to inform our knowledge, it is through practical experience that individuals gain the ability to work with other people in teams. Teams usefully function more effectively if some developmental strategies have been employed to nurture their development. Developing people's team-working AKS undoubtedly makes good sense. Regrettably, it is not commonly employed. Working with other people can also be stressful, and sometimes differences of opinions will occur. Modern organizations use multidisciplinary teams and sometimes there can be tensions and disagreements, so HR specialists and managers alike should be competent in understanding and resolving team-member disputes. Even within a supportive learning environment, I can say with reasonable certainty that each academic year there will be at least one student who will come to advise me that one or other of their team activities is not going as well as they would like, and that it is not their fault. Once people graduate and find employment, the team-working challenges in organizations are similar, except that if projects are not completed correctly, or fail to meet the required standards, there are unlikely to be second chances by way of a resat coursework submission. However, working with other people is an integral part of organizational life, so it is constructive to acquire the appropriate AKS in a safe learning environment such as a business management programme or short course. This can save a lot of unnecessary experiential learning later in professional life.

At college or university, the main object of interest is the students' development, whereas organizations tend to prioritize more task-orientated outcomes. To put the case in the clearest way, it is probably better to learn about working in teams with an empathetic tutor overseeing proceedings than a potentially unsympathetic employer who is likely to be more concerned about getting the job done than nurturing your personal development. It is, however, worth noting that since work is completed by people, the best way managers can ensure that work is completed to a high standard is to train and develop their team of people to be more effective both individually and as part of the organization. This is one of the many reasons that post-experiential courses can make a valuable contribution to management development.

> **Key Point:** Organizations operate by the consent and co-operation of many individuals, so any policy or project relies upon the willingness of colleagues to work together towards agreed aims and objectives.

If we subdivide team-working into AKS, it is evident that the right attitudes are going to be a decisive factor in whether or not a team succeeds. Unless people actually try to make a team function effectively, it is likely to encounter difficulties early on, no matter how knowledgeable and talented they are. The American writer Stephen Covey (1999: 31) has challenged some of the conventional thinking on organizational behaviour by asserting that we can only achieve quantum improvements in our lives by moving from a focus on our behaviour and onto the paradigms from which our attitudes and behaviours are formed. Later in this section there is an opportunity to answer an attitudes questionnaire, which can be used to facilitate personal reflection.

The area of attitudes is a challenging one for those professionals interested in improving the performance of people in organizations because of the three key AKS areas, attitudes are likely to be the most difficult to alter. This presupposes that the individual employees begin by wanting to work together in a team at all. Hence, it is worth acknowledging that there can be no set formula or any one theory which can provide the perfect solution to team-working. Instead, team-working situations can be regarded as an opportunity for on-going personal development. HR professionals often refer to continuous development in learning. This is particularly the case in team-working. There is always something new to learn about working with other people.

In recognizing that attitudes are important, members of a work team should begin by reflecting upon their own motivations and commitment to the team project. Organizations operate by the consent and co-operation of many individuals, so any policy or project relies upon the willingness of colleagues to work towards agreed aims and objectives. Even a good project can fail if it lacks the support of colleagues because passive resistance is as likely to scupper a good plan as outright rebellion. Learning to work in project teams is a key factor in developing the kind of attitudes that are likely to equip us to work with other people in the workplace, recognizing and respecting diversity.

During the last few decades, a wide range of academic research has critically evaluated the question of whether teams can outperform individual decision making (Hoffman and Maier 1961; McGrath 1984; Davis 1992). When viewed collectively, the research evidence tends to indicate that team performance usually depends upon how members interact and their abilities to elicit the best from each other. While it may be true that one highly talented individual may sometimes outperform a team, his or her work is less likely to be adopted in an organization where colleagues have had no opportunity to influence the outcomes or decisions.

There is also growing evidence to indicate that what has come to be described as emotional intelligence influences how successful a person's professional career might be (Goleman 1995; Martinez 1997; Davis et al. 1998; Fisher 1998; Huy 1999). It may therefore be proposed that emotional attributes such as self-awareness, self-discipline, commitment and empathy can be more relevant to working successfully with other people than intellectual capabilities alone.

> **Key Point:** Emotional attributes such as self-awareness, self-discipline, commitment and empathy can be more relevant to working successfully with other people than intellectual capabilities alone. People care less about what you know until they know that you care about them.

This means that people who are able to display the appropriate attitudes are more likely to be hired and more able to gain the approval of others to progress in their career. Hence, the approach we take to team-working situations can have an influence on our own professional success and relationships with others.

A negative and ultimately self-defeating attitude to team-work is called 'social loafing' (Latane et al. 1979; Karau and Williams 1993; Erez and Somech 1996). Supervisors and colleagues soon recognize individuals who simply avoid contributing to the work, which can eventually isolate the social loafer. In organizations, team failures inevitably have consequences for every member of the team because a project of work will not have been brought to a satisfactory completion. The extent to which any one member contributed more or less to that failure is ultimately of less importance than the fact that the team failed. A business course is therefore an excellent opportunity – whether for undergraduates or post experience professionals – to enter into a safe learning area to improve their self-awareness and team-working attitudes.

Activity: Everybody, Somebody, Anybody and Nobody

Over the years, I have worked with some successful project teams in both commerce and universities. The challenge of successful team management

> **Key Point:** Agree what is to be done by which team member, and the standard expected. Then plan a schedule of work for the team-work project to be completed.

often begins with individual commitments to begin the work in time and make a full contribution to the aims of the team. It is therefore prudent to agree a statement of aims and targets early in the team's activity schedule.

This approach also provides an opportunity for team members to recognize each other's areas of strength so that future work can be distributed according to the members with the most appropriate knowledge and skills. Without such forward planning, important tasks may be left inadequate time for completion.

Everybody, Somebody, Anybody and Nobody's team project

There are four people named Everybody, Somebody, Anybody and Nobody. The team had an important project, which Everybody in the team was responsible for completing on time. However, Everybody was sure that Somebody would do it. Anybody could have done it, but Nobody actually got on with the work.

Somebody got angry about the team's poor performance because it was Everybody's job. Everybody thought they could have done better without anybody else. In fact Anybody could have done the work, but Nobody realized that Everybody was waiting for Somebody to do the project for them.

In the end Everybody blamed Somebody when Nobody did what Anybody could have done.

Discussion questions

Think about the teams you have been/are a member of and consider the following questions:

1. How well do you think the team organized itself from the start of the project?
2. Do you think the team membership's responsibility is to improve performance or is it somebody else, such as a manager, training facilitator or lecturer?
3. To what extent would you describe yourself as an active member of your team?
4. If some members are less active than you, what steps have you taken to encourage more involvement in the team's activities?

EVALUATE ISSUES IN TEAM DEVELOPMENT AND PERFORMANCE

This section will consider the key elements of team-working in conjunction with practical self-evaluation and teamwork exercises. Teams move through different stages of development. In this respect, the work of Tuckman (1965) is particularly interesting because he outlined the stages of progression which team members should be aware of. However, to understand teams, your theoretical knowledge requires experimental skills development in team-working learning sets.

Tuckman's (1965) stages of team development:

1. Forming. Finding out about task and your team.
2. Storming. Internal conflict develops.
3. Norming. Team conflicts are settled and co-operation develops.
4. Performing. Teamwork objectives are achieved.
5. Adjourning. Teams (that have worked together well) may have fond memories of the experience and gladly work together on another project.

In the workplace, the team is likely to change as new employees join the organization and others are promoted or leave the organization to develop their careers elsewhere. The management consultant Duncan Christie Miller has commented that managers need to re-evaluate their attitudes to new members of a team. Accordingly, he has observed that when a new person joins a team it is also a new team, not the original team with just a new member. To examine this, consider that the new team member alters the interpersonal relationships within the team. A new team member will have different experiences to offer as well as differences in AKS. There is also likely to be a period of settling in and adjustments to their new organizational culture and environment. Hence, it is a new team, not the old team with a new member. Consequently, all the team members will be need to make adjustments.

In meeting a new group of people, first impressions can shape how they subsequently behave towards each other. Furthermore, the untrained

Key Point: When a new person joins a team it is a new team, not the old team with a new member.

person is more susceptible to continue reinforcing their original first impressions. When people are presented with someone new, they reference back to previous experiences to categorize the new person. This is a process know as stereotyping, which is a psychological process by which humans categorize the complex world (Devine 1989; Hilton and Von Hippel 1996).

Stereotypes may be a convenient means of categorizing the world around us, but the enormous diversity that is humanity makes categories unreliable. The key here is to be aware that you have stereotypes and then alter your perceptions in response to the real person as opposed to the stereotype you may already have in your mind. The early stages of team development are consequently relevant to how members form early impressions of each other. It can also be a pivotal moment for the team because we do not get a second chance at making a really good first impression. It is therefore helpful to enter this early stage prepared to listen as well as contribute to the forming conversations.

How a team is set up in the initial stages of a project can have a considerable influence upon how it progresses later. Even if you are working with people you already know, it is still helpful to set an agreed set of objectives before the project commences. My experience of working with numerous teams would also support the view that those who fail to plan from the start may fail to achieve their full potential. The modularization of many courses can mean that team members have other study commitments which influence the timetabling and schedule of work for you team project. It is better to anticipate and plan for such factors than to encounter them unprepared later. This can be a valuable transferable skill for the workplace where colleagues often have to manage several projects at one time.

The team should agree where to conduct meetings. For example, arrange a meeting place where there are unlikely to be interruptions and which is conducive to study and discussion. Also, be sensitive to team members who may not care to meet in bars or at times of religious significance. Establish communication early on by agreeing on whatever method (telephone, email, meetings) is best to maintain regular contact. Many students work their way through college, so teams need to plan their meeting times in advance. Usually the best time is when you are all together for a timetabled seminar. Many course leaders design a period of team-working within the allocated session time to facilitate teamwork meetings. Be flexible and agree a realistic schedule that the team can keep to.

What are the team's objectives? The aims of the team are relevant to the eventual outcomes. The objectives should be specific, realistic and agreed by the team members. Once the objectives are agreed, write them down and give every team member a copy to sign.

How are we going to achieve our objectives? The team also has to set out a clear commitment to achieving the agreed objectives and prepare a schedule of work for the whole project. The motivation to succeed has to come from inside the team. It is not usually necessary to produce a complicated work proposal. I have seen teams that produced superb flow diagrams to support their projects subsequently fail to complete the work. Nevertheless, a plan of work stages is useful.

How is the project work to be divided? Each team member should have specific tasks. If the division of work is not managed, the team may drift along for weeks in misplaced complacency that someone is doing something, when in reality no-one is doing anything! In such circumstances social loafing may occur (Latane et al. 1979) whereby the feckless member/s may rely upon their more conscientious teammates to eventually get the work done.

> **Key Point:** Remember to include everyone in the team tasks allocation, then create a simple diary of what needs to be done and by whom.

Action   by whom   Date

1.

2.

3.

4.

5.

6.

7.

8.

9.

10.

11.

12.

As the term 'storming' (Tuckman 1965) implies, the research into team dynamics anticipates the possibility of conflicts arising within the team. To some extent, unnecessary storming can be avoided by careful preparations at the initial stage of the project. However, the best-laid plans can go astray, so some adjustments are likely to occur. Although it can be tempting to seek external validation for individual positions from outside the team, it is more helpful to resolve difficulties within the team membership. In the final analysis, it is the team's responsibility to complete a task so the strains and stresses are better resolved internally. It may be more emotionally comforting to blame one person for the team's difficulties, but the sometimes unpalatable truth is that it is more likely that communication failures and problems are the whole team's responsibility. Storming may be the result of disputes regarding objectives, meetings and task allocation. It is for this reason that each member of the team should have a copy of the agreed objectives and the work diary as a starting point for discussions. It is also helpful for team members to recognize and remind each other that the purpose of their working together

> **Key Point:** Team members are usually willing to work with each other if they have agreed goals. However, the extent to which differences are sublimated into the team objectives depends upon the extent to which each team member values the team and its plans.

is to complete a team project. If the project is not progressed successfully, *everyone* fails.

If team members regard the project as important, then they are more likely to invest their knowledge and skills and time to help the team succeed. Be prepared to make adjustments to the work in progress. Do remember to allow for contingencies. For example: computers do sometimes crash, appointments may be delayed, and research can take longer than anticipated. Build 'contingency time' into the schedule so that the final project date can be fulfilled.

As well as different stages in team development, we also tend to perform differing roles when working with other people. The research work by Belbin (1981, 1993, 2000) identified a set of different but equally valuable team roles. Each of the roles provides the team with potentially different AKS, which can combine to promote a more effective team-working situation. Belbin's research indicated that each team member could adapt to more than one team role, so it is not necessary to have a representative for every team role. To use a simple example, in an Olympic team, the weight-lifting members are not required to run races and in football teams the goalkeeper is not generally expected to score goals. Alternatively, it is perfectly reasonable to argue that team members should gain experience of areas in which they do not have confidence in order to build their personal skill base.

Theoretical models provide us with metaphors to categorize and make sense of the world. However, abstract models cannot provide the experience to evaluate the complexity and diversity that is human kind. Everyone is on a learning and experiential journey. The reality is that all human kind does not fit into any set of predetermined categories. Instead, the metaphors can be a useful starting point to adjust our perceptions in response to each person we meet. The work of Belbin (1981, 1993, 2000) provides a useful guide to team roles. However, team roles can assist, but not define, our diverse and multicultural world.

A *chairperson* role requires someone who can be enthusiastic, pleasantly assertive, self-confident. It also calls for impartiality and the ability to consider alternative points of view and approaches. The chairperson in a team also needs to have the trust and confidence of other members.

The *company worker* denotes a person who is hard-working and conscientious. In general, a company worker will present a high degree of self-control and commitment to achieving team objectives.

A *co-ordinator* displays tolerance and draws people towards co-operation. The co-ordinating role encourages team members to participate and work together. The person in this role tends to have a calm disposition and thereby provides a helpful influence on the team's proceedings.

If your team requires momentum then this is likely to come from a *shaper*.

The shaper tends to be energetic, enthusiastic, extrovert, task-orientated. They may also be impatient and argumentative, provoking discussion and critical evaluation of ideas.

The *plant* role is a more reflective and creative team member who brings innovation and new perspectives. In some cases, this creativity can become individualistic, intellectual, and not necessarily team-orientated.

The *resource investigator*, as the term suggests, is willing and able to seek out information from outside the team. They generally display good communication and social skills, and are capable of working independently on a specific external assignment.

The *monitor evaluator* tends to be a logical, rational person/s who may appear aloof, even detached, and yet is capable of evaluating conflicting ideas dispassionately.

The *team-workers* are those who provide the all-important morale boosts to teams by being socially sensitive to the needs of others. Teamworkers tend to be diplomatic and keen to encourage other members to focus on common objectives rather than on differences.

Finally, if you have ever been in a team where the finish of the project lacked refinement, perhaps the *completer finisher role* was not adequately provided. As the term 'finisher' suggests, this kind of role focuses on attention to detail. It requires a calm, controlled and focused approach to the detailed aspects of the team's work, particularly task completion. Such people may irritate other team members with constant references to detail.

The reality of team-working is that tasks have to be distributed so that everyone does something, though not everyone has to work on every aspect of a project. For example, one student may go to the learning resources centre to collect information (a *resource investor*). Another may plan and organize the team's meetings, a (*team-worker*). Yet another will act as facilitator to the meetings, ensuring that each person has a fair hearing (the *chairperson*). The leadership and drive may come from someone who enjoys giving direction and shape to the project (a *shaper*). Creative ideas may come from someone who sits and reflects (a *plant*), while the *finisher* may oversee the final project details and so forth through the team roles. It is likely that one person may fulfil two or more of these team activities. Hence, it is worthwhile investing time initially to identify what knowledge and skills are available to the team.

Each role is different and in its own distinct way provides an important contribution to the team's objectives. Yet team members also need to be sufficiently flexible to adopt additional roles where necessary. It is self-defeating to say, 'That's not my role so I won't help my team'. Team members should also be able to recognize the potential stresses that can arise when significantly different personalities come together. The advantage of teams containing a combination of team roles is that results can be achieved that would be difficult to complete individually. For example, although a *shaper* might be irritated by the pedantic interjections of a *completer finisher*, the former provides momentum to the project while the latter ensures quality. It is therefore possible that, left to their own devices, a *shaper* might complete the project sooner but possibly miss a number of errors, while the *completer finisher* might delay reasonable progress while they reviewed and refined every detail of the work.

Operational managers are more likely to be interested in how theories and models can be translated into useful practices (Currie and Procter 2003). Hence, the research by Janis (1982) and Aldag and Fuller (1993) postulated that it is possible for team-work to fail for a number of reasons, where members cease challenging ideas or refuse to consider alternatives. This is what Janis (1982) described as Groupthink. In essence, it may be possible for a team to become too cohesive and insular to both internal and external criticism so that no-one within the team criticizes decisions. In an extreme form people, can subsume their individuality beneath the constraints and dictates of the group/team's leadership. More commonly, team members may hold leaders in such respect that they are disinclined to offer alternative viewpoints.

Key Point: In hierarchical organizations, or where employees have low job security, Groupthink difficulties occur because employees are disinclined to challenge the management. People are less likely to risk offering alternatives in situations where those in management often penalize people who dissent.

This means that factors such as organizational culture and structure, norms and values can influence how people work in teams, and how willing they may be to offer alternative solutions to the established viewpoint. It is therefore useful to view organizations holistically so that the development of teams is considered in the context of the other forces working upon and influencing people's behaviour.

Activity: *Titanic* – a team-work case study

It is helpful to use a situational model to understand a concept such as Groupthink in action. For this purpose, I shall describe Groupthink behaviour as the *Titanic* case study. The famous early-twentieth-century ship was regarded as being the most technologically advanced of its day. According to historical records, the *Titanic* was divided into 16 watertight compartments and had 15 transverse bulkheads that extended far above the water line with watertight doors. Those doors could also be closed from the bridge by an electrical switch. This would 'make the vessel practically unsinkable', according to official pronouncements (from a Public Records Office document). The technological excellence of the *Titanic* encouraged heightened confidence in the ship's officers who, in the pursuit of greater prestige and success, thought it expedient to drive this powerful ocean liner at full speed through an area known for icebergs. The telegraph warnings of ice, falling temperatures and weather conditions that would make spotting floating ice difficult did not deter the captain from pursuing a fast maiden voyage time to New York. Indeed, Captain Smith was a highly regarded and experienced officer of the White Star Line. The officers on the bridge at the time of the collision, First Officer Murdock, (lost), Fourth Officer Boxhall (survivor), Sixth Officer Moody (lost) and Quartermaster Hitchens at the wheel (survived) did not prevail upon their captain to reduce the ship's speed (from United States Congressional sub-committee hearing 1912: 1150). The deference, or unwillingness of the other officers to request a reappraisal of the Captain's decision to continue current course and speed, indicated that elements of Groupthink may have had a role in the disaster.

For today's organizations, the constantly changing environment in which they operate allows little place for polices formed around 'continuing current course and speed'. *Titanic* is arguably an example of where a combination of external and internal factors can lead to a team making the wrong decisions because alternatives are given too little credence.

If an organization/department/team has a record of success and a strong management culture/structure prevails, it can be difficult for people to raise concerns or offer alternative policies. This is not to devalue the importance of strong leadership qualities, but rather to emphasize the value of listening to other viewpoints. While it is difficult to innovate in a risk-averse environment, risk-taking needs to be tempered by counter-balancing evaluation and reflection upon the potential downside. In the case of the *Titanic*, the potential gain in prestige of arriving in New York a few hours earlier should have been balanced against the possible losses caused by a collision. It is therefore evident that team roles and the diversity which, different people can bring to a team can be a substantial asset to performance. Furthermore, 'storming' (Tuckman 1965), if conducted constructively, can avail teams of valuable opportunities to consider different approaches.

Groupthink becomes more likely if:

1. Members of a team have an illusion of invulnerability.

2. Assessments of performance are over-optimistic.

3. Normal precautions are ignored and a high-risk approach is adopted.

4. The team tends to ignore warning signs.

5. Opposition to or dissent from the accepted viewpoint is dismissed.

6. Team members who persist in challenging accepted values are regarded as disloyal.

Discussion questions

1. What do you understand by the term 'Groupthink'?

2. Why do you think teams can become overconfident?

3. What initiatives/steps can be taken to lessen the occurrences of Group-think?

4. Consider whether a team you are working with may have Groupthink tendencies. What can team members do to challenge Groupthink complacency?

If members of a team share the rewards and responsibility for the team's successes or failures, they have an incentive to work co-operatively. For example, the success of contemporary Japanese companies was supported by a realization of the value of co-operative team-working (Procter and Mueller 2000). If a member ascribes all successes to themselves and all failures to the other members, a team is likely to become dysfunctional. Thus, competition rather than co-operation ensues thereby debilitating the team's ability to operate effectively. If an organization sets individual performance-related targets, then teams are less likely to be as effective because personal aims and ambitions become the focus of employee attention.

It is quite possible, even likely, that teams may experience some difficulties (Rayner 1996). There are also likely to be differences, both minor or major, whenever a group of people with there own perspective on events and priorities comes to work together. This can be healthy and helpful providing individuals respect each other's contributions and retain commitment to the overall success of the team project.

SUMMARY: EMPLOYABILITY, CONTINUOUS PERSONAL DEVELOPMENT AND TEAM BUILDING

(a) The changes in career patterns mean that people do not stay with one employer for many years. There is also more emphasis on each person continually investing in his or her employability as a means of securing future employment.

(b) When an employee leaves to take another position with more pay and greater responsibilities, it is helpful to question whether the former line manager had underestimated her/his potential. This is because the organization has thereby lost talent and will incur costs in recruitment, selecting and induction for a replacement.

(c) Anticipating employees' developmental needs and providing training, which harnesses these positive qualities, can make a real difference.

(d) The major benefits of e-learning are: a reduction in training costs; flexibility of access; greater reach.

(e) Team-working requires the acquisition and practice of a set of inter-personal AKS.

(f) The research evidence tends to indicate that team performance usually depends upon how members interact and their abilities to elicit the best from each other.

(g) Emotional attributes such as self-awareness, self-discipline, commitment and empathy can be more relevant to working successfully with other people than intellectual capabilities alone.

(h) A negative and ultimately self-defeating attitude to team-work is called 'social loafing'.

(i) When a person joins a team it is a new team, not the old team with a new member.

(j) Stereotypes are a means of categorizing the world around us, but the enormous diversity that is humanity cannot be set into categories.

(k) Include everyone in the team's task allocation, then create a simple diary of what needs to be done and by whom.

(l) The research work by Belbin (1981, 1993, 2000) identified a set of different but equally valuable team roles.

(m) Groupthink: A team can become too cohesive and insular to both internal and external criticism so that no-one within the team criticizes decisions.

(n) In hierarchical organizations, or where employees have low job security, there may be a greater chance of Groupthink difficulties because employees may be disinclined to challenge the status quo.

REVISION SECTION

'A secure employment environment is likely to be more conducive to collaboration and creativity than organizational environments where people are less secure'. Discuss.

Evaluate why team-working is key to contemporary organizational performance?

Explain what you understand by the term 'Groupthink'. What actions can managers initiate to encourage open discussion?

TAKING IT FURTHER

Key texts to look up:

Belbin, R. M. (2000) *Beyond the Team*. Butterworth-Heinemann: London.

Covey, S. (1999) *The Seven Habits of Highly Successful People*. London: Simon & Schuster.

Goleman, D. (1995) *Emotional Intelligence*. New York: Bantam Books.

Refer to the books and journals in this references section.

REFERENCES

Aldag, R. J. and Fuller, S. R. (1993) Beyond Fiasco: A Reappraisal of the Group Think Phenomenon and a New Model of Group Decision Processes. Psychological Bulletin. 113(3), pp. 533–552.

Aragón-Sánchez, A., Barba-Aragon, I. and Sanz-Valle, R. (2003) Effects of Training on Business Results. *International Journal of Human Resource Management*. 14(6), pp. 956–980.

Bagshaw, M. (1997) Employability – Creating a Contract of Mutual Investment. *Industrial and Commercial Training*. 29(6), pp. 183–185.

Barrett, A. and O'Connell, P. J. (2001) Does Training Generally Work? The Returns to In-company Training. *Industrial and Labor Relations Review*. 54(3), pp. 647–662.

Bartel, A. P. (1994) Productivity Gains from the Implementation of Employee Training Programs. *Industrial Relations*. 33(4), pp. 411–425.

Begg. D., Fischer, S. and Dornbusch, R. (2000) *Economics*. London: Mc Graw-Hill.

Belbin, R. M. (1981) *Management Teams: Why They Succeed or Fail*. London: Heinemann.

Belbin, R. M. (1993) *Team Roles at Work*. London: Butterworth-Heinemann.

Belbin, R. M. (2000) *Beyond the Team*. London: Butterworth-Heinemann.

CIPD (2011) Focus on e-learning. Available http://www.cipd.co.uk/binaries/e-learning%20SR%20(WEB).pdf [accessed 28 December 2012].

CIPD (2012) E-learning. Available www.cipd.co.uk/hr-resources/factsheets/e-learning.aspx [accessed 28 December 2012].

Clarke, M. and Patrickson, M. (2008) The new covenant of employability, *Employee Relations*. 30(2), pp. 121–141.

Covey, S. (1999) *The Seven Habits of Highly Successful People*. London: Simon & Schuster.

Cox, A., Zagelmeyer, S. and Marchington, M. (2006) Embedding Employee Involvement and Participation at Work. *Human Resource Management*. 16(3), pp. 250–267.Currie G. and Procter, S. (2003) The Interaction of Human Resource Policies and Practices with the Implementation of Team Working: Evidence from the UK Public Sector. *International Journal of Human Resource Management*. 14(4), pp. 581–599.

Davis, J. H. (1992) Some Compelling Intuitions about Group Consensus Decisions, Theoretical Empirical Research and Interpersonal Aggregation Phenomena: Selected Examples 1950–1990. *Organizational Behaviour and Human Decision Processes*. 52(1), pp. 3–38.

Davis, M., Stankov, L. and Roberts, R. D (1998) Emotional Intelligence: In Search of an Elusive Construct. *Journal of Personality and Social Psychology*. 75(4), pp. 989–1015.

Devine, P. G. (1989) Stereotypes and Prejudice: Their Automatic and Controlled Components. *Journal of Personality and Social Psychology*. 56(1), pp. 5–18.

Erez, M. and Somech, A. (1996) Is Group Productivity Loss the Rule or the Exception? Effects of Culture and Group Based Motivation. *Academy of Management Journal*. 39(6), pp. 1513–1537.

Fisher, A. (1998) Success Secret: A High Emotional IQ. *Fortune*, 26 October.

Goleman, D. (1995) *Emotional Intelligence*. New York: Bantam Books.

Hearing Before a Subcommittee of the committee of commerce United States Senate (1912) *Titanic* Disaster. Pt 15. Digest of Testimony. Washington: Government Printing Officer.

Hilton, J. L. and Von Hippel, W. (1996) Stereotypes. *Annual Review of Psychology*. 46, pp. 237–271.

Hoffman, A. B. and Maier, N. R. F. (1961) Quality and Acceptance of Problem Solutions by Members of Homogeneous and Heterogeneous Groups. *Journal of Abnormal and Social Psychology*. 62(2), pp. 401–407.

Huy, Q. N. (1999) Emotional Capability Emotional Intelligence and Radical Change. *Academy Of Management Review*. 24(2), pp. 325–345.

Janis, I. L. (1982) *GroupThink*. Boston: Houghton Mifflin.

Karau, S. J. and Williams, K. D. (1993) Social Loafing: A Meta-analytic Review and Theoretical Integration. *Journal of Personality and Social Psychology*. 65(4), pp. 681–706.

Kleiner, M. M., Nickelsburg, J. and Pilarski, A. M. (2012) Organizational and Individual Learning and Forgetting. *Industrial & Labour Relations Review*. 65(1), pp. 68–81.

Latane, B., Williams, K. and Harkins, S. (1979) Many Hands Make Light Work: The Causes and Consequences of Social Loafing. *Journal of Personality and Social Psychology*. 37(6), pp. 822–832.

Mabey, C. and Finch-Lees, T. (2008) *Management and Leadership Development*. London: Sage.

Martinez, M. N. (1997) The Smarts that Count. *HR Magazine*. November.

McGrath, J. E. (1984) *Groups: Interaction and Performance*. New York: Prentice Hall.

Procter, S. and Mueller, F. (eds) (2000) *Teamworking*. Basingstoke: Macmillan.

Public Records Office (1997) *Titanic: 14th–15th April 1912: The Official Story*. London: Public Records Office.

Rayner, S. R. (1996) Team Traps: What They Are and How to Avoid Them. *National Productivity Review.* 15(3), pp. 101–115.

Revans, R. W. (1982) *The Origins and Growth of Action Learning*. Bromley: Chartwell-Bratt.

Thang, N. N. and Buyens, D. (2008) *What Do We Know About Relationship Between Training and Firm Performance: A Review of Literature*. Proceedings of the 7th International Conference of the Academy of Human Resource Development (Asia Chapter), 3–6 November, 2008, Bangkok, Thailand.

Thang, N. N., Thu, N. V. and Buyens, D. (2008) *The Impact of Training on Firm Performance: Case of Vietnam*. Working Paper Series, Faculty of Economics and Business Administration, Ghent University, 08/538, pp. 1–26.

Towards Maturity (2012). Bridging the Gap, Integrating Learning and Work, Towards Maturity Benchmarking Practice, 2012–2013 Report. Available http://www.towardsmaturity.org/download/2012-bench-mark-full-report-bridging-gap-v2 [accessed 28 December 2012].

Tuckman, B. W. (1965) Development Sequences in Small Groups. *Psychological Bulletin*, 63(6), pp. 384–399.

Tuckman, B. W. and Jensen, M. A. C. (1977) Stages of Small Group Development Revisited. *Group & Organization Management.* 2(4), pp. 419–427.

11
Corporate Social Responsibility and Business Ethics

This chapter provides students of management with the opportunity to study materials and reflect upon business ethics issues. Organizations are no more or less than the decisions which people in them make about how the organization works with the local, national and international community. In areas such as business ethics and corporate social responsibility, each person makes choices about how they behave, so this chapter aims to encourage self-reflection, too. By reading and applying the materials you will become more able to develop the AKS to critically evaluate organizational, ethical and corporate social responsibility.

LEARNING OBJECTIVES

The key learning outcomes for the chapter are below:

- Appreciate the growing importance of business ethics/corporate social responsibility (CSR) in twenty-first-century organizational life.
- Grasp how CSR boosts recruitment.
- Understand the relationship between business ethics/CSR and organizational reputation.
- Reflect upon matters of trust and organizational accountability.

- Reflect upon the challenges of implementing ethical policies in organizations.
- Conducting an ethical audit.

BUSINESS ETHICS/CORPORATE SOCIAL RESPONSIBILITY IN TWENTY-FIRST-CENTURY ORGANIZATIONAL LIFE

To be human is to make choices. Each of us makes hundreds of choices every day which can influence the commercial environment. For example, if people in a local community choose to buy products from a large retail park instead of their local stores, then it is likely that those retailers will eventually cease trading because of a lack of customers. It is a choice. If consumers buy more products from the Internet then shops in their town will close and eventually be replaced by regional/national distribution centres.

Key Point: Business ethics accepts the standards set out by national and international law and often goes further than legal requirements in caring for the interests of the organization's stakeholders.

Another aspect of organizational/stakeholder relations is described as corporate social responsibility (Griseri and Seppala 2009). A CSR-conscious organization accepts that it has responsibilities to a range of stakeholders which are directly or indirectly affected by what it does and how it conducts its business. This includes private, public as well as not-for-profit and non-governmental organizations. CSR is the responsibility of every employee and so it is important to emphasize the value of constructive engagement rather than prescription. This may mean learning through experience, although much can be achieved through case-study evaluations and studying organizations as part of a degree course or managerial development plan.

The history of management has regrettably recorded many high-profile debacles where integrity, both individual and collective, has been called into question. This proposition has resonance with papers in the current academic debate including (Brakel 2000; Hinman 2000; Argandona 2001; Brinkmann 2001; Davidson 2002; Whitehouse 2002). Accordingly, Watson (2003) has commented that more attention should be given to business ethics in organizations.

> **Key Point:** Senior executives have a significant role in establishing their organization's ethical tone. Employees tend to follow the example set by the top management. If the focus is on ethical behaviour and that is rewarded by promotions and salary increases, then people will work to achieve those ethical goals.

Research by Trevino et al. (2003) indicates that senior executives have a significant role in establishing their organization's ethical tone. Their findings further indicate that ethical leadership requires more than personal integrity; it involves using communication and reward systems to guide ethical behaviour. While I was conducting research on senior management and ethical behaviour, I found an interesting example of how a senior executive 'communicated ethical values'. The previous appointment we had agreed had been postponed, so when I arrived to meet the executive later we had a few minutes of introductory conversation. His answer as to why our earlier meeting had been cancelled was illuminating. The executive had personally travelled abroad to dismiss a regional manager who had been regularly and deliberately misleading clients in order to secure more business. Although the region was profitable and there were no specific complaints registered, the senior executive wanted to communicate the message that deliberately misleading clients to increase profits was unacceptable.

Each organization's behaviour reflects the prevailing culture, values and beliefs of the people responsible for defining and implementing policies. Managers also need to balance the competing pressures of profitability, customer service and targets to improve service levels. Accordingly, the senior leadership needs to indicate how it would like managers to respond to these differing requirements.

CSR BOOSTS RECRUITMENT

The next section was prepared for this book by Nina Seppala, who has also co-authored with P. Griseri and N. Seppala (2009) *Business Ethics and Corporate Social Responsibility*.

According to Nina Seppala, in the field of human resource management, there is increasing evidence to show that CSR boosts recruitment. For example, jobseekers are more interested in applying to companies that demonstrate their environmental awareness and social responsibility in recruitment materials. Candidates seem to appreciate CSR because it has a positive effect on the company's reputation and how it is perceived by society as a whole. Moreover, information on CSR increases applications across different types of people irrespective of their personal values. Researchers have argued that this is because potential employees believe that companies that invest in CSR also treat their employees well. The effect of CSR, however, varies across cultures and needs to be explored further.

Activity: business ethics

Let's begin by stimulating some self-reflection and group discussion about the kind of ethical decisions you might make in a number of organizational scenarios.

The questionnaire below provides a set of scenarios where you are required to make ethical choices. In reality, people make ethical choices frequently, on both personal and organizational issues.

Discussion questions

- A salesperson undercharges you for goods you have purchased from a large retail chain. Do you tell them about the error or keep quiet?
- What is your view on employers who give staff so much to do that they need to regularly work longer hours than specified in their contracts without additional payments/rewards/time off?
- If your organization imposed performance indicators, would you spend more time meeting them to impress management/external assessors or

continue doing whatever work was in the overall best interest of your clients/customers/patients/students?

- The company you work for uses low-cost producers in a third-world country who pay very low wages. An important customer asks you about your company's ethical employment policies, as this will influence their decision about whether to place a large order with your company. Do you tell them what you know or keep quiet?

THE RELATIONSHIP BETWEEN BUSINESS ETHICS/CSR AND ORGANIZATIONAL REPUTATION

According to a report by the CIPD, it is the role of HR departments or HR-trained professionals to promote the CSR agenda through their organizations (Watkins 2003: 10). Some stakeholders, such as shareholders, may carry more immediate influence than others, but it is a mistake to disregard sections of the stakeholder community. So, for example a corporation quoted on the stock market might focus on the interests of shareholders while ignoring its employees; or the quality of customer services delivery may eventually influence share-price values.

> **Key Point:** HR should be an integrated service that touches every aspect of an organization's operation from the boardroom to customers.

According to the CIPD, the largest influence on employee attitudes comes from managing people well, by giving them interesting jobs and helping them to achieve a satisfactory life–work balance (Emmott cited in Peasaud 2003: 37). It is difficult to create a climate where the employees care about the long-term interests of other stakeholders when they are insecure and or working to overly demanding targets. For example, the factory worker who is required to produce a large number of units per hour or the manager who has strict financial targets constraining their planning can find it challenging to balance such targets with other stakeholder considerations.

Members of an organization may experience some conflict from to time between their responsibilities to management, colleagues, clients and the

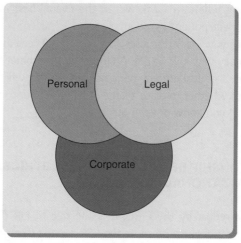

Figure 11.1 The intersections of personal, corporate and legal accountability
Source: Nieto (2006).

> **Key Point:** Avoid worker overload. Each new target, measure, reporting requirement adds to employee workload.

wider society. It is also possible that some of these constituencies may have different requirements. Hence, stereotypically, an employer may seek profit maximization, the professional body may require quality standards be upheld and clients may want the best services/products at the least cost. These do not have to be mutually exclusive and the aspiration of professionals should be to serve the various stakeholders.

TRUST AND ORGANIZATIONAL ACCOUNTABILITY

The reality of corporate business ethics is exposed when there are scandals relating to accounting inconsistencies, mis-selling of financial products, and where global names have been found to have misled authorities to enhance share value and profits. Such incidents are a reminder of the temptations facing organizations which are measured by financial performance.

The victims of such white-collar crimes are the many small investors who lose their savings and, of course, employees who are made redundant when the corporations collapse. The onus of integrity is ultimately upon the individual, although, self-evidently, organizations are composed of the interactions of many individual minds conforming to, or sometimes resisting, the norms and values of the majority (O'Neill 2002a, 2002b; Kitson and Campbell 2008).

Business ethics for the twenty-first century

The following extracts from are from a paper I delivered to The Business Ethics Conference at the University of Surrey, 6 March 2002, entitled 'Business Ethics For the Twenty-first Century'. After reading the extracts discuss the questions that follow.

Academics leading the way

A group of academics from several leading universities was invited to an international management consultancy. The purpose was to form a think tank on business ethics and ethical auditing. Why? My impression was that business ethics is an area of increasing interest to organizations, and consultancies are keen to build their expertise and knowledge in this area. There is also research evidence to indicate that ethical issues in organizations have been steadily moving up the managerial agenda (Chryssides and Kaler 1996). Indeed, as early as 1990, a study by Langlois and Schlegelmilch found that just over 50% of organizations in their study had a written code of ethics (pp. 519–539).

The later part of the twentieth century was influenced by the famous 1980s Thatcherite (Margaret Thatcher, former British prime minister) assertion that there is no such thing as society. If there is no society then organizations are also merely collections of individuals and as such have no identity beyond that which is promoted by the senior management. However, for Albrow (2000: 1) society is back in the frame, although it is not so clear that sociology has illuminated this development, or advanced a counterweight to excessive emphasis on the economy. At an organizational level, it is easier to remain fixated with the economic and the statistically measurable than to include the so called 'soft' indicators like employee morale and commitment.

Reputations and stakeholders

> **Key Point:** Business Priorities
> 1. Staff. 2. Customers. 3. Profit.
>
> Happy employees provide high-quality customer service.
>
> Content customers return to buy again and tell their friends about their positive experiences.
>
> Retaining customers increases profits.

If the image of an organization and its brands can influence profitability, then it is all the more important for organizations to consider how their stakeholders see them. A paper presented by Walsh (2001) on 'Building a Sustainable Business Brand', at Kingston University, argued that in both global corporations and local enterprises, brand is probably what acquires new business while reputation is what keeps it. Organizations which invest in maintaining a positive reputation are more capable of withstanding setbacks and surviving in a competitive market. The research by Nieto (2001: 73–80) with the Virgin Group found evidence that successful commercial performance was achievable when profits were placed in third place of importance, below staff and customers.

Discussion questions

- Why do you think an international management consultancy asked academics to help design an ethical auditing model?
- What are the benefits to organizations of becoming more sensitive to issues of social responsibility?
- Why is brand image not sufficient in itself to maintain organizational reputation?

IMPLEMENTING ETHICAL POLICIES IN ORGANIZATIONS

When there is a news report about an organization whose products or services have in some way been below standard, there are usually demands for tighter regulatory legislation and more externally controlled performance indicators. Modern organizations operate in a complex legal framework of externally and internally regulated corporate governance. Indeed, in recent years, the culture of central control of organizations has proliferated internationally.

The regulatory demands for conformity to procedures and protocols, detailed record-keeping, the provision of information in specified formats and compliance to imposed targets has multiplied. The regulatory culture extends to the work and performance of health trusts and schools, universities, research councils and commercial business. All this certainly produces a lot of additional work for employees.

The interesting question is whether these additional regulations have resulted in much progress being made in the way organizations behave. According to O'Neill (2002), on the contrary, a climate of control can be counter-productive to encouraging trust and improving performance.. For example, does all the documentation generated encourage people to be committed to the espoused standard, or just to comply with the reporting requirements? It may be surmised that external ethical controls alone are unlikely to deliver high standards of integrity in the way organizations operate. If regulations were the answer then the state-controlled economies would be the most successful, yet this is not the case. And innovation often emerges from creativity and entrepreneurs who implement new ways of organizing a business.

Key Point: For a code of ethics to have any real validity, it should proactively influence the way an organization operates day to day.

During, my years of conducting academic research, consultancy and lecturing, I have found it fascinating to listen to the diversity of beliefs expressed by people in organizations and during seminars. The range of acceptable versus non-acceptable behaviours can vary considerably, thereby stimulating some very interesting discussions. By completing the exercise below ('My Ten Commandments'), you can experience some of the issues which organizations face in designing codes of ethics. If, as can be the case, a small group of people find it challenging to agree a list of agreed 'commandments', then it is likely to be even harder for large organizations to agree and then apply national and transnational codes of ethics.

For a code of ethics to have any real validity, it should proactively influence the way an organization operates day to day. Alternatively, an ethical code may become no more than a piece of public relations material. In such cases, the code of ethics and other documents such as 'mission statements' may pronounce admirable, attractive virtues to be aspired to, but actually have little impact upon daily organizational life.

This is not, however, an argument for excessive compulsion or organizational regulation, whether internally or externally imposed. Indeed, organizational life is so complex that it would be difficult to attempt to codify a specified behaviour for every eventuality. In the classic science fiction novel *Brave New World*, Aldous Huxley (1932/1975) presented the reader with a world in which everything was controlled and individual choice had been replaced by complete social conformity. However, humans with free will are likely to be less compliant. Although codification of behaviour may be imposed, employees who are required (by company regulations) to comply, but without any personal sense of ownership, are unlikely do work with any commitment to management's objectives.

Activity: 'My Ten Commandments'

Form a small group of between two and ten people. Each member prepares a list of ten personal rules which they believe are the most important ones governing their behaviour. Once completed, the group can discuss the individual lists and try to create one collective set of ten rules which everyone can agree to. The group discussion should also assess the extent to which the agreed set of rules could be applied to an organization. Individual list:

- ....
- ....
- ....
- ....
- ....

- ....
- ....
- ....
- ....
- ....

Group list:

- ....
- ....
- ....
- ....
- ....
- ....
- ....
- ....
- ....
- ....

One of the learning outcomes of the exercises may be for group members to recognize the personal commitment they have to make in order for collective organizational behaviour to reflect whatever codes of ethics they have agreed to.

The role of reputation is an important factor in the long-term success of an organization. The passing of time and fashions may dictate changes in products and services, yet a sound reputation can serve as a valuable constant factor in maintaining stakeholder loyalty. A good reputation is therefore a valuable asset in its own right and endows credibility upon an organization's products and services. Hence, organizations invest large amounts of money enhancing their image with consumers. It therefore follows that organizations should consider how their stakeholders see them and act in ways that add to a positive reputation.

In a global economy where there is more choice, consumers can elect to buy similar products or services elsewhere. Accordingly, some organizations are aware of the need to actively take steps in communicating positive messages, not just about their services or products, but also about who they are. However, unlike a product or service, which can be replaced, reputations are entwined within the network of interpersonal messages transmitted by employees and their interaction with both each other and the organization's stakeholders.

The extent to which organizations accept and practise ethical policies can vary according to what fits into the organizational plans and policies. Although, to use the American colloquialism, organizations recognize the PR benefits of *talking the talk*, on ethics, there is some evidence to suggest that not all organizations *walk the walk*. For example, a report by the think tank Demos, reported by Tomlinson (2002), found that – despite the rhetoric of social responsibility – the FSSE 100 companies gave only 0.4% of their pre-tax profits to charity and community projects. Stakeholders are quite able to recognize the differences between corporate PR and operational reality, and it is ultimately upon their interactions with their stakeholder that the organizations' reputations will rest. Organizations are rightly expected to convey information about their products and services in an honest and transparent manner. It would be interesting to consider how organizational communication policies might change if they sought to ensure that their products and services were not hyped to the point where consumers might be disappointed by the gap between advertisements and reality.

The first impression of brands might be that they are something of an illusion. Yet to understand the influence of brand values, it is necessary to reflect upon the context. In the postmodern affluent nations, many people already have most of their needs and wants satisfied. For example, in wealthy nations, it is taken for granted that owning a pair of shoes is attainable, so the issue then becomes which brand of shoe conveys the right image about the wearer. The product itself and any utilitarian purpose it has therefore become less important than the image it conveys about the user. According to Legge (1995: 85), from a postmodernist perspective, it is inappropriate to regard rhetoric, the brand illusions, as less important than reality. In a brand-driven environment, the rhetoric *is* the real world. Products are differentiated more by image than substance. However, can an organization sustain a good reputation on little more than product brand image? The values ascribed to the organization, how it interacts with the community, local and global, the environment and its employees and clients/consumers may provide a more sustainable basis for reputations.

CONDUCTING AN ETHICAL AUDIT

As organizations become more aware of the how their behaviour can impact upon public perception, there is a growing need for independent audits. Audits can also provide benchmarking of what other organizations are doing in a similar environment. However, the act of comparing an organization's behaviour within their market does not, in itself, validate its actions and operating policies. After all, just because others behave in a similar manner does not absolve an organization from its own misdemeanours, where they occur. More usefully, research can provide a catalyst for organizational reflection and re-evaluation of behaviour.

It is possible, with appropriate tutorial support, for a team of HR students to conduct an ethical research audit and gain valuable insights into an organization's ethical life. In most cases, it is usually possible to gain some access to organizations for this type of research work, although confidentiality is crucial. If necessary, materials can be presented with the names removed or as a case study with fictitious job titles to protect anonymity. This is necessary because it is ultimately the organization that decides whether or not to grant researchers access. The anonymity of respondents should be respected.

SUMMARY: CORPORATE SOCIAL RESPONSIBILITY AND BUSINESS ETHICS

(a) Business ethics and CSR are the responsibility of every employee, and so it is important to emphasize the value of constructive engagement rather than prescription.

(b) The research indicates that senior executives have a significant role in establishing their organization's ethical approach.

(c) According to a report by the CIPD, it is the role of HR departments or HR-trained professionals to promote the CSR agenda through their organizations.

(d) HR should be an integrated service that touches every aspect of an organization's operation from the boardroom to customers.

(e) According to O'Neill (2002), a climate of control can be counter-productive to encouraging trust and improving performance. Instead, O'Neil has observed that the additional administrative controls of institutional and professional life do not necessarily bring about the quality improvements intended.

(f) Employees who are required (by company regulations) to comply, but without any personal sense of ownership, are unlikely to be committed to management's objectives.

(g) Reputation is an important factor in the long-term success of an organization. The passing of time and fashions may dictate changes in products and services, yet a sound reputation can serve as a valuable constant factor in maintaining stakeholder loyalty.

REVISION SECTION

What is the difference between legal compliance in an organization and corporate ethical behaviour?

If there is such a thing as society, what responsibilities do organizations have as 'corporate citizens'?

Organizations should share more of their profits with the workers who produce the goods and services. Discuss.

TAKING IT FURTHER

Key texts to look up:

Griseri, P. and Seppala, N. (2009) *Business Ethics and Corporate Social Responsibility*. Andover: Cengage.

Kitson, A. and Campbell, R. (2008) *The Ethical Organization*. Basingstoke: Palgrave Macmillan.

Refer to the books and journals in this references section.

REFERENCES

Albrow, M. (2000) *Sociology After the Third Way in the UK and USA.* Lecture at City University, London, 13 October.

Argandona, A. (2001) Managing and Acting 'Beyond the Call of Duty'. *Business Ethics A European Review.* 10(4), pp. 320–330.

Brakel, A. (2000) Professionalism and Values. *Business Ethics: A European Review.* 9(2), pp. 99–108.

Brinkmann, J. (2001) On Business Ethics and Moralism. *Business Ethics: A European Review.* 10(4), pp. 311–319.

Chryssides, G. and Kaler, J. (1996) *Essentials of Business Ethics*. London: McGraw-Hill.

Davidson, H. (2002) How to Make Vision and Values Work. *People Management.* 26 September. CIPD.

Griseri, P. and Seppala, N. (2009) *Business Ethics and Corporate Social Responsibility*. Andover: Cengage.

Hinman, L. (2000) *Integrity.* Paper from Department of Philosophy, University of San Diego.

Huxley, A. (1932/1975) *Brave New World.* London: Penguin Modern Classics.

Kitson, A. and Campbell, R. (2008). *The Ethical Organization*. Basingstoke: Palgrave Macmillan.

Legge, K. (1995) *Human Resource Management: Rhetorics and Realities.* Basingstoke: Palgrave Macmillan.

Nieto, M. L. (2001) *Marketing the Human Resource Function.* Oxford: Chandos Press.

Nieto, M. L. (2006) *An Introduction to Human Resource Management: An Integrated Approach*. Basingtoke: Palgrave Macmillan.

O'Neill, O. (2002) *A Question of Trust: The BBC Reith Lectures*. Cambridge University Press.

O'Neill, O. (2002a) *Is Trust Failing?* Reith Lecture. *BBC Radio 4*. 17 April.

O'Neill, O. (2002b) *Licence to Deceive*. Reith Lecture. *BBC Radio 4*. 17 April.

Peasaud, J. (2003) In Good Company. How can Organisations Encourage Their Employees to Absorb and Adopt the Message of Corporate Social Responsibility? *People Management*. July. CIPD.

Tomlinson, H. (2002) Ethics Treated As PR Exercise. *The Independent*, Sunday 21 July.

Trevino, L. K., Brown, M. and Hartman, L. P. A. (2003) Qualitative Investigation of Perceived Executive Ethical Leadership: Perceptions from Inside and Outside the Executive Suite. *Human Relations*. 56(1), pp. 5–37.

Walsh, J. (2001) *Building a Sustainable Business Brand: Effective Communication to Stakeholders on Environmental and Social Performance*. Conference paper presented at Kingston University, 6 December.

Watkins, J. (2003) HR Must 'Deliver On CSR'. *People Management*. August. CIPD.

Watson T. J. (2003) Ethical Choice in Managerial Work: The Scope for Moral Choices in an Ethically Irrational World. *Human Relations*. 56(2), pp. 167–185.

Whitehouse, (2002) *The Global Compact-Corporate Citizenship in Action. But Is It Enough?* Global Studies Association. 2nd Conference. Global Ethics and Civil Society. University of Surrey, 22–24 July.

12

Emerging Issues: Global Workplace, Management in the Information Age and Life–Work Integration

INTRODUCTION

In this final chapter you are encouraged to open your imagination and explore what the key emerging issues may be for the middle of the twenty-first century. The chapter also draws upon your learning from the preceding chapters to evaluate the interlinking connections between personal development, organizational change and the opportunities for employment within the global labour market. Societal changes, managing business in a mid-twenty-first-century environment and the emerging global markets, each have implications for human resources. Therefore, this chapter explores how the way we work is changing, the implications for work in a global workplace, working in the information age and life–work integration (LWI). LWI differs from the late-twentieth-century work–life balance discussion and goes beyond the revised life–work balance (LWB) that I introduced in 2003.

The chapter also includes practical activities and discussion topics and two interesting contributions by students on the value of conducting business research.

LEARNING OBJECTIVES

The key learning outcomes for the chapter are below:

- Emerging economies in the global environment: implications for employment.
- Trust, staff development and employment stability.
- Short-termism.
- Managing in the information age.
- Life–work integration.
- Research: the students' perspective.
- Wellbeing and mentoring.
- Intra networking and our brand.

EMERGING ECONOMIES IN THE GLOBAL ENVIRONMENT: IMPLICATIONS FOR EMPLOYMENT

The global context of work is more prevalent in the twenty-first-century workplace than at any other time in human history. This means more employment mobility, changes to where work is done and what kind of work is required.

Key Point: The emerging economies in Latin America, the nations of Eastern Europe, India and China (to name but a few) have a generation of new affluent consumers who are able to buy a wide range of products and services. Hence, the mid-twenty-first century is likely to benefit from an expansion in global markets for products and services.

For example, Chapter 1 traced the progressions from pre-industrial society, industrialization and collectivism and on to the contemporary workplace. By the end of the twentieth century, the changes in information technology had transformed what people do at work and where they can be based in ways which would have been difficult for people 50 years earlier to have envisaged.

Hence, the mid twenty-first century is likely to benefit from an expansion in global markets for products and services. This expansion will also create infrastructure requirements for public services. For example, the expansion in emerging economies is generating employment opportunities in areas such as transport systems, communication infrastructure, hospitals, schools and universities.

Interestingly, these opportunities are emerging at the same time as some of the western nations have reduced their expertise pool in public-service areas. An alternative approach may be for organizations with expertise in areas such as transport systems, communication infrastructure, renewable fuel resources, hospitals, schools and universities to turn their attention towards bidding for projects outside their traditional national boundaries. They could thus develop new income streams. In other words, an organization which was established as a national public service can provide expertise to growing nations. That expertise is in the minds of the experienced employees who have accumulated decades of experience. This can already be seen in universities around the globe which attract international students to their campuses and also offer partnerships with like-minded institutions in other countries. For governments, this approach provides an opportunity to share public-sector expertise internationally and generate revenues to support their services at home.

The global access to information has created an unanticipated transparency about how organizations behave and the quality of their services and products. Consequently, organizational reputations can no longer be managed by advertisements and public relations campaigns. The implications for organizations – be they public, private or not-for-profit – is that concepts such as people being the most valuable asset or corporate social responsibility are more likely to be scrutinized by potential customers around the globe (Nieto 2002). This moves the debate about quality standards and governance outside the arena of professional standards and quality assurance audits and into the wider public domain (O'Neill 2002a, 2002b). The question then becomes not whether an organization has complied with the audit requirements, but whether interested stakeholders trust the services or products it delivers. With

> **Key Point:** For the twenty-first century, what employees think of their organization has become more significant because those opinions can be exchanged among social networks on a global scale.

such public transparency comes also the need to deliver on areas such as employee welfare, job security and pay and rewards (Reid et al. 2008).

For employees, the ability to disseminate information brings new responsibilities too. Hence, if an employee unfairly criticizes their workplace, their misinformation may deter customers from using that organization, which in turn reduces revenues and employment security for the employees.

Key Point: The new global citizens are educated, internationalist and mobile.

What does this mean for employment? The global community and emerging markets offer new opportunities for the new global citizens. The future of work is likely to be more globally focused than it has been in times past. Organizations – including public and private organizations in areas of education, health, transport, communications and infrastructure – will benefit from thinking beyond their home-country boundaries.

TRUST, STAFF DEVELOPMENT AND EMPLOYMENT STABILITY

Employers need to be able recruit and retain people both locally and internationally from a talent pool of educated and well-trained people. To have such a talent pool requires investment in the provision of education.

Key Point: Organizations need to invest more in training young people and retaining their employees.

This means more education for people in this century to enter the workforce and continually update their knowledge and skills to retain employability. Hence, there are opportunities for education and career development providers to deliver affordable, continuous, professional development. Furthermore, governments may need to revise their financial support and loans to create lifelong learning opportunities for people who need further qualifications and training to remain in the workforce.

The changes in the demographic balance between those aged under 35 and those in their 70s and beyond means that more people will need to continue working into their 70s and beyond. To make the best use of experienced employees, organizations will probably need to revise their employee retention strategies, including the wellbeing of employees (Kossek et al. 2012). In practice, this requires a commitment to promoting and nurturing talent from inside their organizations and to prioritizing the retention of employees. Such steps should encourage employees to have confidence in a future career with their current employer, and will require mutual trust and mutual commitment (O'Neill 2002a, 2002b). Such initiatives could also reduce the talent drain whereby an organization's competitors benefit from the talents of people who leave due to a lack of career prospects. For example, if an employee can trust that they have a future with the organization, then they are more likely to stay. This emerging issue differs from the current psychological contract, which places the responsibility for retaining employability onto the individual employee (as discussed in previous chapters). However, if the employer choses to offer low commitment to retention and promotion then the employees are likely to reciprocate the same values and with low trust, too.

> **Key Point:** Organizations will need to create employee-retention strategies to keep experienced employees in a competitive, global, employment environment.

The research by Bélanger et al. (2003) indicated that it is helpful to trust employees and allow more self-determination. This is because when people feel trusted they are more engaged by exercising some control over how they complete their assigned tasks. A study by Harter et al. (2002) of 7,939 business units within 36 companies evaluated the relationships between employee satisfaction and their engagement with their work, staff retention and the possible relationships these factors might have with levels of customer satisfaction, productivity and profitability. The paper indicated that management initiatives which raised employee satisfaction could positively improve organizational performance and profitability. This is interesting because the trend in the late twentieth and early twenty-first century has been towards less job security and more reorganization of structures within organizations with consequences for employees' sense of security and wellbeing (Baptiste 2008). A question thereby arises concerning what influence multiple changes of managers, structures, reporting systems, targets, performance indicators, strategies and policy initiatives might have on levels of employee satisfaction and security, which – according to Harter et al. (2002) – can reduce productivity and profits if lessened,.

> **Key Point:** Employee satisfaction and security improves customer service and profitability

In Maslow's (1943) hierarchy of needs, the foundation of a person's motivation begins with safety and security. Consequently, unless the basic needs are assured, the higher levels of motivation are unsupported.

According Harter et al. (2002), it therefore follows that if the employees' psychological contract is short-term due to insecurity of tenure, the organization will be less successful than it could be with a more secure stable workforce. This has implications for HR in setting the future pathway for employee relations because, in a highly competitive global business environment, the best resources an organization has in innovating and changing to remain successful are the talents, innovation and skills of its people. This includes everyone in the organization and at all levels. A boardroom strategy, however well conceived, can only succeed if those responsible for its delivery believe in the strategy and have the knowledge and skills to communicate the new initiative to the organization's stakeholders. Hence, the employees require the necessary AKS to deliver the strategy. This requires communication, motivation and staff development, all of which have been discussed in earlier chapters of this book.

The future trend is therefore likely to include a reappraisal of what is understood by employee benefits to address issues such as trust and security for long-term careers as people stay in the workforce longer than was the case in the twentieth century. Employment is also likely to last longer in the twenty-first century as governments continue to raise the retirement age (in the mid-60s, during the later twentieth century) in order to retain experienced workers in the workforce instead of funding unsupportable unemployment and retirement benefits. As such, HR is not a cost but an investment in creating an organization that works, whatever that 'work' might be.

SHORT-TERMISM

Short-termism can be defined as an overly short-term focus on immediate outcomes which may not serve the longer-term sustainability of an organization. A focus on short-term profitability and stock-market values tends to encourage decisions which might accrue a short-term profit gain but also medium to long-term losses (Davies el al. 2013; Thanassoulis 2013). According to the report by the CFA Centre for Financial Market Integrity and Business Roundtable Institute for Corporate Ethics (2006), one of the contributing factors to the global economic downturn in the first decades of the twenty-first century was short-termism.

An organization needs to invest for the coming decades rather than the next stock market valuation. For example, while conducting the primary research and background case studies for this book, I have interviewed people in many different organizations. It was interesting to learn about what objectives people were expected to achieve in their organizations and the timescales. Here is one example from a City stock-market trader. In reply to the question 'What is a long time in your area of work?', one City of London stock trader reflected and then replied: 'Ten minutes'.

> **Key Point:** The job life expectancy of many of the managers I met was estimated as less than five years and often managers had been replaced in less than two years. Managers reported being in acting roles awaiting an appointment, which in practice means they can be removed at any moment, producing instability, insecurity and short-termism.

Another of the areas which I was keen to learn about was how long senior managers remained in an organization. It was also interesting to hear from senior managers in not-for-profit organizations such as the health service and education. Short-term objectives and pressures appeared to be quite common in both for-profit and not-for-profit organizations. With the not-for-profits, the drivers for short-termism were 'efficiency savings' (often a term which disguises simple cost cutting) and performance targets, such as league tables.

Accordingly, for many managers who realize that they may not remain in post for a year,, there is pressure to do something in the first few months, even if the medium-term impact of those changes damages the organization's performance. This kind of employment insecurity and instability debilitates organizational sustainability, reduces employee wellbeing and wastes human capital.

The research for this book found indications of short-termism in organizations where the more obvious pressures of the stock market were not prevalent. For example, in some public-sector organizations such as the Health Service in the UK, employees were exposed to restructuring programmes which in practice meant applying to keep their jobs. In such circumstances, people described feeling under pressure to 'do something' which would enhance the possibility of keeping their role.

In the education sector, a significant number of posts were reported as temporary, acting or for just a two or three-year contract, instead of permanent. The imposition of employment insecurity discourages long-term strategic planning with employees who, of necessity, need to offer a short-term justification to retain their employment. For example, if the senior team of an organization wished to create a five-year strategic plan, the success and follow-through would rest upon how many of the team remained in post for five years. And five years is hardly long-term, so what if the planning were to extend to ten, twenty or thirty years? Instability of employment renders such strategic planning operationally impractical.

When I discussed teams and planning with the consultant Duncan Christie Miller (see Chapter 9), we concluded that when a new person joins a team, it is a new team. This is because the interpersonal dynamics inside the team have changed. Each new team member also brings their unique personality and their personal attitudes, knowledge and skills sets. The new team therefore needs to progress through the team-forming process to the performing status whereby each member understands their role in the team and is working in harmony towards agreed objectives (Tuckman 1965). It follows that the more often a team changes during a process of implementing a strategic plan, the more team readjustments and delays are likely to

> **Key Point:** An environment where employees are sufficiently secure to create and deliver plans is in the long-term interests of their organization.

be incurred, which thereby disrupts performance and increases costs.

Accordingly, there is an interesting paradox with organizational team stability and a constantly changing environment. The only constant which we can be certain of is change. The global environment – be it for industries, banking, services, education, health care or communications – is constantly changing as new markets emerge and new services and products are created. So, if an organization has an insecure workforce based on short-term contracts then employees are likely to be focusing on either short-term successes to support the renewal of their temporary contract, or an exit strategy to find a new job or both, neither of which benefits longer-term planning. Indeed, the research by Maslow (1943) indicated that employees focus on securing the means to maintain employment as their priority when they lack job security (Tay and Diener 2011). So in a working world where constant change is producing new requirements for innovation, creativity and cooperative teams, the competitive advantage is likely to reside with those organizations which have the strategic vision to stabilize their teams by providing secure employment.

MANAGEMENT IN THE INFORMATION AGE

It is interesting to recall that the technologies – such as telecommunications, the computer and the Internet – which underpin the information age were created in the twentieth century,. The modern manager probably spends hours reading and replying to multiple systems of communication. It is worth noting here that change is a value-neutral word, and that perhaps some of the additional workload created by the multiple forms of communication might be adding little value or even detract from productive management activity. I have described this expansion of communications as Information Inflation.

In a constantly changing environment, managers no longer have the twentieth century's respite opportunity to organizationally re-freeze; instead,

> **Key Point:** Information Inflation. Managers receive multiple sources of electronic information as well as meetings in person. This increases managerial work's complexity in terms of its volume, content and speed of response to stakeholders.

the rapid changes in the global business environment require regular adjustments in terms of products or service delivery. The metaphor for such constant change is described as the Slush Model (Nieto 2006) instead of the twentieth-century 're-freeze' stage in the change model (Lewin 1951). The Slush Model refers to continuous flexibility of product and service adaptations. If the past rate of change indicates the future trend, then the next 50 years are going to see more shifts in markets as well as what we do and how we do it. The complexity of the new business environment means that employability is becoming less about qualifications, though that is one element, and more about what people can do. This includes actual experience of working in different organizations and an attitude of wanting to learn more – continuous personal development (CPD).

The opportunities to reach new customers in emerging economies may be achieved via international alliances and organizational networks. By increasing trust and security, employees are more likely to innovate, to create new services and products that can serve the emerging market opportunities.

Organizations will need to review policies so that employees can move up the motivational pyramid (Maslow 1943). In practice, this means management policies which seek to create stability internally and less insecurity about tenure, thereby facilitating a climate of trust between management and employees (Wong and Law 2002; Nieto 2003; Bakker and Heuven 2006; Brunetto et al. 2011). This approach enables organizations to focus on strategies which generate revenue externally, instead of an inward focus on restructuring which seeks to reduce costs internally. Whilst cost cutting can provide a short-term profitability spike, it quickly falls away as the repercussions reduce staff morale, productivity and performance.

It is likely that the complexity of management work is going to continue to increase, which bodes well for graduates trained at business school and members of the CIPD and the CMI. For example, managers will need the capacity to negotiate with complex local, global organizational alliances, while balancing constant change with employees who also need stability and security of tenure and a sense of wellbeing about their workplace (Nieto 2002; Grant et al. 2007; Baptiste, 2008).

LIFE-WORK INTEGRATION

'To everything there is a season, and a time to every purpose' (Ecclesiastes: 3, 1).

Time management

The time we have is the most value of our personal assets because it cannot be replaced. While money, jobs and personal possessions may be upgraded or replaced, time cannot be. The opportunity is therefore to find ways of using time more efficiently to achieve the things we want in life. For example, I wrote parts of this chapter sitting on a comfortable bench overlooking the river Thames in London where HMS *Belfast* is moored. It was a relaxing environment and a perfect opportunity to practise the skill of managing time efficiently, prior to attending an appointment. If, instead, I had chosen to wait until I had a few hours to work on the chapter continuously, the new ideas which came to me at that time might not have been included. Furthermore, local inspirations sometimes stimulated interesting ideas which might not have emerged by sitting in my university study.

The choices of how or where to work of course vary according to each person's personal preferences and occupation. In terms of managing your time it is therefore worth reflecting on when and how you can improve your time utilization. How to improve the way you manage time in an increasingly busy work environment is a key topic discussed later in this chapter.

In the twentieth century, academic papers and textbooks took the perspective that there ought to be a work–life balance. However, in 2003 I argued that an alternative model, which presented life first and then work, better described the intentions of most people's approaches to their workplaces. In general, the majority of people would agree that they work to live, not live to work. In 2013, I have reflected upon the many changes since 2003 and would like to offer that in managing complexity, life and work have become more blended. For example, new technologies mean that working can happen on a riverside bench or at home or on a beach. The technologies that enable us to do this have been in use for a couple of decades. As such, those technologies have become integrated into our working practices.

> **Key Point:** Life–work integration. The boundaries of work and personal life for many workers have become blurred.

Indeed, home-based workers could be working longer hours than they might have done within the more socially interactive environment of a traditional workplace environment. Each situation has its advantages, so it is possible that some forms of work are improved by the synergy of social interaction in a workplace-type environment, while other forms of work may benefit from periods of uninterrupted concentration.

There are balances to be explored in where and how to work: hence, life–work integration (LWI). The LWI concept reflects the constantly interconnected nature of contemporary working, whilst retaining the recognition that life still comes first. For example, the older model of a work–life balance (Nieto 2003) created an impression of two sides of a scale where life's personal activities are weighed on the one side and counter-balanced by a person's work requirements. Instead, the LWI model more accurately identifies the interconnected life and work environment in which many people function. Personal life interests and work are no longer so easily divided into time in the workplace and time away from the work environment. Indeed, for some employees, the work environment may be contained in their pocket in the form of a mobile device which has multiple modes of communication, including a telephone! Of course you can switch all the mobiles and devices off. This is then a choice as to how much integration of work a person decides to have in their life.

With an increasingly diversified workforce (full-time, part-time, workers 65+ years of age, contractors, self-employed, new-career entrants, single parents, carers for family members, this list is not exhaustive), what each employee wants from work may be very different. This means that HR policies and practices need to reflect that diversity. In this area, the choices of how to integrate life and work can be facilitated by the technologies, if employers so decide. In harmony with the integrated HR philosophy which underpins this book, the nature and design of LWI is specific to the person and situation (Nieto 2003, 2006).

People invest a lot of their time at work so it is makes sense for them to enjoy what they do and feel that it is useful and valued. My experience of working with organizations and developing time management plans is that a review of priorities is a valuable first step towards improvements in time management, performance and LWI. So, this chapter considers time management and LWI with practical initiatives that HR (and other management students) can apply to their workplaces/HR study projects.

The level of process input does not necessarily have a positive correlation with successful outcomes. For example, in the British public sector, a common criticism of successive governments is that they have interfered by prescribing how work should be carried out. According to Smith and Cracknell (2002) the King's Fund, (a health think tank) criticized the numerous policy documents, regulations, advice and guidance that had been issued by the Department of Health because such interventions wasted time and resources on the front line and demoralized doctors and nurses. Interestingly, at the time of writing in 2013, the NHS was undergoing yet another major reorganization.

An executive with a major international organization based in the US advised me that one of his French executive colleagues applies a simple question to test whether an activity is worth investing time in: 'To which key area of this organization's work does this task contribute value?' By contribution he meant tangible improvements to the delivery of service to internal and external customers. If the answer to that question was 'not sure'

> **Key Point:** Reorganizing an organization may not produce much positive improvement and may reduce productive outcomes if it reduces employee security, commitment and motivation.

Key Point: Reduce the number of meetings, emails, reports and reviews that do not make a direct contribution to key activities. Less monitoring, reviewing and more productive work.

then the activity was curtailed. This approach reduced a significant amount of processes, paperwork, emails and general bureaucracy, thereby increasing profitability by focusing the organization's efforts on front-line productive service.

Activity: work efficiency audit

It is useful to analyse the key activities of a job role and to examine what is essential to its performance, what is desirable, and also to identify activities which take up time but contribute little to the organization's customers. If you are/have been employed in full or part-time, paid or voluntary work, it is helpful to review the work you do/did and create an efficiency audit.

List the tasks you were required to complete in your job under one of the three headings below. Once you have made the lists, estimate how much time was dedicated to each item.

Cumulate your allocations to a total of 100 per cent of your working time.

Essential to job performance

Item	Percentage of time
	Subtotal of percentage

Desirable to job performance

Item	Percentage of time
	Subtotal of percentage

Unnecessary to job performance

Item	Percentage of time
	Subtotal of percentage

Totals of time invested:

Essential to job performance   %
Desirable to job performance   %
Unnecessary to job performance   %

This exercise is also of practical value to HR specialists who are asked to appraise performance and design job descriptions because it provides specific job information and encourages employee reflection upon how and where they are investing their time or where the organization is wasting their time. Team leaders and others responsible for directing workloads can also reflect upon the findings and then discuss where the priorities should be.

> **Key Point:** Less is more. It is important to recognize that every new IT system, management report, set of compliance requirements, external inspection, internal observation, team review, data presentation your people are asked to work on means that they have less time to deliver on core areas of productivity.

The only part of a person's itinerary that is not flexible is the number of working hours available. Hence, the removal of unnecessary work can significantly enhance performance by releasing valuable time to invest in value-adding activities. The process of agreeing such priorities is best affected through consultation and mutual agreement. In most cases, the person who is actually doing the job will be best placed to identify the essential and desirable tasks.

Twenty-first-century HR professionals are likely to encounter a variety of issues arising from LWI, which differ according to the personal circumstances of employees, workers or volunteers. The conventional practices of reward management, which concentrated on financial remuneration and hierarchically structured benefits systems, may lack sufficient flexibility to sustain employee motivation and retention within a modern diversified workplace. It is therefore possible that a paradigm shift in HR philosophy may be required, away from employee relations, with its tendency to paternalism, towards a more empowering employee partnership (Nieto 2003).

Activity: LWI questionnaire

Answer the questions below as a seminar activity and discuss the results in a study group. If you are conducting primary research for a course, seek permission to circulate the questionnaire to employees in the organization.

Responses to each item are measured: (1) strongly disagree; (2) moderately disagree; (3) slightly disagree; (4) neither agree nor disagree; (5) slightly agree; (6) moderately agree; (7) strongly agree.

1. Life work integration issues are important to this organization.

 1   2   3   4   5   6   7

2. I am happy with the balance of work and personal interests I have been able to achieve as an employee of this organization.

 1   2   3   4   5   6   7

3. My career is the most important aspect of my life.

 1   2   3   4   5   6   7

4. I would prefer to have more time to follow interests outside the workplace.

 1   2   3   4   5   6   7

5. I am prepared to work long hours when it is necessary to get a job completed.

 1   2   3   4   5   6   7

6. I regularly work longer hours than specified in my contract.

 1   2   3   4   5   6   7

7. Work pressures have contributed to creating difficulties in my personal life.

 1   2   3   4   5   6   7

8. I think my colleagues are happy with their life–work integration.

 1   2   3   4   5   6   7

9. My manager takes an active interest in helping me to achieve a sustainable LWI.

 1   2   3   4   5   6   7

10. My immediate manager has been supportive of my participation in personal/ career development activities.

 1   2   3   4   5   6   7

11. The three main benefits of the life–work integration in this organization are:

(i)

(ii)

(iii)

12. The three recommendations I would like to offer are:

(i)

(ii)

(iii)

Activity: LWI – planning your time allocation

Identifying priorities

It is quite easy to be very busy, but it takes planning to be busy doing the value-adding activities which contribute to the success of the organization. According to Covey (1999), it is important to organize schedules around the priority activities. The system below is designed to encourage a clearer evaluation of what is and is not important in the daily work schedule. When I run time-management courses, people often tell me that they are already managing their time well and that in their situation it would be difficult to change anything. Yet when I ask them how they are coping, it becomes clear that some of them are experiencing problems handling their workloads. The first step is to accept that a change in working methods is both possible and achievable. It is also possible that time management may not be the key issue, but rather other factors such as a need for training. It may also be appropriate to review staffing levels after the study in time management is completed. The time management system shown below can provide a simple record of activities so that it is clearer where time is being invested. If after trying the system for a month it is still evident that there are too many high-importance tasks to be completed, then the possibility of recruiting more staff could be evaluated.

Before you fill in the sections below, read the descriptors which follow. Then fill in the tasks you have into the area which best identifies their urgency and importance.

High urgency–high importance	Low urgency–high importance
1. ...	1. ...
2. ...	2. ...
3. ...	3. ...
4. ...	4. ...
5. ...	5. ...
High urgency –low importance	Low–urgency–low importance
1. ...	1. ...
2. ...	2. ...
3. ...	3. ...
4. ...	4. ...
5. ...	5. ...

High urgency–high importance

The high urgency status means these tasks need to be dealt with immediately and the high importance denotes their key value. It is worth noting that unless time is managed properly, this section can soon become overfilled. The key to success is to carefully select what is placed in this must-do list as opposed to doing whatever is interesting or simply on top of a pile of papers. What is included will vary according to your job role and may also be affected by seasonal variations. If there are genuinely too many of these tasks, then it may be time to consider having more people available to perform them.

Low urgency–high importance

The types of tasks which are likely to come under this category are those that require work over a longer period of time. It is important to allocate time in the daily/weekly schedule for these because their low urgency status can sometimes mean they are left unattended until the deadline date looms near. For example, any activity which requires research and discussion will be time-consuming. Preparing a management report can easily be put aside as day-to-day pressures mount, but it is these medium to long-term projects which have to be *planned* into the work schedule. Do consider home/social activities as well as work.

High urgency–low importance

There are certain activities which can overrun a work schedule and are really quite unimportant. It is therefore not surprising that one of the most common causes of poor time management is the time spent dealing with the high urgency–low importance tasks. Exactly what these are will differ for each person, but they are guaranteed to devour time. One of the most common problems of the information age is that, while is has become easier to communicate, this does not necessarily improve the quality of the messages. The modern flow of electronic information can fill a working day before it has begun.

It may be useful to set aside some time each day for working on important projects without interruption. The extent to which this can be achieved again depends on the nature of the job and the type of organization. It is worthwhile trying to negotiate times when people can focus on important tasks.

Low urgency–low importance

This section includes all the activities which add little or no value to the business and objectives of the organization. Such activities will vary enormously from one occupation to another. However, most people know which elements of processes add little or no value to the outcomes of their organization. Ask the question: Why do we do this? Then make the necessary adjustments in policy.

WELLBEING AND MENTORING

Employee wellbeing is an important area in the increasingly complex and demanding work environment of the twenty-first century, and is likely to continue to move into the high importance–high priority area of management activity. If not managed properly, wellbeing may be set aside as work becomes integrated into the personal as well as professional life of professional workers (Hall et al. 2012). However, giving attention to the wellbeing of people in an organization can improve the quality of each person's time with the organization and can thereby enhance the harmony and success of the organization itself.

A study by Axtell and Parker (2003) indicated that membership of an active improvement group and personal development could influence confidence in performing interpersonal tasks. The Confidence and Competence Model (Nieto 2006) discussed in the present volume (Chapter 4) can help you evaluate your self-perception and identify where you may like some support and development.

The Confidence and Competence Model can be used developmentally in mentoring and coaching situations. For example, in one of the HRM modules I have worked with, students in their second year at university are encouraged to mentor a small team of students who have recently started their studies. The model is used to identify where the mentored require support and where they may have confidence yet need to be encouraged to improve their competence. The tasks which can be mentored may be anything where AKS may require development. For example, presentation skills, CV preparation, study and research skills or employability. The mutual learning process thereby benefits the mentors, who reinforce their own learning by teaching others, and the mentored, who are supported through their first semester at university by a small team of students who have already successfully completed their first two semesters.

INTRA NETWORKING AND OUR BRAND

Networking with people for both professional and social purposes has been common for centuries. Networking can be seen throughout history as a means of improving social status and for securing employment. The electronic communications of the modern age enable that networking to reach a wider audience. In this section we consider closer relationships with colleagues and professional networks; for example, those people in

> **Key Point:** Intra-networking. The workplace is a space for building connections with people within your current employment: intra-networking. This is a valuable source of connections for your present or future employment opportunities.

your immediate workplace who can be a source of advice and support. Accordingly, the way we interact with our immediate circle of people creates an image of us, a brand status of how the people who meet us regularly perceive us. It is therefore worth investing in those interpersonal relationships and nurturing the friendships which may emerge. The social environment of the workplace can also be a space for building connections with people within your current employment: intra-networking.

SUMMARY OF EMERGING ISSUES: GLOBAL WORKPLACE, MANAGEMENT IN THE INFORMATION AGE AND LWI

(a) The emerging economies of Latin America, the nations in Eastern Europe, India and China (to name but a few) have a generation of new affluent consumers who want to buy products and services. Hence the mid-twenty-first century is likely to benefit from an expansion of global markets for products and services.

(b) Global citizens: people with employability are able to move to jobs around the planet.

(c) The question is not whether an organization complied with the audit requirements, but whether interested stakeholders trust the services or products it delivers.

(d) The future of work is likely to be more globally focused than it has been in times past. Organizations will benefit from thinking beyond their home country boundaries including public, private organizations in areas of education, health, transport, communications and infrastructure.

(e) In order to reduce the costs of state pension provisions, people in this century are going to need to continue in the workforce into their 70s and possibly beyond. Hence, there are opportunities for education and career development providers to deliver affordable, continuous, professional development.

(f) Encouraging employees to have confidence in a future career with their current employer requires mutual trust and mutual commitment.

(g) If the employer chooses to offer low commitment to retention and promotion, then the employees are likely to reciprocate the same value with low trust.

(h) If the employees' psychological contract is short-term due to insecurity of tenure, then the organization will be less successful than it could be with a more secure and stable workforce.

(i) Information inflation: the expansion of communications. Managers receive multiple sources of electronic information as well as attending meetings in person. This increases the level of complexity of managerial work in its volume, content and speed of response to stakeholders.

(j) Slush Model: the metaphor for constant change is 'slush' instead of the twentieth-century 're-freeze' stage. The Slush Model refers to continuous flexibility of product and service adaptation.

(k) HR policies, which seek to create stability internally and less insecurity about tenure, thereby facilitate a climate of trust between management and employees.

(l) It is likely that the complexity of management work is going to continue to increase, which bodes well for graduates trained at business school and professionally qualified members of the CIPD and the CMI.

(m) The time we have is the most value of our personal assets because it cannot be replaced. While money, jobs and personal possessions may be upgraded or replaced, time cannot be.

(n) The LWI concept reflects the constantly interconnected nature of contemporary working, while retaining the recognition that life still comes first.

(o) Restructuring? Continually reorganising internally may not produce positive improvement and often reduces employee morale, thereby reducing productivity.

(p) To reduce reports and meetings, ask yourself a simple question: 'To which key area of this organization's work does this task contribute value?'

(q) The Confidence and Competence Model can be used developmentally in mentoring and coaching situations.

REVISION SECTION

Evaluate the opportunities for expansion into global markets by public services and not-for-profit organizations; for example, public services such as transport systems, communication infrastructure, hospitals, schools and universities.

Global interconnectedness has made managing more complex in a time of multiple information sources. Discuss the implications for managers of 'Information inflation'.

Evaluate the advantages and disadvantages of LWI.

TAKING IT FURTHER

Key texts to look up:

Davies, R., Haldane, A. G., Nielsen, M. and Pezzini, S. (2013) Measuring the Costs of Short-Termism. *The Economist*. United Kingdom. July 2013.

Grant, A. M., Christianson, M. K. and Price, R. H. (2007) Happiness, Health, or Relationships? Managerial Practices and Employee Well-being Tradeoffs. *Academy of Management Perspectives*. 21(3), pp. 51–63.

Kossek, E., Kaillaith, T. and Kaillaith P. (2012) Achieving Employee Wellbeing in a Changing Work Environment: An Expert Commentary on Current Scholarship. *International Journal of Manpower*. 33(7), pp. 738–753.

Refer to the books and journals in this references section.

REFERENCES

Axtell, C. M. and Parker S. K. (2003) Promoting Role Breadth Self-Efficacy Through Involvement, Work Redesign and Training. *Human Relations*. 46(1), p. 113.

Bakker, A. B. and Heuven, E. (2006) Emotional Dissonance, Burnout, and In-Role Performance among Nurses and Police Officers. *International Journal of Stress Management*. 13(3), pp. 423–440.

Baptiste, N. R. (2008) Tightening the Link between Employee Wellbeing at Work and Performance: A New Dimension for HRM. *Management Decision*. 46(2), pp. 284–309.

Bélanger, J., Edwards, P. K. and Wright, M. (2003) Commitment at Work and Independence from Management: A Study of Advanced Teamwork. *Work and Occupations*. 30(2), pp. 234–252.

Brunetto, Y., Farr-Wharton, R. and Shacklock, K. H. (2011) Using the Harvard HRM Model to Conceptualise the Impact of Changes to Supervision upon HRM Outcomes for Different Types of Public Sector Employees. *International Journal of Human Resource Management*. 22(3), pp. 553–573.

CFA Centre for Financial Market Integrity and Business Roundtable Institute for Corporate Ethics (2006) *Breaking the Short-Term Cycle: Codes, Standards and Position Papers*. Symposium Series on Short-Termism. July.

Covey. S. R. (1999) *The 7 Habits of Highly Effective People*. London: Simon & Schuster.

Davies, R., Haldane, A. G., Nielsen, M. and Pezzini, S. (2013) Measuring the Costs of Short-termism. *The Economist*. United Kingdom. July 2013.

Grant, A. M., Christianson, M. K. and Price, R. H. (2007) Happiness, Health, or Relationships? Managerial Practices and Employee Well-Being Tradeoffs. *Academy of Management Perspectives*. 21(3), pp. 51–63.

Hall, D., Lee, M., Kossek, E. and Las Heras, M. (2012) Pursuing Career Success while Sustaining Personal and Family Well Being: A Study of

Reduced-load Professionals over Time. *Journal of Social Issues.* 68(4), pp. 741–765, Special Issue on Sustainable Careers.

Harter, J. K., Schmidt, F. L. and Hayes, T. L. (2002) Business-Unit-Level Relationship between Employee Satisfaction, Employee Engagement, and Business Outcomes: A Meta-Analysis. *Journal of Applied Psychology.* 87(2), pp. 268–279.

Kossek, E., Kaillaith, T. and Kaillaith P. (2012) Achieving Employee Wellbeing in a Changing Work Environment: An Expert Commentary on Current Scholarship. *International Journal of Manpower.* 33(7), pp. 738–753.

Lewin, K. (1951) *Field Theory in Social Science.* New York: Harper & Row.

Maslow, A. H. (1943) A theory of Human Motivation. *Psychological Review.* 50(4), pp. 370–396. Nieto, M. L. (2002) *Business Ethics for the Twenty-first Century.* Paper delivered to Business Ethics Conference at the University of Surrey, 6 March.

Nieto, M. L. (2003) The Development of Life Work Balance Initiatives Designed for Managerial Workers. *Business Ethics: A European Review.* 12(3), pp. 213–215.

Nieto, M. L. (2006) *An Introduction to Human Resource Management: An Integrated Approach.* Basingstoke: Palgrave Macmillan.

O'Neill, O. (2002a) *Is Trust Failing?* Reith Lecture. *BBC Radio 4.* 17 April.

O'Neill, O. (2002b) *Licence to Deceive.* Reith Lecture. *BBC Radio 4.* 1 May.

Reid, M. F., Riemenschneider, C. K., Allen, M. W. and Armstrong, D. J. (2008) Information Technology Employees in State Government: A Study of Affective Organizational Commitment, Job Involvement, and Job Satisfaction. *American Review of Public Administration.* 38(1), pp. 41–61.

Smith, D. and Cracknell, D. (2002) *The Gamble that Will Cost Us All. The Sunday Times.* 14 April.

Tay, L. and Diener, E. (2011) Needs and Subjective Well-being around the World. *Journal of Personality and Social Psychology.* 101(2), pp. 354–365.

Thanassoulis, J. (2013) Industry Structure, Executive Pay, and Short-termism. *Management Science*. February, 59, pp. 402–419.

Tuckman, B. W. (1965) Developmental Sequence in Small Groups.

Psychological Bulletin. June, 63(6), pp. 384–399.

Wong, C. S. and Law, K. (2002) The Effects of Leader and Follower Emotional Intelligence on Performance and Attitude: An Exploratory Study. *Leadership Quarterly*. 13(3), pp. 233–274.

INDEX